Walking Ireland

25 Superb Walking Routes

from Wicklow to Connemara

WALKING IRELAND

25 Superb Walking Routes from Wicklow to Connemara

TOM LAWTON

Photographs by the author
Diagrams by Dr William Rouse

Gill & Macmillan

Gill & Macmillan Ltd
Goldenbridge
Dublin 8
with associated companies throughout the world

0 7171 2692 7
Diagrams by Dr William Rouse
Design and print origination by Design Image, Dublin
Printed and bound by Edelvives, Spain

A catalogue record for this book is available from the British Library.

Cover Photographs

front: Time to relax on the sunny summit of Mount Brandon, Co Kerry
back (top): The view northwards across Galway Bay seen from Abbey Hill, Co Clare
back (bottom): Walkers admiring the view down from Devil's Ladder, Carrauntoohil, Co Kerry

This book is dedicated to the wild, untamed, mountainous countryside of Ireland, that which stretches in a semi-circle through the attractive counties of Wicklow, Tipperary, Waterford, Cork, Kerry, Clare, Galway and Mayo; and to the dedicated, congenial and vastly experienced Irish walking guides who have shown me many of the adventurous ways up these high, formidable slopes and, more importantly still, have then got me down safely again.

CONTENTS

INTRODUCTION

When I started this journey, I intended undertaking a walking tour of the Irish coastline which would include only a few adventurous ascents along the way. However, people who knew better than me, together with the many-splendoured mountains of Ireland, persuaded me to raise my sights, to allow my spirits to soar and to venture onto higher ground. In the end it meant placing my feet on some of the loftiest spots in the whole country.

There is a link between my original intentions and their subsequent execution. Much of the higher ground that I eventually trekked across is located either along the coastline or relatively close to it. This is part of the fascinating attraction of Ireland.

As it turned out, I am very pleased and happy about this upwards change of direction. It enabled me to experience the unique joy, fulfilment and exuberance of standing on many of Ireland's high mountain peaks stretching from Co Wicklow to Connemara and Co Mayo. I was fortunate to experience these delights with a number of local walking guides. They and their friends generously shared their expertise, knowledge and warm companionship with me. I doubt very much whether I could have persuaded these energetic ladies and gentlemen to remain beside me for very long simply by walking along the coastal fringe! I, therefore, have much to be grateful for and I do hope that some of you will also benefit from this know-how should you decide to follow in our adventurous footsteps.

Having been lured away from paddling in the sea, it fairly quickly became apparent that to do even scant justice to exploring the vast and varied mountainous landscapes of Ireland, where peaks of every shape and size pop up all over the place, it would be sensible to place some realistic constraints on the extent and sequence of what might otherwise become haphazard and uncoordinated wanderings. This I reluctantly did by limiting the area covered to those mountains which lie to the south, south-west and (roughly) west of Dublin.

The subsequent, thrilling tour of these mountains is presented and described as a clockwise circuit, commencing from Dublin. It includes my exploration of the Wicklow Mountains, the mountains surrounding the Nire Valley, the mountains of the far south-west peninsulas of Beara, Iveragh and Dingle, the limestone pavements of the Burren and the mountains of Connemara and Co Mayo, in that exciting sequence.

From these extensive and dedicated wanderings, 25 walks of varying degrees of challenge and difficulty have been selected for the book, although there are many other deserving candidates which vied for inclusion. These walks range from demanding climbs to some of the highest peaks in Ireland where walkers can stand above 3000 ft to strolling on the flat around a sandy promontory. Thus, the book contains walks which will appeal most to strong, vigorous and experienced walkers, those which are fine for most reasonably fit walkers, those which will be more suitable for less energetic people and those which will be enjoyed by family groups. This is befitting, for although many of us are able to experience the great elation and share the unique ambience generated from standing with others on the tops of high mountains, not everybody is physically capable of achieving this. Fortunately, much joy and excitement may also be experienced by simply looking up at these towering heights.

The walks are presented area by area in sequence, commencing with the four routes amongst the Wicklow Mountains. The 25 walking routes are disclosed in accurate, factual, easy-to-digest descriptions. Here, relevant information is provided to enable you to follow each route with minimum uncertainty and thus to identify and appreciate the main features of the landscapes through which each walk passes. Of course, in this I am assuming favourable weather along the way.

Additionally, an introduction is provided for each of the seven separate mountain areas covered. This is written in a contrasting anecdotal style which discloses pertinent background information as seen through my own eyes and agreeable experiences. I intend this to be helpful to walkers and to enable them to obtain the maximum benefit from the attractions and amenities of each region. These disclosures include some opinions which, whilst given in good faith, may not always be shared fully by all those who follow! However, the contact names and addresses provided are factual, and in particular the expert walking guides listed will greatly aid, facilitate and augment your own walking explorations if you give them the opportunity to do so.

This conveniently brings me to the crucial matter of safety. Many of the high, mountainous regions covered in this book are composed of really rugged terrain which can quickly generate needless difficulties and cause unnecessary exposure to the unwary adventurer, particularly in deteriorating weather conditions. Often, the mountains and surrounding high places contain an assortment of such features and potential dangers as precipitous cliff faces, rocky ledges, boulder fields, steep scree slopes, narrow ridges and arêtes, expansive peat bogs (some with sinkholes in them) and, on hot days, tempting, icy-cold, deep corrie lakes. All of these features need to be treated with appropriate respect and they should be places which you either avoid or negotiate exercising the greatest care and discipline.

An additional hazard is posed by the climate. In Ireland, influenced by a predominantly moist or wet south-west air flow from across the Atlantic Ocean, the weather is exceptionally fickle and changeable, particularly in the high mountains. Suppose the day is fine and clear when you set out; suppose the weather appears settled; further suppose that these favourable conditions are confirmed by the latest weather forecasts: you should still be wary. Never get caught out! Blanketing mist can come down very quickly and bad weather conditions may then follow equally suddenly, especially when blown in by a strengthening, south or south-westerly gale, the exact timing and course of which the meteorological experts may have unfortunately misjudged! Therefore, learn to read the signs and leading indicators. When it appears fairly likely that weather conditions are going to deteriorate rapidly, get down as fast as possible — but always moving at a controlled, safe pace.

The sensible advice for most walkers when venturing into a challenging, high mountain area with which they are unfamiliar is to consult, or better still undertake their first walk with, an expert, local walking guide who is adequately trained in mountaincraft and who knows that particular area exceptionally well. Not only will such persons ensure that you walk safely but they will show you features of interest that you might otherwise pass by unnoticed, thus adding greatly to the overall attraction of each route.

I did just this, even though for some time now I have walked between one and two thousand miles each year in the mountains of Great Britain and also explored many Alpine peaks. Compared with the high places of England and Wales, walking in the mountains of Ireland raises two important safety issues to which all walkers familiar with these other regions should be alert. First, there are significantly fewer paths spanning Irish mountains and, generally speaking, much of the terrain there is rougher and more remote. Secondly, there are fewer other walkers with whom to pass the time of day, or from whom to seek advice or even help. To exemplify this, one of our extremely well-guided routes in the Wicklow Mountains, barely 30 miles from the sprawling environs of Dublin city, took us to the vast summit area of Lugnaquillia along a quite superb walking route starting out from Glenmalure (this walk will be disclosed in a future book!), and during the entire day we met just four other walkers — a party of people on the top of 'Lug' who just happened to come from Cumbria in England!

The message is clear. Only walk amongst the mountains if you are well prepared and equipped, always wearing comfortable boots, appropriately clothed (with additional warm clothing stowed away in your rucksack) and carrying robust waterproofs with you. Take more than adequate food and drink, and also carry a torch, whistle and survival bag just in case of unforeseen emergencies. The three absolute essentials are: detailed maps of the area, a reliable compass and a clear but flexible route plan in your head as to where you are going that day! Know how to use and adapt this formidable combination properly.

For most walking routes, probably the two most important items of outdoor clothing are boots and waterproofs. Fortunately, nowadays there are several excellent makes at competitive prices for both these indispensable items. For the record, I wear either Brasher or Wainwright mountain boots, rotating these when walking for a prolonged period on consecutive days, and Sprayway protective clothing. I am well satisfied with this combination, having tested them exhaustively in the conditions and extremes (excluding ice and heavy snows, which are rare in these parts) that walkers exploring the mountains of Ireland are most likely to experience.

Also, at appropriate times of the year and when necessary, take at least factor 12 sun cream, sun-glasses, protective headgear, insect repellent, isotonic drinks and the like. I carry a warm, woollen ski hat and mittens with me at all times, even during the hottest days of summer. I am always pleased when these items prove to be superfluous!

My wish is that, thus prepared and equipped, you enjoy each walk described in this book and many more besides to the full and that you always return safely, well pleased with your explorations into the mountains, uplifted and elated by what you have achieved and eager for more of the same. I shall be flattered if you will allow my thoughts and good wishes to go with you, all the way there and back. Good luck with whatever heights this book motivates you to reach.

TOM LAWTON

ACKNOWLEDGMENTS

Many people, most of these Irish, have contributed to this book. They have given generously of their time and expertise; I thank them all for this valuable input and wish to record my warm appreciation for the agreeable manner in which it was delivered.

In particular, the following individuals and organisations who specialise in arranging and guiding walking holidays and other outdoor activities in Ireland, together with a delightful hillfarmer from Beara, have shaped and helped determine the final collection of walks chosen. In addition, they have often located accommodation for my wife and I at places where the proprietors are particularly empathetic to the simple but extremely important needs of walkers; my grateful thanks for this are due, therefore, to (these names listed in the sequence they appear in the book) Christopher Stacey, Michael Desmond, Connie Doyle, all at Go Ireland and South West Walks Ireland Ltd, Christopher Browne, Shane Connolly and Gerry Greensmyth.

I believe the outcome of these generous contributions of invaluable local expertise and knowledge is 'our' book rather than 'my' book and, as a consequence, the only contents which I feel able to take full responsibility for are any unfortunate residual mistakes! These I do hope are minimal and are veiled in the mists of obscurity!

In addition, the following have either subsidised or reduced my expenditures on getting to Ireland and accommodating my family and I whilst there: Irish Ferries Ltd, Stena Line Ltd, Swansea Cork Ferries Ltd, Maura Byrne, Des and Liz, Seamus and Mary Wall, and Ann Black; Tommy and Kay Woods and Teresa Clery in conjunction with Go Ireland and Glencar House Hotel in conjunction with Countryside Tours; Robert Ashe, Kathleen and P J O'Connor, Kitty Brosnan, James and Carol Cullinan, Bríd Casey, Theresa McDonagh, Rose Rima, and Gerry and Bernie Greensmyth. My thanks are due to you all and, in particular, to Maura Byrne from Co Wicklow, Mary Wall in the Nire Valley and Rose Rima from Connemara who have been exceptionally kind and generous.

Several executives at Bord Fáilte and at various regional tourism organisations have taken an active, helpful interest in my endeavours, have pointed me in the right direction when this was needed and have opened doors which might otherwise have remained closed. These persons to whom I am indebted include Matt McNulty, Liam Campbell, Bill Morrison, Anne Melia and Ray O'Connor.

My thanks are due to Dr F Broadhurst for his expert contributions, including the 'Geological Perspective' contained in the introductory sections to each of the mountain groupings. Fred is an infectious enthusiast and his geology lectures at Manchester University were invariably full to overflowing, with his students, like volcanos, always on the point of 'erupting' in glowing appreciation of his perceptive disclosures.

My dear friend and walking companion for many years, Bill Rouse, has expertly produced the precision, computer-generated diagrams included in the book, and once again it is appropriate to record that whilst I am considered something of a perfectionist, Bill is much harder to please!

As with my several other books, Eddie Fidler and Bob Carter have checked the manuscript and proof stages of the book and I am indeed fortunate to have access to such thorough and professional auditing expertise. Many thanks also to my copy-editor, Finbarr O'Shea, for his meticulous and perceptive editing.

My final acknowledgments must be to my wife Bridget who happens to be of Irish parentage and to our two daughters Katrina and Helen who have accompanied me on many of the walks included in the book and who have allowed me to go off either alone or with others on this prolonged labour of love amongst the high places of Ireland. They have also graciously accepted the inevitable, subsequent long hours when I neglected them whilst I was closeted away recording these joyous walking experiences to share with others of similar inclination.

IRELAND
THE WALKING AREAS COVERED

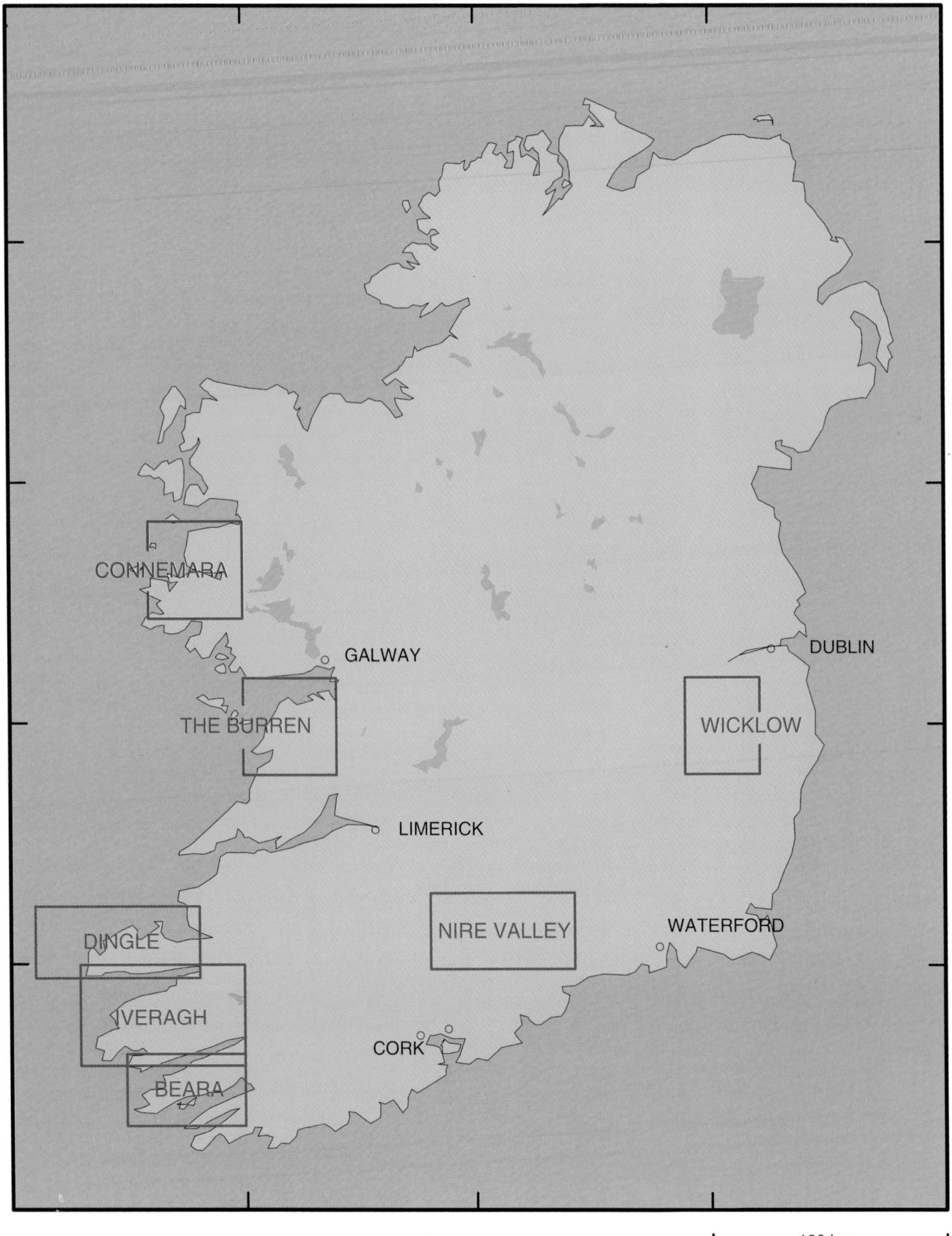

Using the Book

The main objective of the book is to provide a collection of interesting walking routes which comprehensively covers the varying landscapes of the mountains of Ireland stretching from Co Wicklow in the east to Connemara and Co Mayo in the west and looping through the southern part of the country *en route*. The walks are presented clearly and concisely with diagrams and photographs to provide an authoritative and appealing compilation of routes, some familiar and others relatively new. The text describes these walks in some detail and points out features of interest as these are first observed, given favourable weather, along the way.

Arrangement and Composition

In all, 25 walking routes spread over seven separate areas are covered, and these have been distributed across the mountainous terrain of Ireland as shown in the following table.

Walking Area	**Number of Walks**
The Wicklow Mountains	4
The Nire Valley and the surrounding Comeragh, Knockmealdown and Galty Mountains	4
The Mountains of the Beara Peninsula	3
The Mountains of the Iveragh Peninsula (Ring of Kerry)	4
The Mountains of the Dingle Peninsula	4
The Mountains of the Burren	2
The Mountains of Connemara and Mayo	4
Total	**25**

In selecting the walks, apart from the wide geological coverage, a balance has been struck between including 'firm favourites' and incorporating some less well-known routes in the hope of introducing some 'new friends'. The collection of walks also encompasses as wide a range as possible of routes of varying challenge, and this extends from walks which are graded as easy/straightforward to routes which are classified as difficult/strenuous. Most of the walks start from a conveniently located car park or lay-by, and details of the size of these and of other facilities available there, such as toilets, picnic areas and information centres, are also provided.

In total the 25 walking routes cover 285 km (177 miles), which is greater than the road distance from Dublin to Cork. The cumulative height climbed is approaching 16 500 m (over 53 500 ft), which is about twice the height of Mount Everest!

The range of pertinent features of the 25 walks is summarised in the following table.

Feature	From	To
Grading	Easy/straightforward	Difficult/strenuous
Walking time allowance – hours	$2\frac{1}{2}$	9
Distance		
– kilometres	3.9	21.8
– miles	2.4	13.5
Total height gained		
– metres	20	1140
– feet	70	3740
Principal height		
– metres	10	1039
– feet	35	3410

Introduction and General Information

At the start of each of the seven walking areas there is an introduction together with some pertinent information which should be helpful to both walkers and more general tourists alike. This is arranged under the subheadings of Getting There; Geological Perspective; Present-Day Landscapes and Opportunities for Walking; Choice of Walking Routes; Local Walking Guides; and Accommodation, Eating Out and Local Transport.

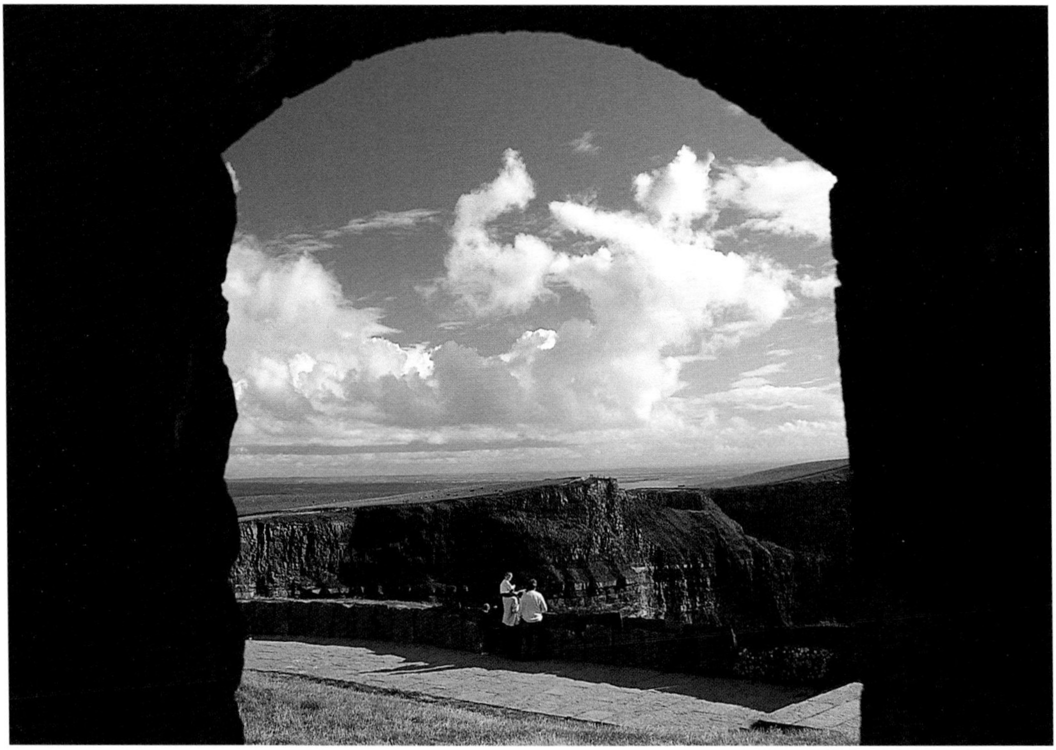

The Cliffs of Moher observed from O'Brien's Tower, Co Clare

The dramatic cliffs cupping Coomasaharn Lake, Co Kerry

Walking Routes

Each walking route commences with a concise 'Factfile' which, in easy-to-assimilate, tabular format, provides details of the walk's Start/Finish; Grading; Walking Time Allowance; Distance; Total Height Gained; and Principal Heights. All distances and heights are stated first in exact metric measurements, followed by their imperial equivalents which have been rounded off.

A 'Digest of Walk' follows, and this provides summary information and disclosures covering Parking; Overview/Interest; Gradients; Maps, Footpaths and Waysigns; and Getting Started.

A 'Summary Description of Walk' follows, and this provides detailed route instructions together with features of interest encountered along the way.

Grading

For obvious reasons there is no universally accepted definition of how walking routes should be graded. What is an exhilarating challenge to a fit, experienced walker who knows a particular walking area well and who undertakes a meticulously planned walk in that area in fine weather, is a totally different proposition from the same route undertaken by a casual walker who is not particularly fit and who sets out on a day when atrocious weather then closes in and the walker enters unfamiliar territory! There are also large variations in the hours of daylight, depending upon the time of year during which the walk is undertaken and the prevailing weather conditions.

However, there are a number of physical features of each walking route which, in total, are likely to determine the ease or difficulty of that walk and which, therefore, might be sensibly summarised into an overall grading indicator that will provide most walkers with a helpful benchmark as to what they may expect to encounter along the way. The physical factors of each walking route which have been given consideration in determining the three selected gradings for the purposes of this guide are:

- length
- total height gained
- steepness and difficulty of slopes, both up and down
- spacing of these gradients
- whether some elementary scrambling is necessary
- overall roughness of terrain
- drainage and the extent of waterlogged areas
- the crossing of peat hags
- the degree of exposure to the elements
- the extent and state of footpaths
- the extent and quality of signposting, waymarkers, cairns etc.

A qualitative judgment has been made of each of these factors, and based on this assessment each walk has been allocated to one of the three following categories. These are based more on relative than on absolute values.

- **Easy/straightforward** (colour-coded GREEN). Distance usually below about 12 km (8 miles). No sustained long or severe slopes. Climbing well spaced out. No dangerous exposure or difficult terrain of any consequence. Minimum waterlogged ground and no difficult peat hags. Route finding presents few problems and the way is either adequately signed or fairly obvious. Route frequently suitable for family groups, with often plenty of general interest in addition to the surrounding views and landscapes.
- **Moderate** (colour-coded BLUE). Walk eminently suitable for all reasonably fit walkers who wish to follow a route which could occupy up to a full day. A combination of some features which are more exacting than those on which the previous category is based, such as perhaps some fairly demanding climbing, together with a longer route, sections of which are not as clearly defined as might be expected. A category midway between the extremes of easy/straightforward and difficult/strenuous.
- **Difficult/strenuous** (colour-coded RED). Route includes a combination of features which in total make the walk a challenging one, even for experienced and fit participants. These walks either will be relatively long or will contain steep gradients, or even both. Sections of the terrain covered will quite often be rough, waterlogged, treacherous, and/or exposed. Paths will not exist in many places and route signing will often be incomplete.

Routes which straddle two categories have been appropriately bracketed. Additionally, the allocated category may be either downgraded or upgraded by selecting one of the suggested escape or extension variants provided at the end of the route description.

Diagrams

There is a diagram for each route giving a plan and a cross-sectional relief of the walk. These diagrams have been computer generated and are based upon grid reference points downloaded from Ordnance Survey of Ireland maps, the Discovery Series 1:50 000 — 2 cm to 1 km ($1\frac{1}{4}$ inches to 1 mile).

The relief cross-section is based upon the contour lines provided on the Ordnance Survey maps. This relief commences from the starting location and accurately follows the exact line of the route.

Camera symbols locate the position and direction of take of each photograph. These have been allocated a distinctive number identical to that referenced beneath each photograph as part of its caption. The first part of the number indicates the route, whilst the second part refers to the sequence of the photographs within each route. Photographs taken along the route are indicated by the camera symbol pointing either along or away from the line of the walk, whereas photographs taken of the route from other locations are identified by the camera symbol pointing inwards from outside of the plan.

The panoramic view northwards towards the Mweelrea Mountains observed from the rugged slopes above Gleninagh, Co Galway

Walking Time Allowance

Estimates of walking time have been provided, and these include allowances for all stops including lunch. The estimates have been calculated by allowing a generous 1 hour to walk each 2 miles, plus a further 1 hour for each 2000 ft climbed, plus 1 hour for lunch and all other stops *en route*, and a final adjustment of up to ± ½ hour per walk, depending upon additional factors, such as difficulty of route finding, state of the paths and type of terrain. You can adjust these estimates to suit your own walking speeds and preferences.

Photographs

On average each walk is illustrated by two colour photographs. These photographs are keyed in to the route, making them additional aids to route finding. The photographs have been taken throughout the seasons and a balance has been struck between photographs depicting walkers and their accoutrements and those showing landscapes and other features of interest.

The photographs have been taken with a Canon EOS 650 camera using a standard 50 mm lens and a 35–135 mm zoom lens, in each case with polarising filters. Fujichrome, Sensia 100 colour slide film has been used exclusively.

Abbreviations

Abbreviations are used sparingly in the book, and then only to avoid constant repetition. These are listed below, and include the familiar directional signals, compass bearings and measurements.

Abbreviations		**Abbreviations**	
L	left	cm	centimetre(s)
R	right	ft	foot/feet
N	north	hrs	hours
NNE	north-north-east	km	kilometre(s)
NE	north-east	m	metre(s)
ENE	east-north-east	mm	millimetre(s)
E	east	sq	square
ESE	east-south-east	MR	map reference
SE	south-east	OS	Ordnance Survey
SSE	south-south-east	YH	youth hostel
S	south		
SSW	south-south-west		
SW	south-west		
WSW	west-south-west		
W	west		
WNW	west-north-west		
NW	north-west		
NNW	north-north-west		

Looking down on Lough Dan from the heights of Knocknacloghoge, Co Wicklow

Geological and Associated Terms

The following list explains geological and associated terms which are used in the book or may be encountered.

anticline upfold of rocks

arête sharp-crested, serrated or knife-edged ridge separating the heads of abutting valleys that previously contained glaciers

bog (blanket) accumulation of plant material (sphagnum, grasses, sedges, trees) across poorly drained areas where decomposition of organic matter is slow; the surface of the bog may be fairly level or undulating

bog (raised) accumulation of plant material (sphagnum, grasses, sedges, trees) across poorly drained areas where decomposition of organic matter is slow; the surface of the bog is arched upwards towards its central region

cavern large natural space or chamber underground

clay sediment particle with a diameter less than 0.004 mm; also the name of a group of minerals

clint limestone block usually less than a square metre in area, enclosed by fissures (grykes)

coal combustible, organic, black sedimentary rock produced by very deep burial of peat

col	sharp-edged or saddle-shaped pass
combe	an elevated, steep-walled, semi-circular basin or indentation associated with the erosive activity of a mountain glacier
country rock	a general term for the older rock containing an igneous intrusion, also called 'host rock'; country rock may be sedimentary, metamorphic or older igneous rock
crinoid	echinoderm, commonly called the 'sea-lily'; their fossilised stem plates form crinoidal limestone
dale	valley
dolomite	rocks, and the mineral, with the composition calcium magnesium carbonate
drumlin	mound of debris formed at the base of a moving glacier
edge	steep cliff
erratic	pebble or boulder composed of a rock type different from that of the immediate surroundings; usually associated with deposits formed by the action of ice during the Pleistocene (Great) Ice Age, when rocks were carried large distances from their source
fault	fracture in rocks the opposite sides of which have been displaced relative to one another, vertically or horizontally
fjord	flooded glaciated valley
glacier	river of ice draining the region of permanent snow cover
glen	valley
gorge	deep, narrow, steep-walled valley
granite	white, grey or pink rock with conspicuous large mineral grains, formed by cooling of a large molten mass at great depth below the surface
grit	coarse-grained, sandy sediment; ill defined
gryke	deep fissure in limestone separating the rock into blocks or clints
hag/grough	natural channel or fissure in a peat moor; a deep drainage ditch in a peat bog
hause	summit of narrow pass, col
heath	large, open area with scrubby vegetation, usually comprising heathers
Hercynian (fold system)	belt of deformed (folded and faulted) rocks extending from Ireland to England through France and into Germany (this deformation is believed to be related to the closure of an ocean between the African and European plates)
karstic	limestone topography containing clints, grykes and sinkholes
knoll	small, rounded hill
limestone	sedimentary rock composed almost entirely of calcium carbonate, mainly as calcite
lough	lake or arm of the sea
moraine	accumulation of rock material that has been carried or deposited by a glacier
Namurian	the bottom series of the Silesian (Carboniferous)
nunatak	isolated peak of bedrock that protrudes above a glacier or icecap
peak	topmost point of a mountain; less commonly of a hill

peat	compacted remains of vegetation which has accumulated under wet conditions where organic decomposition is slow
pike	pointed summit
Pleistocene	the lower division of the Quaternary, the most recent period of geological time
quartz	mineral with the composition silicon dioxide (silica); quartz is hard and resistant to most chemical weathering
quartzite	rock composed mainly of the mineral quartz
ria	flooded river valley
sandstone	sedimentary rock of sand and/or silt bound together by a cement, often calcite or silica; quartz grains predominate in the average sandstone
scree	loose, shattered rock on mountain slope
shale	fine-grained sedimentary rock formed dominantly of compacted clay
Silesian	the upper subsystem of the European Carboniferous
Silurian	division of geological time extending from 440 to 410 million years ago; the sedimentary rocks laid down in this period are mainly marine and include shales, muddy sandstones and limestones
sinkhole	area, especially in limestone, where a surface stream sinks underground
sphagnum moss	accumulation of sphagnum material in poorly drained areas where decomposition of organic matter is slow
stalactite	conical mineral deposits, usually calcite, which hang from the roof of limestone caves or caverns
stalagmite	water dripping onto a limestone cave floor builds stalagmites, which are usually blunter than stalactites
summit	topmost point of a mountain; less commonly of a hill
syncline	downfold of rocks
tarn	small lake often occupying a concave floor gouged out by rock debris contained in a retreating glacier
tor	core of unweathered, harder rock standing above a surrounding area of weathered rock
tower	tall, squarish structure of unweathered rock, usually located on or near the steep slopes of rocky gorges
turf	covering of grasses and associated material
well	spring or stream

Maps

No guidebook is an adequate substitute for maps and a compass but should be used in conjunction with these. Use the Ordnance Survey of Ireland Discovery Series maps, scale 1:50 000, previously referred to and a reliable compass at all times when you are walking in these mountains. Be sure that you know how to use this combination correctly. The full complement of Discovery Series maps needed to cover all the walks listed in this book are

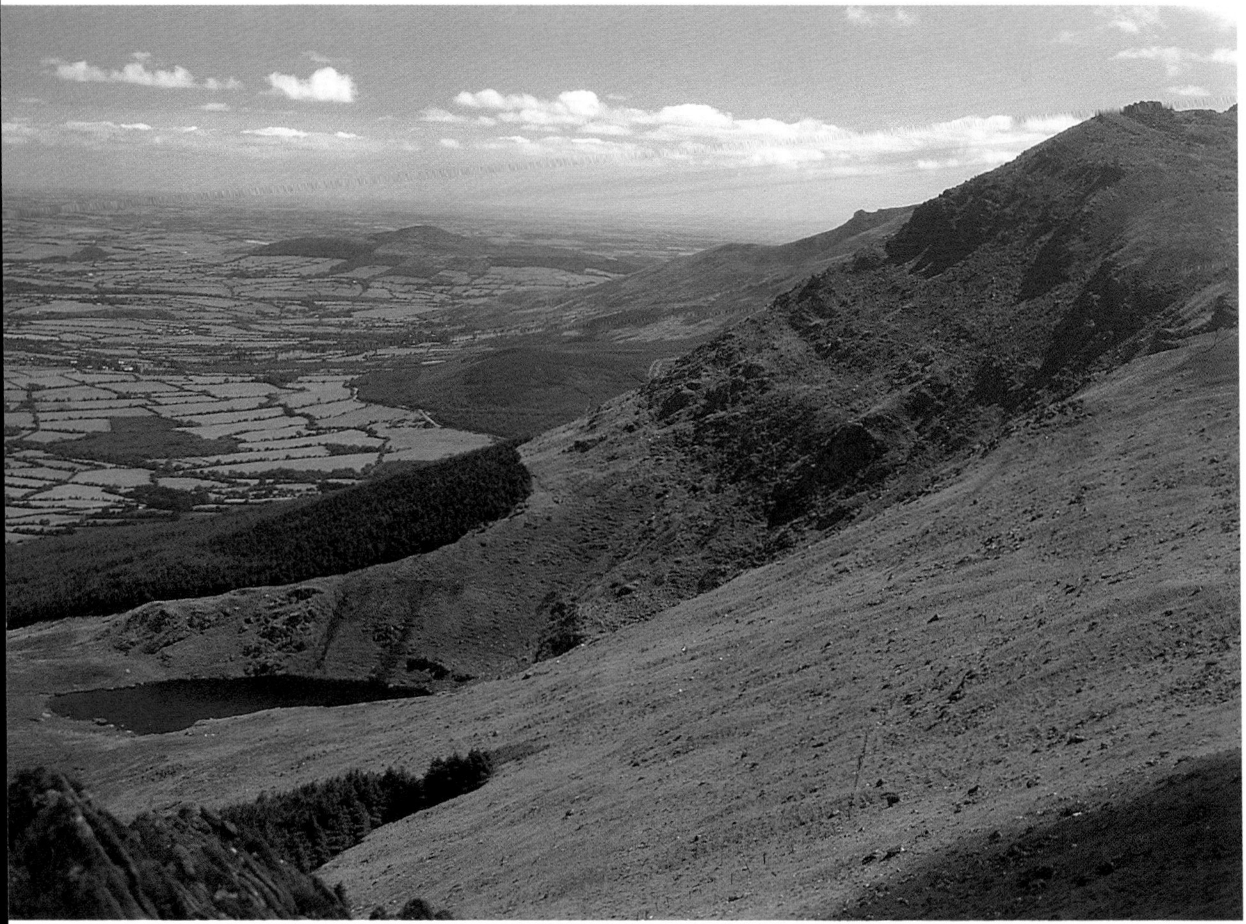

CONTRASTING HIGH AND LOW GROUND OBSERVED FROM THE KNOCKANAFFRIN RIDGE, CO WATERFORD

Numbers 37, 44, 51, 56, 70, 71, 74, 75, 78, 83 and 84. In addition, there are two larger scale maps, 1:25 000, of the MacGillycuddy's Reeks and the Killarney National Park which it is recommended are also used.

The Ordnance Survey maps are excellent but not infallible! On the rare occasions where there are differences between the route descriptions in this book and the paths shown, or not shown, as the case may be, on the OS Discovery Series maps, rely on the route descriptions!

Additionally, the Ordnance Survey produces four holiday maps, scale 1:250 000, which disclose in broader bands than the Discovery Series maps the relief of the countryside. These are ideal for completing the motoring journeys between the various mountain areas, and for this purpose you will require Numbers 2, 3 and 4.

Compass Bearings

All compass bearings have been given to the nearest $22\frac{1}{2}$ degree point, for example N, NNE, NE. This is considered to be sufficiently accurate over the relatively small distances travelled between the taking of successive readings. Get into the habit of taking frequent compass bearings, particularly when visibility is poor or you are not sure of your exact position.

Human Constructions

The human-constructed features of the Irish countryside are constantly changing: fences appear and disappear, gates replace stiles and vice versa, additional waymarker signs appear, some signs get removed and so on. Therefore, should you come across isolated differences between the route and what is described here, presume that these have occurred since the book went to press and proceed with confidence to the next certain feature described.

Recorded Heights of Mountains

The heights of the major mountains are given in both metric and imperial measurements. The metric heights have been extracted from the relevant Ordnance Survey Discovery Series maps. The imperial equivalents have been calculated from these using a conversion factor of 0.3048 m equals 1 ft. These equivalents have then been rounded off to the nearest 5 ft.

Spelling of Place-names

Often there is more than one version of the spelling of place-names. In such instances the spelling which appears on the Ordnance Survey Discovery Series maps is used, unless otherwise indicated.

Getting Started and Suggested Itineraries

Following the descriptions of the 25 walking routes, advice is given on getting started and suggested itineraries are provided for undertaking walking holidays in that part of Ireland covered by the book.

Overleaf: The Lower Lake, Glendalough

Wicklow Mountains Walks

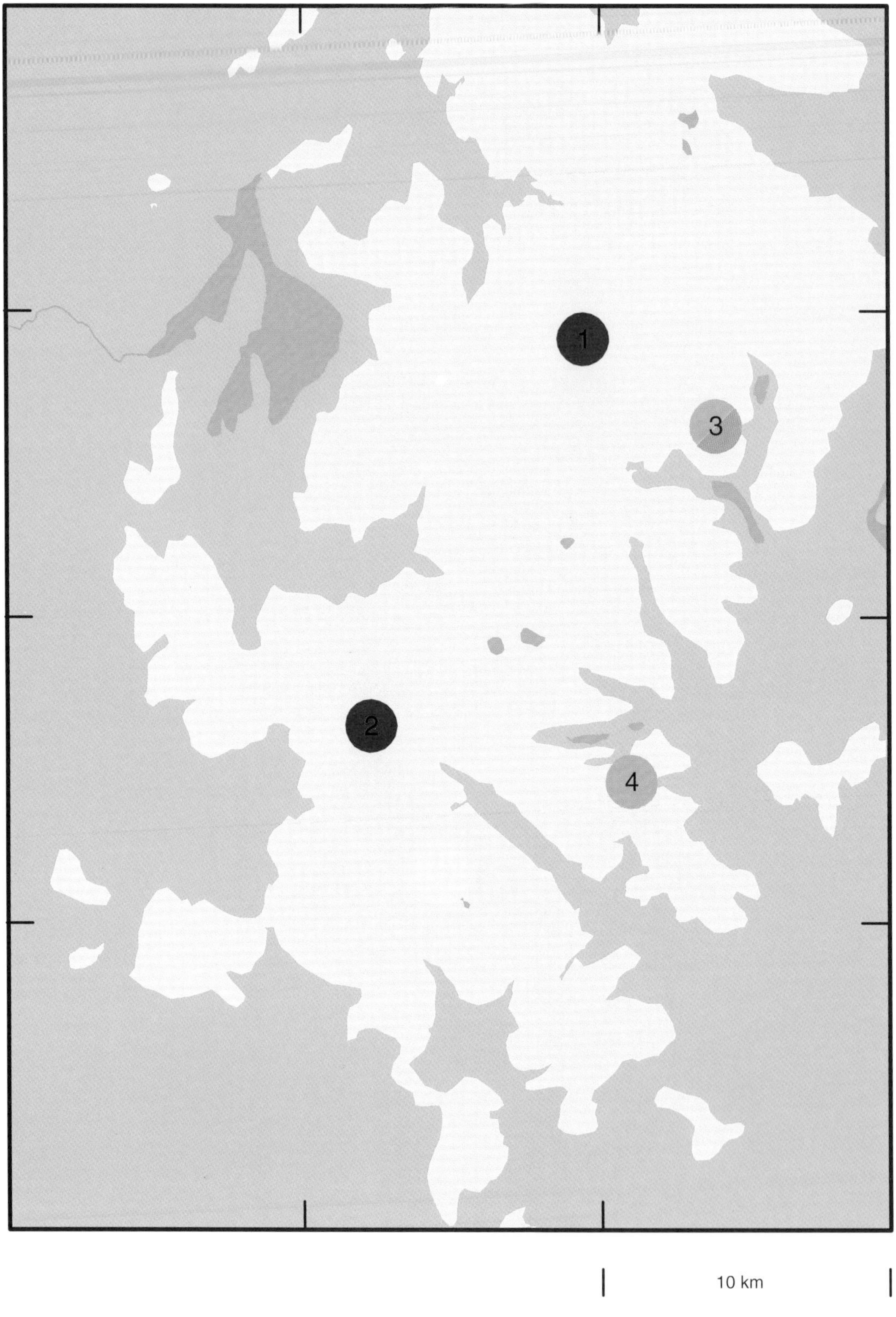
1
2
3
4
10 km

The Wicklow Mountains

Getting There

The Wicklow Mountains are located a short distance to the S of Dublin and the most popular destinations in and around this upthrust crust of granite are within 1 to 1½ hours' drive from the city. However, even Dubliners will admit that their fair city is not one of the best-signposted capitals of the world and, therefore, getting away from the city centre and travelling through the sprawling suburbia does merit some careful advance planning!

Most visitors from abroad who are not familiar with Dublin are advised to travel down either the W or the E flank of the Wicklow Mountains, this choice depending on the place of arrival, and then use the R759 road via Sally Gap or the R756 road over the Wicklow Gap to cross through the mountains should this prove necessary. The three more usual entry points for overseas visitors are Dublin Airport, Dublin Port and Dún Laoghaire Port. Should you arrive at either the airport or Dublin Port, make a beeline for the M50 motorway which arcs around the city to the W and then travel along this to its southern terminus. Turn R here onto the N81 road and this will take you down the western side of the mountains towards Blessington. Should you arrive at Dún Laoghaire, travel down the eastern side of the mountains, initially motoring S along the major N11/M11 highway and then branching off right up the R755 road towards Roundwood.

Geological Perspective

The Wicklow Mountains are composed of the so-called Leinster Granite which is tough and more resistant to erosion than most of the surrounding rocks. This granite was formed approximately 400 million years ago as a mass of molten rock which accumulated several kilometres below the surface. This molten mass cooled slowly, the heat loss causing much alteration to the surrounding rocks. Mineral deposits such as lead and zinc ores were also formed and these have since been mined in the Wicklow Glens.

Subsequent uplift of the region has brought about erosion which has exposed the granite in the rock outcrops visible today. In places, remnants of the original surrounding country rocks may be seen on the surface of the granite, as in the summit area of Lugnaquillia, the highest point in these mountains. Some of the altered rocks have also proved resistant to erosion and these are evidenced in the deep gorges of the Slaney River near Tinahely and Shillelagh in the S of the area.

During the Great Ice Age, commencing about two million years ago and ending about 10 000 years ago, the Wicklow Mountains like most northern parts of Britain and Ireland experienced phases of glaciation. The impressive glacial corries of Lugnaquillia and Kippure were formed during this period. Additionally, the straight, U-shaped valleys of the Wicklow Glens, for instance Glendalough, Glendasan, Glenmacnass and Glenmalure, result from erosion by valley glaciers, whilst many of the lakes such as Lough Dan and Lough Tay also owe their origin to the action of glaciers, this by overdeepening the valley floors or by depositing material to form dams.

Present-Day Landscapes and Opportunities for Walking

The Wicklow Mountains are the largest land mass rising to above 2000 ft in the whole of Ireland. The highest mountain is Lugnaquillia towards the S of the area; this commands a height of 925 m (3035 ft) and is one of only 12 peaks in Ireland soaring to above the 3000 ft mark. The mountains occupy a compact rectangle which extends for about 1200 sq km (nearly 500 sq miles), this being broadly referenced to Naas in the NW and Avoca in the SE.

The main spurs and the highest ground, again based on meaningful simplifications, run diagonally NE to SW from Kippure and Djouce Mountain to mighty Lugnaquillia. This is wild, undulating, upthrust country composed of a range of impressive peaks linked together with long, high-level ridges which form the broad shoulders of many of the interlocking mountains. The ground covering hereabouts is a mixture of rocky granite outcrops and acid moorlands which stretch for miles around. Heathers and bilberry cover vast areas of land but these are riddled with boggy ground where channels and hags have been cut deep into the covering of peat, and these features present formidable challenges even to the fittest and most experienced of hillwalkers.

This high ground falls fairly uniformly to the W, where the gentler, lower terrain includes rounded hillsides, some of which are covered with coniferous forest plantations. Wide, sheltered valleys and the large and attractively located Pollaphuca Reservoir complex near Blessington, which has become a major tourist attraction, also feature. These hills and valleys offer extensive and relatively easy walking opportunities and this countryside is popular with more casual walkers and with family groups, as is motoring around and picnicking beside the reservoir.

By contrast, the eastern flanks of the mountains are punctuated by a number of steep-sided, glaciated valleys of which Glendalough, with its famed archaeology and association with St Kevin, is world famous. This magnificent countryside, with its corrie lakes, gushing streams, flat valley floors, spectacular cliff faces and forested hillsides, is a walker's paradise which offers a tremendous variety of routes ranging from short, sheltered strolls along the valley bottoms beside lakes and streams to standing on the tops of impressive mountain peaks marvelling at the scenery above, around and below.

All in all, the Wicklow Mountains offer something for everybody who enjoys exploring the great outdoors with boots and camera, be this those who are content with a leisurely saunter on the flat or dedicated hillwalkers who enjoy energetic climbs to over 3000 ft.

Choice of Walking Routes

Whilst in Ireland I had the pleasure of attending one of the Wicklow Walking Festivals which featured, amongst other offerings, a strenuous, two-day, linear walk from Sally Gap, via the Wicklow Gap, over Lugnaquillia and then down into the Glen of Imail. This route traverses most of the high-level spine of the Wicklow Mountains; it was a superb choice made by those who know best, and it is presented here as Walks 1 and 2. The other two routes are less demanding. Walks 3 and 4 explore two of the glaciated valleys on the eastern side of the mountains, ascending to modestly sized peaks where the surrounding countryside may be observed and appreciated from strategically located vantage points. In total the four walks will provide an introduction to exploring these formidable but friendly mountains which have so much to offer all well-equipped walkers who venture with care into their seductive embraces.

LOCAL WALKING GUIDES

The author has had the good fortune to explore extensively these mountains with Christopher Stacey, a forester by trade and a member of the local mountain rescue team. Christopher operates a professional guiding service and arranges walking holidays under the banner 'Footfalls'. This congenial forester knows every nook and cranny of these mountains; he is widely experienced in mountaincraft and has a wide, in-depth knowledge of and enthusiasm for the geology, flora, fauna, archaeology and folklore of the area. Most importantly, he knows how best to apply this extensive know-how for the benefit, interest, comfort and safety of all those in his care. Moreover, Christopher is great fun to walk with and all those who do this will return from each day's walk fulfilled, happy and exhilarated, and contentedly exhausted just up to the point that they wish to be. Then there are the evenings, for which you will need a completely different combination of stamina!

CONTACT DETAILS
Christopher Stacey
'Footfalls'
Trooperstown
Roundwood
Co Wicklow
Tel/Fax: 0404 45152
Email: cstacey@iol.ie

ACCOMMODATION, EATING OUT AND LOCAL TRANSPORT

ACCOMMODATION

The village of Laragh is probably one of the best and most central venues for staying in or around and using as a base for walking amongst the Wicklow Mountains. Other excellent places for doing this are in the Blessington, Valleymount, Hollywood and Donard area to the W of the mountains, in and near to Roundwood in the E, and Rathdrum and along the Vale of Avoca to the SE.

My family and I have stayed at superior guest houses located at Valleymount and at Laragh. Maura Byrne, who is also involved with the organisation of one of the Wicklow Walking Festivals, kindly looked after all our needs at her splendid Escombe Country Home at

Valleymount, whilst Liz and Des pampered us at their spacious and select Tudor Lodge at Laragh. At both of these places it is guaranteed walkers will receive a warm and friendly welcome, will enjoy peace and quiet in the most comfortable, tranquil surroundings, will sleep soundly, will tuck into hearty breakfasts and almost certainly will come back for a second helping and more besides on some future occasions.

These guest houses, together with a selection of other accommodation establishments which have been recommended to the author and which have a special empathy towards the needs of walkers, are listed in the table below.

ACCOMMODATION REGISTER

Hotel/Guest House	**Rooms en suite**	**Rooms other**	**Charge B&B**	**Open**	**Visited by Author**
Maura Byrne Escombe Country Home Lockstown Valleymount Glendalough Road Co Wicklow Tel: 045 867157 Fax: 045 867450	F 4 D 1 T 1 S 0	F 0 D 0 T 0 S 0	£18	All year	Yes
Des and Liz Tudor Lodge Laragh Glendalough Co Wicklow Tel/Fax: 0404 45554	F 3 D 4 T 1 S 2	F 0 D 0 T 0 S 0	£18–20	All year	Yes
Pat and Ann Dowling Glenmalure Lodge Glenmalure Rathdrum Co Wicklow Tel/Fax: 0404 46188	F 0 D 2 T 7 S 0	F 2 D 0 T 0 S 1	£17	All year	Yes
Mary Byrne Ballyknocken House Glenealy Ashford Co Wicklow Tel: 0404 44614/44627	F 1 D 2 T 4 S 1	F 0 D 0 T 0 S 0	£ 18	March to Nov	No
Caroline and Tony Buch Old Farm House Greenane Rathdrum Co Wicklow Tel/Fax: 0404 46676	F 0 D 2 T 1 S 0	F 2 D 1 T 1 S 3	£13–20	Feb to Nov	Yes

Hotel/Guest House	Rooms en suite	Rooms other	Charge B&B	Open	Visited by Author
Regene Clarke Forest Lodge Lacken Co Wicklow Tel: 045 865565	F 0 D 2 T 0 S 0	F 0 D 1 T 0 S 0	£17.50	All year	No
Annette and Patrick Fanning Tochar House Bar/Lounge Roundwood Co Wicklow Tel: 01 2818247	F 1 D 3 T 1 S 0	F 0 D 0 T 0 S 0	£18	All year	No

Rooms: F = Family; D = Double; T = Twin; S = Single

EATING OUT

There are plenty of good, value-for-money eating places dotted in and around the Wicklow Mountains. Those we have tried and enjoyed include Tulfarris House Hotel and Country Club overlooking Pollaphuca Reservoir (Tel: 045 864574), Wicklow Heather Restaurant at Laragh (Tel: 0404 45157), The Coach House at Roundwood (Tel: 01 2818157) and Glenmalure Lodge near Rathdrum (Tel: 0404 46188).

The elegant, up-market Tulfarris serves substantial bar meals, the spacious Wicklow Heather Restaurant has a wide menu of delicious dishes to choose from and in particular the set Sunday dinner is exceptionally good value, whilst the huge, tender steak and mountains of chips served at the charming Glenmalure Lodge will keep even the hungriest of walkers contentedly well fed for several hours to come after they have descended into this remote and sublime valley.

LOCAL TRANSPORT

Unless you have the luxury of belonging to a two-vehicle walking group, you will almost certainly need supporting transport for Walks 1 and 2 which are linear routes starting and finishing at different places. Reliable taxi and minibus services are operated throughout the Wicklow Mountains by Maurice O'Sullivan, Blessington (Tel: 045 865114) and William McCoy, Laragh (Tel: 0404 45475).

Sally Gap to Wicklow Gap

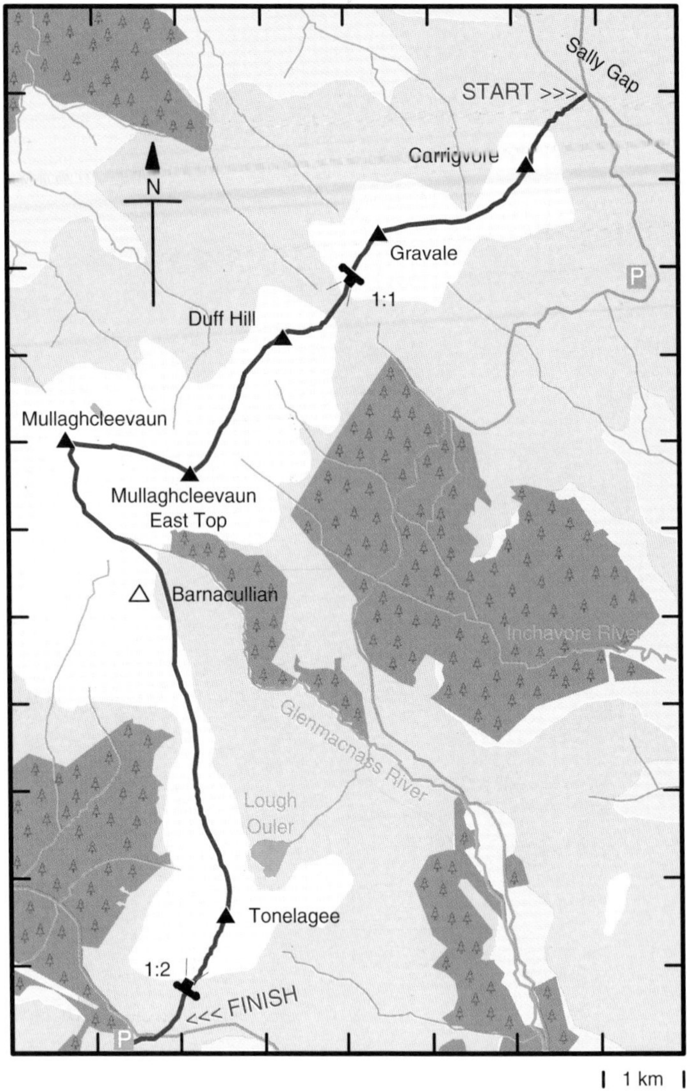

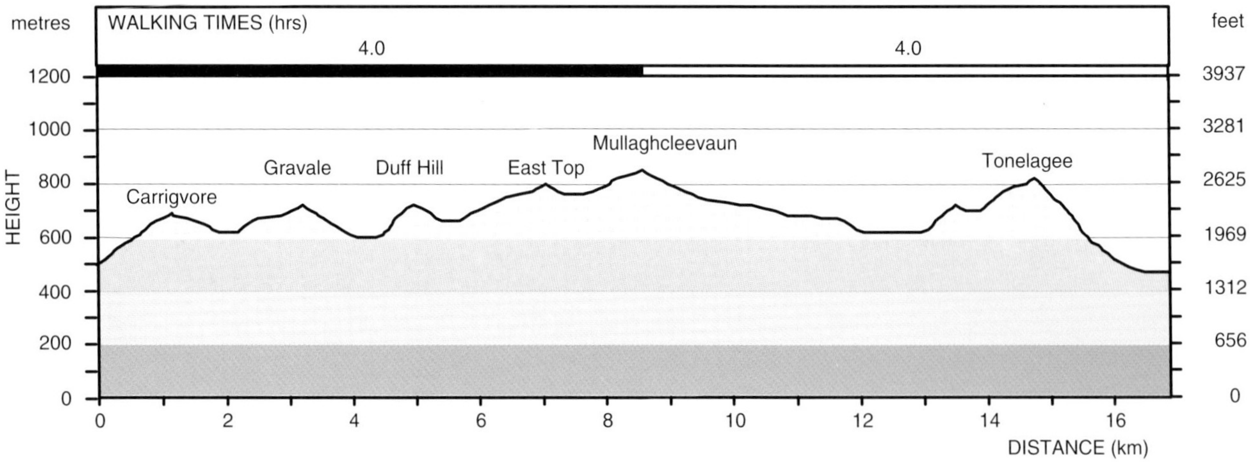

TRAVERSE OF THE WICKLOW MOUNTAINS

PART 1

SALLY GAP TO WICKLOW GAP

fact file

START/FINISH

Start at Sally Gap — MR 130110

Finish at Wicklow Gap — MR 076002

GRADING

Difficult/strenuous (colour-coded RED)

WALKING TIME ALLOWANCE

8 hours

DISTANCE

16.8 km (10.5 miles)

TOTAL HEIGHT GAINED

860 m (2820 ft)

PRINCIPAL HEIGHTS

• Carrigvore	682 m (2240 ft)
• Gravale	718 m (2355 ft)
• Duff Hill	720 m (2360 ft)
• Mullaghcleevaun East Top	795 m (2610 ft)
• Mullaghcleevaun	849 m (2785 ft)
• Tonelagee	817 m (2680 ft)

digest of walk

PARKING

Scattered parking along verges at or near to Sally Gap with room for one or two cars in each of several separate places. (Note: This is a linear walk and, therefore, ideally two vehicles should be used, the second one positioned in one of the two large car parks at the Wicklow Gap. Otherwise, arrange transport to collect you from the end of the walk at your estimated time of arrival there.)

OVERVIEW/INTEREST

- A high-level, switchback route over difficult, peaty terrain.
- Series of challenging ups and downs over heathers and through bogs, including some of the oldest blanket bogland in Europe, dating back 10 000 years.
- Several mountain tops are scaled, these located along a winding ridge amongst magnificent, vast, undulating landscapes.
- Superb, panoramic views during the entire walk in favourable weather.
- Route will appeal most to strong, sturdy walkers who enjoy a demanding day traversing wild and remote mountainous countryside.

GRADIENTS

The route is a series of ups and downs with virtually no flat sections! The slopes are fairly rounded and, therefore, the gradients are not too severe; however, with difficult terrain to cross for most of the way, the going is formidable, so pace yourself accordingly, particularly when gaining height.

MAPS, FOOTPATHS AND WAYSIGNS

OS Discovery Series 1:50 000 — Number 56 (Wicklow, Dublin and Kildare)

Footpaths are a mixture varying from non-existent for lengthy sections to reasonably well defined in a few places where they appear to be moderately well trod. In between these extremes there are a variety of narrow tracks and intermittent paths; these are of varying length and assistance, as several of them, no sooner located, deviate from your intended direction of travel a short distance further on! For the most part the route is uncharted, across exposed, peaty uplands which contain numerous deep hags oozing wet, clinging slurries.

There are no signs, but helpful guiding cairns, additional to those marking the key summits, appear sporadically.

GETTING STARTED

Sally Gap may be reached by particularly scenic minor roads from several compass points. A former military road (R115) passes through the gap, winding roughly N to S and linking the southern outskirts of Dublin with Laragh to the S, whilst the R759 tracks NW to SE connecting the N81 and the area around Blessington with the R755 to the E in the vicinity of Roundwood. These two approach roads intersect at Sally Gap.

From Sally Gap walk southwards along the R115 road and at some convenient and encouraging point turn off this to your R, to commence climbing through the clinging, open heathland on a SSW bearing until you come to a narrow path ahead. Veer L along this welcome, clearly defined way and continue SW.

Summary Description of Walk

THE WAY TO MULLAGHCLEEVAUN — MR 068071 (Allow 4 hours)

The walk starts amidst vast, expansive, wild countryside stretching for miles in all directions. The rounded summit of Kippure (Cipiúr) rises serenely to the NNW, its location confirmed by a major communications aerial which does not enhance its already perfect profile. Long

1:1 Participants in the Wicklow Walking Festival crossing the high ground between Sally Gap and Tonelagee

ridges appear on the skyline to the ESE rising to the peak of Djouce Mountain (Dioghais). These landscapes are of high, undulating, largely heather-covered slopes with few distinctive rock features. These views remain with you as you progressively gain height, continuing SW, until you reach the summit of Carrigvore at 682 m (2240 ft). This mountain top is characterised by a scattering of weathered, rectangular-shaped boulders and some of these are quite large. From this elevated vantage point new vistas open up to the SW and these include your next objectives, the successive peaks of Gravale, Duff Hill (An Cnoc Dubh) and Mullaghcleevaun (Mullach Cliabháin). The isolated, symmetrically rounded shape in the far distance to the WNW is Sorrel Hill.

The route continues to the SW veering WSW and descending gently across vast, uncharted, peaty slopes which contain plenty of deep hags that will progressively sap your energy levels. In places, an intermittent path reappears, and further on a broad, shallow hause has to be crossed where it can be particularly wet and soggy traversing its wide, flat basin. Look ahead to your L as you descend and cross the level ground to sight, in favourable weather conditions, the vast slopes of Tonelagee (Tóin le Gaoith) rearing up to the SSW. This is the final summit on your itinerary. Climb to the W from the saddle up bilberry- and heather-covered slopes, making good use of a peaty path which weaves along a shallow, sheltered furrow for part of the way. More peat hags have to be crossed higher up, where you will do well if you manage to escape sinking up to your knees in the more difficult, oozy places, before the temporary respite of the summit rocks of Gravale are reached!

The top of Gravale, located at 718 m (2355 ft), is composed of large, rocky outcrops of granite. The views from here add little new to what has been observed previously, that is unless bad weather has obscured these and suddenly this clears. A gradual descent follows over more rough, peaty ground interspersed with easier rocky sections as the way drops to the SW to cross another shallow hause. Towards the bottom of this downhill slope, bear first L to track further SW towards and then up more hag-laden slopes ahead, looping up these by curving back to the R. This climb is not too demanding, particularly if you locate and follow a narrow, indistinct path which conveniently zigzags upwards in your direction of travel. During this ascent when visibility is good, part of Lough Dan (Loch Deán) may be seen to the SE, down to your L. Head more to the W as the steepish gradient levels off, and then over the next brow ahead the welcome sight of the rounded summit area of Duff Hill appears. This high spot stands at 720 m (2360 ft) and is marked by a substantial cairn positioned within another scattering of rocks.

From the cairn, head SW towards your next objective, Mullaghcleevaun East Top. This involves negotiating another lofty cleavage between seductively rounded mountain tops, walking across fairly rough terrain which again is laced with peat hags. A long, gradual climb

1:2 Time for a pause amongst the heathers during the descent from Tonelagee

follows, but the going underfoot does become easier higher up as rockier ground is penetrated and the gradient simultaneously slackens off. Another assortment of large boulders is then reached, and these together with a cairn signify that you have reached the flattish summit area of Mullaghcleevaun East Top. This commands an elevation of 795 m (2610 ft), with views similar to those previously seen.

Veer R at the cairn on East Top and walk westwards towards the higher, more prominent peak of Mullaghcleevaun, heading initially downhill across relatively walker-friendly terrain. This is a mixture of rocks separated by short grasses. However, more familiar peaty ground with its usual characteristics is soon once again encountered as the terrain flattens out into yet another broad hause. Another uphill section follows, and you will have to do some weaving about whilst climbing up this in order to avoid the worst of the hags, achieving this by hugging the grassy shoulder of the mountainside. The final part of the ascent is quite easy up a gently sloping, massive escarpment, as you head W across ground covered with a mixture of grasses and lichen. There is a combined trigonometrical point and cairn on the top of Mullaghcleevaun, which at 849 m (2785 ft) is the highest point of the entire walk. A short distance from these features is a plaque inscribed with a poignant, permanent memory to three Wicklow hikers — Peter Purfield, Joseph O'Gorman and Mathew Porter — who drowned at Clogher Head, Co Louth, in 1945. Extensive new vistas to the S are revealed from here. These contain a more detailed sighting of Tonelagee and many peaks further away, including to the SSW that of Lugnaquillia Mountain (Log na Coille), the highest mountain in Co Wicklow.

THE WAY TO WICKLOW GAP — MR 076002 (Allow 4 hours)

The next part of the navigation demands some extra care, for it is best to avoid crossing the summit of Barnacullian with its treacherous mounds of peat in which unwary walkers could quickly become ensnared! To do this turn L at the summit of Mullaghcleevaun to head initially S and then be vigilant to locate and follow a grassy gully, which additionally provides protection from any wind. A stream meanders along this channel, perpetually eroding a deeper V-nick in the grove, and you will have to hop across this infant watercourse, the source of the Glenmacnass River, on numerous occasions during your gradual descent which changes course to veer SE.

The channel and stream eventually reach a steeper fall-away located at MR 076058. At this point cross over the rivulet once again and then bear R away from the watercourse to locate and use a stile in a wire fence ahead. From here, continue southwards along the edge of the higher ground, maintaining a fairly constant height and passing over the tips of massive mounds of peat to your R, these morasses spilling down from the upper slopes of Barnacullian which you have now successfully outflanked. A longish traverse then follows, heading S towards the final climb of the day, the ascent of Tonelagee. The scar ripping into the hillside to your L and to the SE as you head for Tonelagee widens lower down to form a long, wooded valley which extends all the way to Laragh.

The ensuing, gentle descent leads to yet another massive, wide hause with plenty more peat-filled hollows to test your resolve as more exacting terrain has again to be crossed. Fortunately, easier ground lies ahead as a distinct path leading your way becomes established. This peaty path then climbs up a moderate slope covered with grass and heather, and as you trek uphill once more you should be able to reposition Djouce Mountain, this the highest peak on the horizon to the NE. Once more the severeness of the upward slope eases as you approach the top and another assortment of granite outcrops marks this next peak, the rounded top of appropriately named Stoney Top. Another shallow hause has to be crossed, still tracking southwards, before you scale the final, vast slopes leading to the summit of Tonelagee, some 100 m (330 ft) above.

During the final winding climb of the day there is a bird's-eye view of the heart-shaped Lough Ouler (Loch Iolar), tightly embraced by the north-easterly cliff faces of Tonelagee. Wander over to the L to carefully position yourself on the edge of the steep fall-away in order to obtain the best view of this breathtaking corrie lake nestling serenely below in its scooped-out basin. The summit of Tonelagee is situated at 817 m (2680 ft) and it occupies a commanding position above the Wicklow Gap, threading below it to the S. The mountain has been nicknamed 'Backside to the Wind', and this is something which perhaps you have already experienced for most of the day so far! This expansive summit area contains another trigonometrical point and this represents the final high spot from which to savour, lingeringly, the impressive views of the surrounding Wicklow Mountains.

Start your final descent to the SW, heading across flattish ground to reach a group of rocks. From here, take an exact 220 degree bearing which when followed will lead you to a faintly defined track that winds down towards the road below. The ensuing long descent, towards the end of a tiring day, does appear to go on a bit but this leads across mostly easy, well-drained, only moderately sloping ground. However, watch out for the sting when you have almost reached the road, this lying in ambush for you in the form of a deep drainage ditch which you need to cross with considerable care when it is waterlogged. Trim your final approach to arrive at the road opposite the car parks, where hopefully your transport will be patiently awaiting your arrival on time!

Alternative Ways

ESCAPES

It is possible to shorten the walk by descending from several places along the undulating ridge, but connecting transport could then be a problem unless such an abridged route has been planned in advance. The most obvious evasion is from Mullaghcleevaun, tracking downhill over Carrigshouk to the SE to reach the R115 road between Sally Gap and Laragh. At most reasonable times of the day you should be able to obtain a lift in either direction from here.

EXTENSIONS

The described route is demanding and will satisfy the appetites of most walkers, even strong, resilient ones. Therefore, no further extensions are either recommended or offered.

PART 2

WICKLOW GAP TO FENTON'S

factfile

START/FINISH

Start at Wicklow Gap — MR 076002
Finish at Fenton's — MR 973935

GRADING

Difficult/strenuous (colour-coded RED)

WALKING TIME ALLOWANCE

9 hours

DISTANCE

21.8 km (13.5 miles)

TOTAL HEIGHT GAINED

750 m (2460 ft)

PRINCIPAL HEIGHTS

- Conavalla 734 m (2410 ft)
- Camenabologue 758 m (2485 ft)
- Lugnaquillia Mountain 925 m (3035 ft)

digest of walk

PARKING

Extensive parking in two car parks at the top of the Wicklow Gap. However, these are very popular at weekends and during holiday periods. (Note: This is a linear walk and, therefore, ideally two vehicles should be used, the second one positioned at the intended finish of the walk (see Alternative Ways below). Otherwise, arrange transport to collect you from the end of the walk either at your estimated time of arrival there or when you anticipate wishing to leave the pub!)

Wicklow Gap to Fenton's

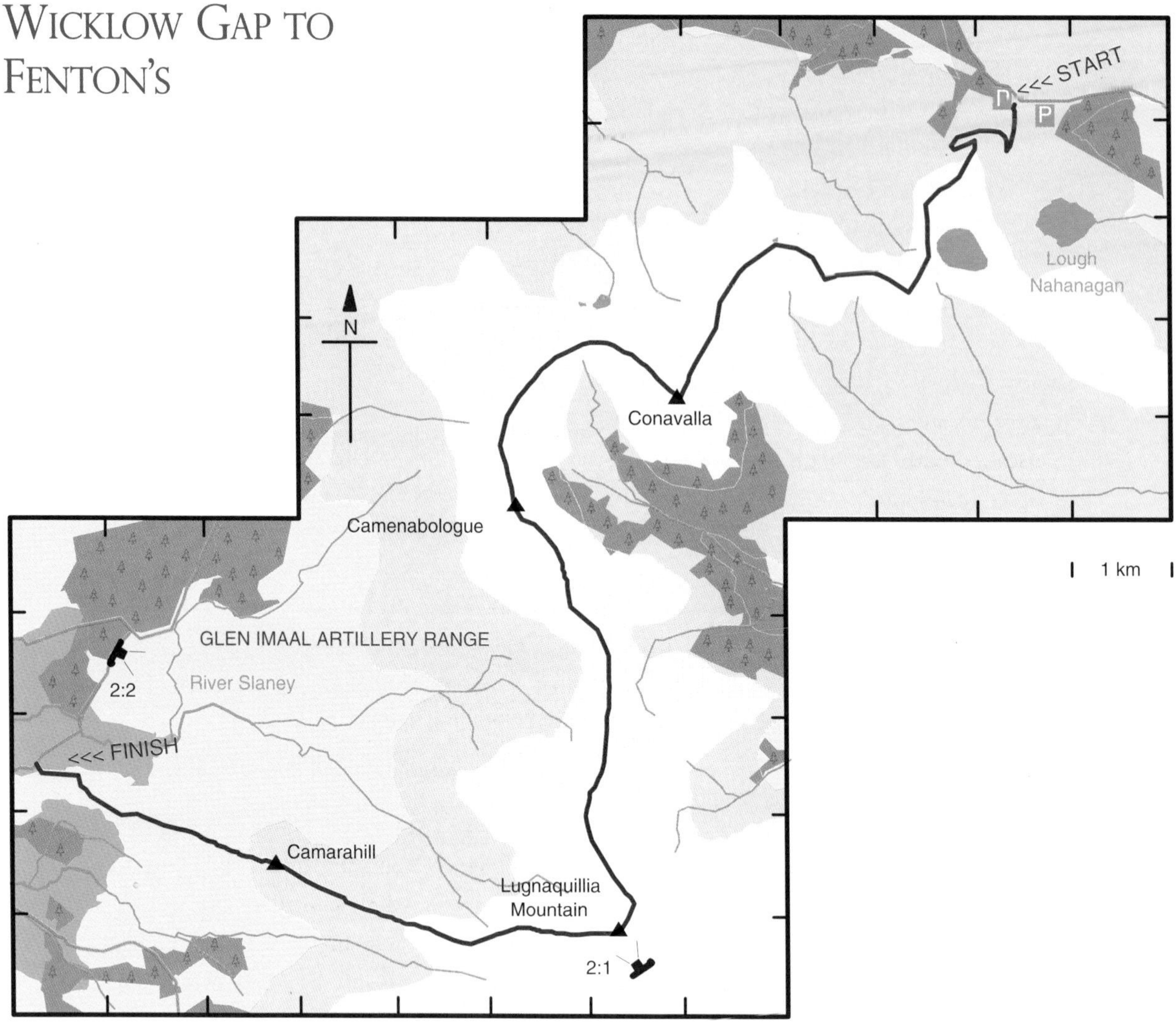

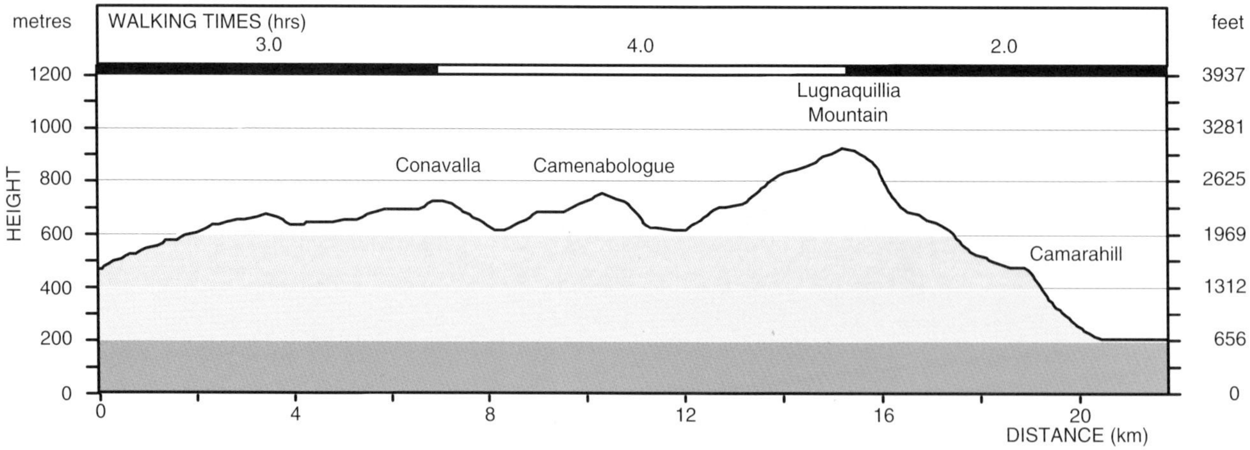

OVERVIEW/INTEREST

- A continuation of Walk 1 through very similar terrain with comparable, challenging characteristics.
- Another high-level traverse of a formidable, undulating mountain ridge, this sprawling SW from the Wicklow Gap.
- The vastness of Lugnaquillia, the highest summit in the Wicklow Mountains, is scaled *en route*.
- Again the way is through expansive, remote landscapes with fascinating views of high, rugged mountain countryside for miles around in all directions, given good weather.

GRADIENTS

Very similar to Walk 1 with again virtually no level sections. Few of the gradients, either up or down, are particularly steep, but with rough, demanding ground to cover almost all of the way, the route presents a continuous contest. Therefore, maintain a pace which you find comfortable and which will conserve your energies over the entire walk.

MAPS, FOOTPATHS AND WAYSIGNS

OS DISCOVERY SERIES 1:50 000 — NUMBER 56 (WICKLOW, DUBLIN AND KILDARE)

The walk starts and finishes along good access roads, tracks and paths where fast progress is possible. In between these assisted ways, much of the route is across exposed, open countryside where in many places testing peat bogs and rough, heather-clad slopes provide the footing and where there are few, if any, clearly defined paths.

Apart from a few waysigns towards the end of the route, the only signs are, in sequence of approach, those warning you of the proximity of disused quarry workings and the Army Artillery Range.

GETTING STARTED

The Wicklow Gap lies at the high point of the R756 road which, running W to E, connects the N81 and the Blessington area with Glendalough and Laragh.

From the westerly of the two car parking areas situated at the gap, head S up the twisting, surfaced access road towards the huge reservoir located above.

CAUTIONARY NOTE

The final sections of this challenging route track beside and then into the Army's Glen Imaal Artillery Range. This is along a permissive way (Route 2) which is open to the public when the range is not in use. Please check with the helpful Warden Service, Army Information and Advice Centre, Seskin School, Glen of Imaal (Tel: 045 54653/54626) when planning a date for this walk.

SUMMARY DESCRIPTION OF WALK

THE WAY TO CONAVALLA — MR 039972 (Allow 3 hours)

There are revealing views downwards to both the W and E from the high-level vantage point of the Wicklow Gap. Forested slopes fall gently to the W and these broaden out into wide, fertile lowlands stretching away in a pleasing latticework of walled fields and groups of trees towards the flatness of Kildare as far as the eye can see. In the opposite direction, the Glendasan

River flows through a wilder landscape, this a narrow, winding valley its sides lined with interlocking mountains whose lower slopes are partly covered with forestry plantations as they regress towards Glendalough and Laragh. High above to the N the vast slopes of Tonelagee sweep down to the pass, whilst the hillsides you are now climbing are part of a wide ridge running from Fair Mountain in the NW to Camaderry and beyond to the SE.

Fast, easy progress is possible along the access road leading to the reservoir above and this will allow you the opportunity of observing, at comparative leisure, the rugged setting of Lough Nahanagan (Loch na hOnchon) down below to the SE. Further up, be careful to keep straight on, thus avoiding a branch road to the L which leads directly to the reservoir. Still heading S, the way penetrates a wild, barren landscape where rocky outcrops abound, and as the terrain flattens off evidence of abandoned quarry working is passed on the R. The road bends around to the L towards the far end of the reservoir and when it does so, abandon it by turning off R along a wide, gravel-surfaced path. The changed direction is to the W, veering SW for a short distance and then reverting to W, and this continuation route necessitates you leaving the comfort of the track when it reaches a level section. This is accomplished by turning off to the R to head across open ground, passing by a marker post informing you of the dangerous ground of the disused quarry.

The continuation route then threads across granite outcrops and you have your first close encounter with laborious peaty ground underfoot. The peat intensifies as a shallow hause — criss-crossed with formidable, boggy, deep hags and furrows — is negotiated. Cross this ground with care, planning the next part of your route in order to avoid the worst of the soggy quagmires. This morass is left behind as you climb up onto firmer, drier, grassy slopes. On reaching these, bear around to the R to avoid walking through a continuation of the peat hags. Further progress to the W is then achieved by walking along a shallow channel which provides a more comfortable walking surface.

From here, follow a narrow path that climbs towards the skyline on your L, gaining further height by walking through bracken and heathers. Above this, the route threads further W along connecting wide channels partly floored with granite blocks but also filled with clinging, oozing mounds of peat. This cocktail of firm ground and slippery, sliding slopes will lead you to the delightful trapped waters of tiny Lough Firrib located at 655 m (2150 ft) and at MR 049988. This is a convenient, and deserved, spot to stop briefly for refreshments before skirting around the south-eastern shore of the lough to continue your journey towards Conavalla.

Further height now needs to be gained to the SW by crossing more, and even deeper, peat hags which will do their best to form a slide on the way down and cause you to slip into them as you attempt to mount their steep, slippery, overhanging edges. Following a slight downward section, the route continues climbing until it reaches the summit of Conavalla at a height of 734 m (2410 ft). This rounded summit rises above the tree line to the NW of the beautiful Glenmalure valley and it commands extensive views in most directions including the long spur which contains Lugduff and Mullacor to the SE, a recapitulation of much of your approach route from the NE and revelations of your continuation way over Camenabologue and then on to Lugnaquillia Mountain (Log na Coille).

THE WAY TO LUGNAQUILLIA MOUNTAIN — MR 032918 (Allow 4 hours)

Descend from Conavalla along the ridge which leads NW and then sweep around and above the upper reaches of forested Glenmalure, gradually veering to your L to cross rather featureless landscapes, particularly so when this area is shrouded in clinging mist. This part of the way drops slightly to pass over — for a welcome change — springy, well-drained, heather-covered slopes. The rugged incline rearing up ahead now has to be scaled, and to achieve this head towards it on an initial WNW bearing and then progressively bear further L, changing your direction of progress to SW. Be vigilant to look out for, spot and avoid the deep bog holes which are prevalent on these upward slopes. (Note: Bog holes, as the name suggests, are potentially dangerous cavities formed below the surface of the ground. They result from swift-flowing underground watercourses carrying away the peaty subsoil and are definitely places where not to place even just one of your footsteps!)

Next, follow a narrow path which connects with a wider track that you bear R along, still climbing to the SW. The summit of Table Mountain, above on your R, is by-passed, and as you continue to swing around to your L you bisect another path which connects the Glen of Imail

2:1 LOCAL GUIDE CHRISTOPHER STACEY WITH A GROUP OF WALKERS ON THE SUMMIT OF LUGNAQUILLIA

2:2 Spring snows lightly covering the upper slopes of Lugnaquillia

to the W with Glenmalure to the E. Here you are warned that you have reached the eastern extremities of the Glen Imaal Artillery Range, which you then track S along making maximum use of a shallow hollow that leads further uphill in your established direction of travel to scale Camenabologue at a height of 758 m (2485 ft). A long, gentle descent follows; keep to an intermittent path which is quite well defined in places and this will lead you further S in the lea of the spur, passing by a number of reassuring marker cairns.

Following this, the final climb to the summit of Lugnaquillia Mountain may be commenced. This is S veering SE and then SW across wide, expansive slopes up a relatively shallow gradient which eventually levels off to the flat-topped high spot of the Wicklow Mountains, an area of enormous size. Should you be making your approach in misty weather, be extremely vigilant to avoid being lured towards the steep fall-away, 'North Prison', on your R. Lugnaquillia Mountain commands a height of 925 m (3035 ft) and its exposed summit is marked by a great mound of stones on top of which a trigonometrical point has been positioned. The rocky outcrop is named Percy's Table after an early eighteenth-century landowner. There is also a revealing observation compass mounted on a stone plinth which discloses the extensive mountain features to be observed from this splendid viewing platform, given good visibility. To give you some idea of the extent of these magnificent panoramas, the author has observed from here, with reliable witnesses present, the distinctive shape of Slievenamon, many miles away in Co Tipperary, and with keen vision he also treasures an unconfirmed sighting of the vague, shimmering, purple profile of the Comeragh Mountains even further away still! See what you can see or conjure up in your fertile imagination from here.

THE WAY TO THE FINISH AT FENTON'S — MR 973935 (Allow 2 hours)

Depart from the vast summit area of Lugnaquillia to the W. This bearing will remain your predominant direction of travel during the ensuing long descent. The gradual downward slope will lead you to a group of rocks, locally christened 'The Whore's Gate'. In this vicinity, take evasive action to avoid awkward, rocky ledges and then locate and follow a broad, grassy path which tracks further westwards down the descending broad spur. The rounded mountain ahead to the WSW is Keadeen Mountain which presents a steep, formidable climb but, fortunately, this is for another day.

Keep descending along the broad spur, following the clearly defined path that hugs its crest. For the most part the relatively easy way down is across grassy slopes, but on occasions the path threads through groups of scattered boulders. The final part of the descent from Camarahill steepens and this is down a grassy band where areas of gorse are penetrated. The waysigned path then passes through walling to your L, beyond which a ladder stile is used to scale a wire fence. After this, an enclosed track continues the westerly descent, though at a significantly shallower angle. Another track is crossed at right angles and, after this, the now broad track flattens off completely and leads into the Glen of Imail. Turn R at the minor road ahead and Fenton's Bar on your R is as good a place as any to finish this adventurous walk and allow the congenial host, Robert Foley, to slake your thirst — although this could take some time!

Alternative Ways

ESCAPES

The most sensible point of escape is at MR 021967 where a well-defined path crosses your way. This path may be followed to the SW to lead you down to the finishing location of the route as previously described or alternatively, by turning L, you may use it to lead you SE into Glenmalure. You will have to plan this second option in advance in order to have transport waiting to collect you towards the head of the long valley.

EXTENSIONS

The route is a challenging one across rough and exposed terrain. Therefore, no extensions are advocated. However, in good weather during the longer days of summer, 'tiger' walkers could consider more interesting and adventurous descents from Lugnaquillia. These are to the E and NE either via the spur above Kelly's Lough (Loch Uí Cheallaigh) or via Art's Lough (Loch Airt). However, never attempt the latter descent in poor visibility, for the critical start of the path leading down to the lake from the northern rim of Clohernagh is difficult to locate! Additionally, either extension will have to be planned in advance with a vehicle in position below at Glenmalure — otherwise you will need to be equipped with camping gear!

Lough Dan and Knocknacloghoge

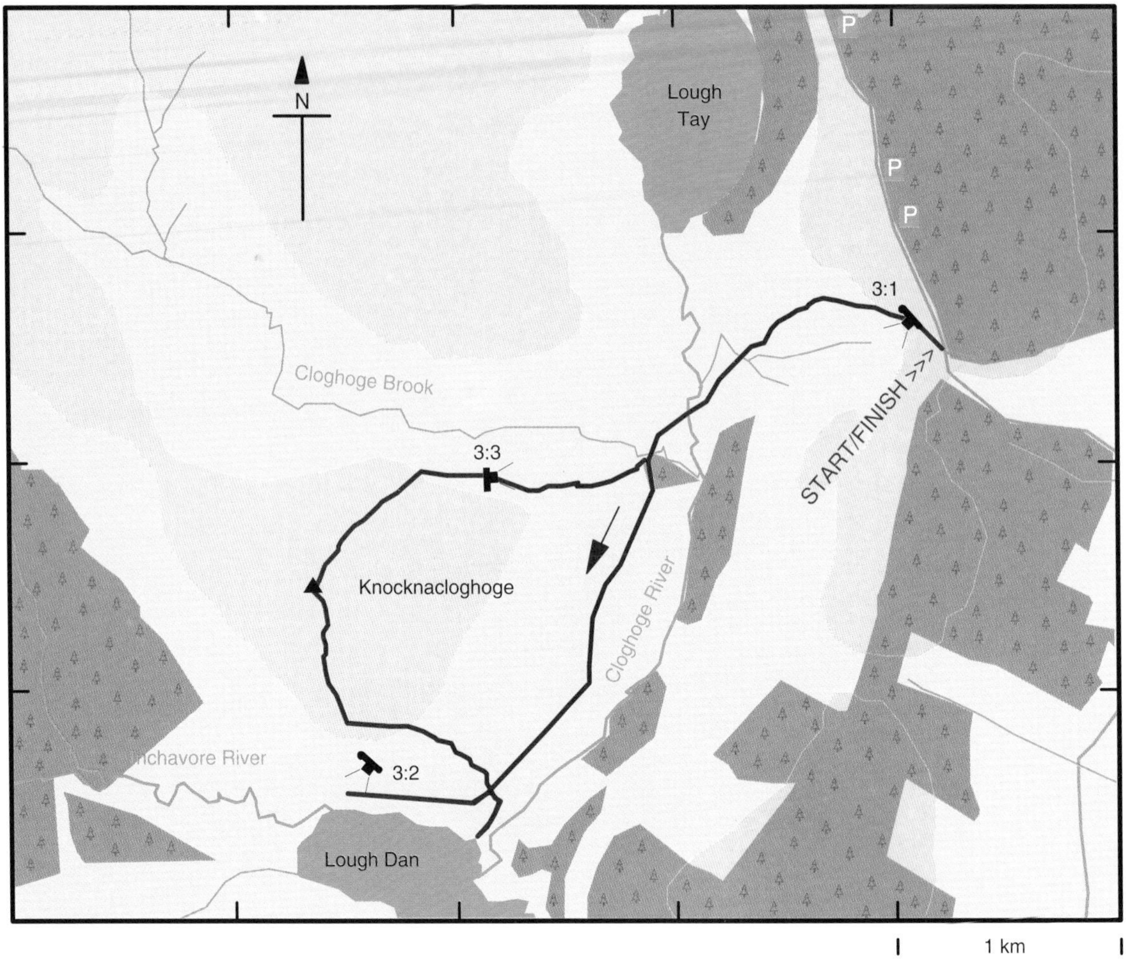

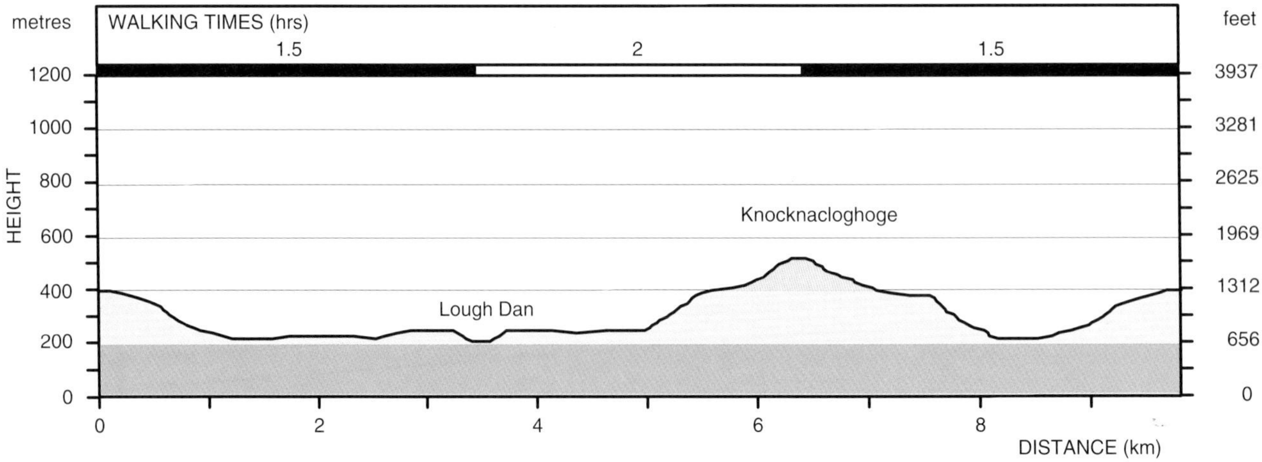

LOUGH DAN AND KNOCKNACLOGHOGE

fact file

START/FINISH
From one of several parking areas beside the R759 road — at or near to MR 172065

GRADING
Easy/straightforward (unless the weather is bad!) (colour-coded GREEN/BLUE)

WALKING TIME ALLOWANCE
5 hours

DISTANCE
9.8 km (6.1 miles)

TOTAL HEIGHT GAINED
540 m (1770 ft)

PRINCIPAL HEIGHTS
- Knocknacloghoge 534 m (1750 ft)

digest of walk

PARKING
Plenty of parking in a number of nearby lay-bys. However, this area is very popular with walkers and more general tourists, and at weekends and during holiday periods these spaces fill up rather quickly.

OVERVIEW/INTEREST
- Fantastic, glaciated landscapes with magnificent scenery all round.
- Sheltered waters of Lough Dan with a safe, shaded beach area.
- Adventurous climb to the top of Knocknacloghoge with its splendid, craggy viewing platform.
- Plenty of wildlife including sika and red/sika hybrid, badgers, foxes, mountain hares, red squirrels, grouse, kestrels, peregrine falcons (26 pairs recorded in Co Wicklow) and brown trout.

GRADIENTS

The walk commences with a moderate descent which has to be reclimbed at the end of the route. Then it is all flatness until the steep, rugged slopes of Knocknacloghoge have to be tackled, only for the height then gained to be surrendered almost immediately on the return journey.

MAPS, FOOTPATHS AND WAYSIGNS

OS Discovery Series 1:50 000 — Number 56 (Wicklow, Dublin and Kildare)

Service roads and then excellent, clearly signed footpaths will lead you to Lough Dan. From here a good path snakes up the initial, grassy slopes of Knocknacloghoge but this regresses to a much narrower and less well-defined track higher up. The final part of the ascent is over rough, rocky ground devoid of pathways in places, and this applies also to the first part of the subsequent descent. However, further down another well-defined, broad, grassy track is reached, and this leads you back to the sanctuary of the quality paths and roads used on your outward route.

GETTING STARTED

It is a short, easy journey from Roundwood by way of the R755 and R759 to any of the convenient parking spots from which the walk may be commenced. Alternatively, this area may be approached from the NW along the R759, and also the R115 which intersects the R759 at Sally Gap. These provide approach routes from Dublin and Blessington.

To get started on the walk, simply go through the gateway which is flanked by stone pillars located at the top end of the most convenient parking area and proceed down the surfaced driveway, walking briskly WNW.

Summary Description of Walk

THE WAY TO LOUGH DAN — MR 151043 (Allow $1\frac{1}{2}$ hours)

Spectacular scenery greets you from the very start in the form of the formidable cliff faces of Luggala (Fancy Mountain) rearing up directly ahead as you walk towards them. Over on your L, to the WSW, the inviting, pointed summit of Knocknacloghoge, which is the main objective for the day, pierces the skyline. On the far-away horizon, just to the L of Knocknacloghoge, the massive escarpment-like shape of Tonelagee which oversees the Wicklow Gap stands high and proud, whilst the straight edge of the high-level reservoir near Camaderry completes a wonderful, mountainous panorama.

Proceed through a wrought iron gate and carry on down the winding driveway where further on Scarr Mountain first comes into view over to the SW. This is followed by revealing views of the wooded valley of the Cloghoge River, one of several streams flowing into Lough Dan. Just prior to the road bending R, turn off down the grassy path on your L, heading directly towards the white-painted estate buildings directly below, which you will shortly pass by. Your narrow path reconnects with a continuation of the roadway further down; here you bear L and at the far end of the buildings below, follow the continuation track signed to 'Lough Dan (Loch Deán)', still surrendering marginal height.

3:1 THE VIEW FROM NEAR THE START OF THE WALK TOWARDS LOUGH DAN AND KNOCKNACLOGHOGE

The continuation way follows the course of the tumbling waters of the Cloghoge River. Walk along the lane signed to 'Lough Dan' and cross over a bridge but refrain from mounting a stile on your R. The route continues SW down the valley along a walled lane which entails crossing over Cloghoge Brook and then climbing over an impressive stile. This way of sheer perfection continues along the beautiful, deciduous-wooded valley which is a veritable haven of peace and tranquillity. Further on, when the track curves distinctly to the L, look above on your R to observe a dilapidated building in which a group of sinister-looking elder trees flourish. There are at least three prophecies that counsel against having anything to do with this unloved species: if you hit somebody with it, you will not grow any taller; if you burn the wood from it, you will see the devil dancing in the flames; and if you place a baby in a cot made from elder, the fairies will replace your fair child with one of their own bad seeds!

Beyond two metal gates, the northeasterly shores of Lough Dan are soon reached, and what sublime views there are across these expansive, trapped waters as your grassy path and the gurgling river on your L converge on the lake at virtually the same spot, near to an attractive, white-painted, disused cottage. Avoid crossing the river by the stepping stones and instead continue down to the tree-lined lake shore where there are sandy beaches, safe for children to splash about on whilst under watchful supervision. However, do be aware of the deep pools in the river over on the L and keep all those in your care well away from these hazards!

To your R the waters of the lough penetrate into rugged, mountainous country, whilst in the other direction they flow serenely towards the more sheltered pastures and forested areas leading down to Annamoe to the SE. Walk a short distance along the path which hugs the north bank of the lough before returning to the vicinity of the white cottage to commence your ascent of Knocknacloghoge, this perhaps after you have allowed yourself some time for refreshments. This short diversion will enable you to look down on a sand bar formed by the silt carried down into the lough by the Inchavore River. Trees and gorse have established themselves on this narrow strip of sedimentary land and these enhance an already attractive setting.

THE WAY TO KNOCKNACLOGHOGE — MR 143054 (Allow 2 hours)

3:2 Looking down on the sand bar at the western tip of Lough Dan

Pass through a gap in the stone walling situated to the L of the isolated cottage. Then select the second and narrower of two grassy paths which snake up the rounded hillside that forms the lower slopes of Knocknacloghoge, and start climbing NW up the mountainside. This is across fairly steep, bracken-covered slopes. Higher up, your path connects with another one; at this point bear L along the merged ways to continue heading NW, but now experiencing less exacting gradients. Turn around when you have gained sufficient height to observe the whole length of Lough Dan curving majestically below you like some gigantic boomerang. More paths join your way higher up still, and you just keep on climbing along your established NW diagonal.

Eventually the way leads, somewhat disconcertingly, towards a dense group of prickly gorse thickets and it becomes less well-defined as it does so! Fortunately, there is an escape route around to the L in the form of a narrow path which traverses along the edge of the higher ground and allows you to avoid tangling with the unwelcome gorse. This important traverse to the W is more or less level but it does require care due to the steep fall-away on your L. Some distance further on, fork R away from the edge to continue climbing to the NW up the easier, higher ground above. When you reach a steep, rocky gully falling rather precipitously on your L and positioned high above the far end of the lough, veer further R across the extensive heather, bilberry and tufted grasses, then heading directly towards the two craggy mounds which signify you have reached the summit area of Knocknacloghoge. This final, pathless-in-places approach is towards the NNW, and you should head towards the L and more westerly of the twin peaks along a re-established path. The mountain commands an elevation of 534 m (1750 ft) and it provides further revelations of the surrounding magnificent scenery which has previously been described.

THE WAY BACK TO THE PARKING AREA — MR 172065

(Allow 1½ hours)

Depart from the summit area to the NE, initially following a distinct path. Unfortunately this clearly defined way soon loses its identity amongst the overgrown heathers, bilberries and long, tufted grasses. However, be vigilant to maintain this NE bearing, making whatever use you can of sections of the path which sporadically appear for short distances. Lower down, track to the R of a predominant grass circle which is visible on the opposite hillside, in line with three rocks, over the brow of the slope you are now descending.

Watch out for drainage ditches on the way down and where necessary take evasive action to avoid tumbling into any of these. Lower down, cross over an inviting track and maintain your established NE diagonal line of descent. Then, after about a further 150 paces, turn R along a well-defined grassy track which leads E down into the valley. Thereafter, allow this to escort you off the mountain by means of a high-level downward traverse followed by a steeper zigzag to the L which will bring you to a metal gate set into a stone wall. There are more lovely views during this easy descent. These include looking down into the valley on your L to observe the tumbling catchment waters of the mountain stream, Cloghoge Brook, racing you effortlessly down the hillside and meandering over a rocky bed towards the mixed conifer plantations and deciduous woodlands below.

Through the gate, turn L and simply retrace your outward steps back to where you have left your vehicle, with a second chance along this way to admire in more detail the stunning surrounding scenery.

Alternative Ways

ESCAPES

Family walkers with young children are advised to venture no further than the interesting shore of Lough Dan.

EXTENSIONS

Strong walkers could consider climbing Luggala as well. If you plan to do this, allow yourself plenty of time and extend the route to come off Luggala to the NNW, thereby keeping away from the dangerous cliffs which line the easterly flank of this exciting mountain. Then cross the Cloghoge River above Lough Tay (Loch Té) before joining the R759 road to the N. Turn R along the road and use this to return to your parked vehicle.

3:3 Nearing the end of the descent from Knocknacloghoge

GLENDALOUGH, MULLACOR AND DERRYBAWN MOUNTAIN

fact file

START/FINISH

Visitor car park at Upper Lake, Glendalough — MR 111963

GRADING

Moderate (colour-coded BLUE)

WALKING TIME ALLOWANCE

6 hours

DISTANCE

11.6 km (7.2 miles)

TOTAL HEIGHT GAINED

560 m (1840 ft)

PRINCIPAL HEIGHTS

- Mullacor 657 m (2155 ft)
- Derrybawn Mountain 474 m (1555 ft)

digest of walk

PARKING

Extensive parking in a well-appointed area with information office, toilets, refreshment facilities and picnic places nearby. However, since Glendalough is a major tourist attraction and is very popular with both walkers and more general visitors, the advice is get there early!

OVERVIEW/INTEREST

- The delights of the glaciated topography of Glendalough located in the Wicklow Mountains National Park.
- Engrossing heritage of Glendalough with many historical monuments dating back to the time of St Kevin in the sixth century.
- Superb visitor centre nearby with excellent presentations.

GLENDALOUGH, MULLACOR AND DERRYBAWN MOUNTAIN

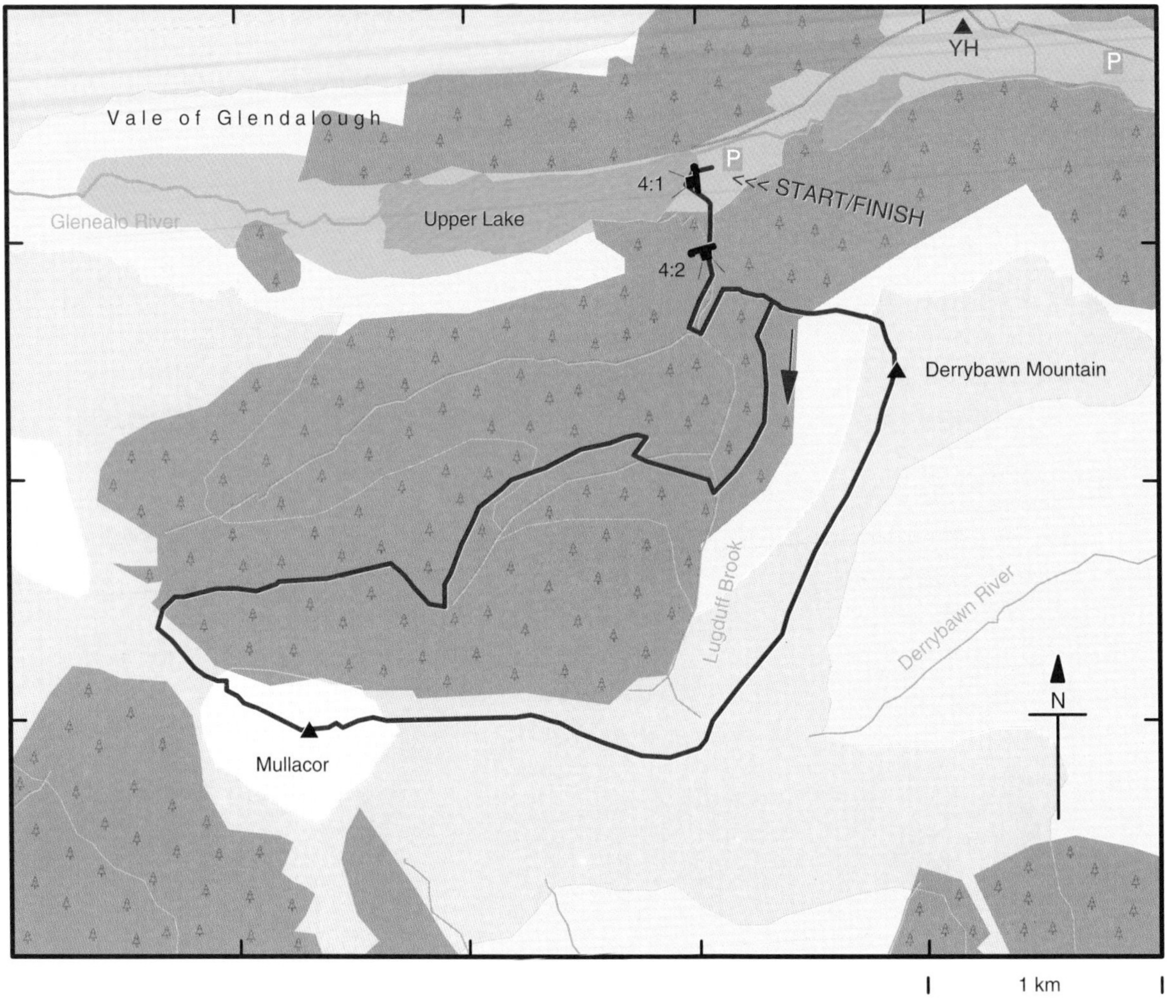

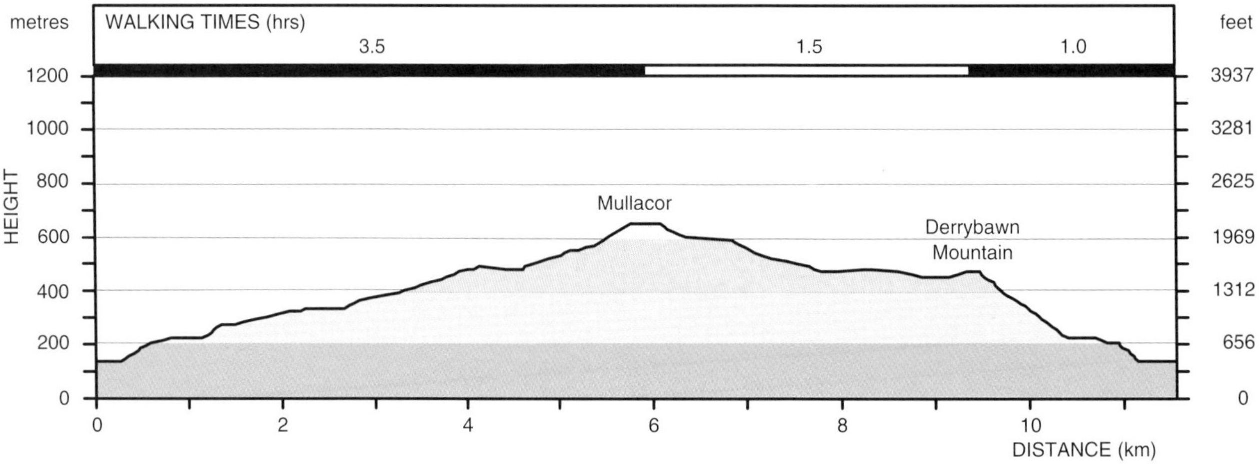

- The airy, open spaces of Mullacor and Derrybawn Mountain will allow your spirits to soar above the activities and sightseeing going on down below.
- Conifer forests and deciduous woodlands with plenty of wildlife including rare peregrine falcons (kings of the high mountains).

GRADIENTS

There is a long, gradual climb from the lake shores to the top of Mullacor with some steeper sections towards the beginning and end. A gradual descent to the summit of Derrybawn Mountain follows, partly along an undulating, narrow ridge. The final descent back into and through the forested area of Glendalough is fairly steep most of the way down.

MAPS, FOOTPATHS AND WAYSIGNS

OS Discovery Series 1:50 000 — Number 56 (Wicklow, Dublin and Kildare)
Almost the entire route is along a combination of connecting paths, forest roads and mountain tracks with virtually no crossing of uncharted countryside.

Signs both around Glendalough and along the forest roads and trails are plentiful, almost too many during that part of the route which coincides with the Wicklow Way! Whilst crossing the mountain tops you will not pass any guiding signs, the correct paths hereabouts are always fairly obvious.

GETTING STARTED

Glendalough may be reached from the W along the R756 road which threads through the Wicklow Gap or from the E through Laragh, which is a minor junction for roads coming from other directions — the R115 from the N and the R755 from the E and S.

Commence the walk by wandering down to the easterly shores of the Upper Lake in order to absorb the fantastic views beyond the blue, lapping waters of the lough, its sides squeezed together by the vice-like jaws of the steep, craggy cliffs which fall precipitously and spectacularly into its hidden depths.

Summary Description of Walk

THE WAY TO MULLACOR — MR 092939 (Allow $3\frac{1}{2}$ hours)

Turn away from the water's edge and cross over the surfaced drive to locate a path signed 'Cathair agus Crosa (Stone "Fort" and Crosses)' and use this to proceed to the helpful information office, inspecting the fort and crosses *en route*. The way leads through a grassy picnic area, after which turn R along the surfaced drive to reach the information office. After looking around the displays and obtaining any information you require there, turn R to continue along the wide, gravel-surfaced, waymarked path and follow this as it bends to the L. Near here there is a well-signed, minor diversion to the site of St Kevin's Cell and the Reefert Church. The interesting remains of the church and surrounds which contain a burial ground of local chieftains (mainly members of the O'Toole clan) are well worth a short visit.

Return to the main path and turn R along it to head gently uphill towards the waterfalls above, signed 'Poll an Easa'. Then branch off L up the steps clearly signed to 'Poulanass

4:1 Springtime arrives at the Upper Lake, Glendalough

Waterfall', venturing southwards up steeper, wooded slopes with the river, Lugduff Brook, crashing down noisily in a series of falls through a narrow, rocky ravine to your L. Further up, there is a spectacular view of these falls with their deep catchment pools, this from a prepared, safe observation place. Keep walking uphill along the railed path and fork R before turning L when you reach a T-junction as indicated by the waysign. The route continues near to and above the course of the stream.

The obvious, wide gravel track loops up the slopes utilising a shallow gradient. Higher up, turn L to cross over the brook by means of the sturdy bridge provided. After this, fork R, keeping to the signed way and then be extra vigilant to locate and follow a narrow path on your R which leads more steeply uphill. This important turning is about 100 paces beyond the bridge and is located at MR 112958. Your changed direction is then to the SE for a short distance. Turn around as you scale the steeper slopes to absorb the fantastic views now opening up behind and below you. These include the rounded dome of Camaderry to the NW. Ahead, vast, wooded landscapes appear in all directions above you.

Within a short distance, the rough, narrow path reconnects with the wider track; turn R here to penetrate further into the vast, mountainous countryside which is now beginning to encircle you. To the SW the slopes of Mullacor — one of your principal objectives — rise serenely, Lugduff spreads across the ground to the W, Camaderry rises to the NW and the pointed peak to the N is Brockagh Mountain. The continuation way bends gracefully to the R in a gigantic sweep before it bends more decisively in that direction to immediately recross the stream. Further on, ignore the branch track leading uphill on your L, opting instead for the certainty of the signed way.

A short, upward traverse through sapling trees follows, and after this an area of recent forest harvesting is entered. Turn sharp L to continue along the signed way, now heading more directly towards the summit area of Mullacor, its forested slopes towering above to the SW. The uphill way along the wide track continues, and following an acute bend a tiny indistinct watercourse is crossed. After this, keep walking along the main track as it bends around to the R, avoiding the narrower way which leads off straight ahead and which you pass to your L. The route curves further to the R, tracking uphill along a particularly wide section of the way that could accommodate a bus!

Keep to the signed way which then bears L and along here ignore a narrower path leading downhill on your R. Further up the slope, avoid a temptation to the L, again trusting the waysigned route which leads you further W. After all these twists and turns along the wide forest tracks it will come as something of a pleasant relief for you to eventually step along a narrower, more natural path which leads, still upwards, towards the ridge ahead. Following a further sharp turn to the L, this ridge is attained at a shallow hause which separates Lugduff to the NW from Mullacor to the SE. This point is at MR 086944.

Rougher ground now provides the footing as more exposed slopes are crossed above the densely packed conifer tree-line, and hereabouts the first areas of peat appear. When you reach the high point of the connecting spur, turn full L to head more steeply uphill, gaining height to the SE up now quite peaty slopes, these laden with heather and bilberry. Beyond a group of quartz outcrops, the rounded summit area of Mullacor is eventually reached, the final approach to the top being along a well-used, clearly defined path. This ground lies at 657 m (2155 ft) and it provides a splendid viewing platform in clear weather. The 360 degree mountainous panorama deserves time for you to absorb and to identify the many separate peaks which provide riveting skylines in all directions. Start this pleasant task by looking WSW to position Lugnaquillia Mountain (Log na Coille), at 925 m (3035 ft) the highest of them all.

THE WAY TO DERRYBAWN MOUNTAIN — MR 119955 (Allow $1\frac{1}{2}$ hours)

The summit of Derrybawn Mountain now lies about 3.5 km (2 miles) away. The route there is along a pleasant, narrowing, undulating ridge, from which in fine weather there are majestic views of the immediately surrounding landscapes that fall away in all directions. Depart to the E from the summit area of Mullacor, walking down a clearly defined path which hugs the crest of the falling ridge. The way bends gradually around to the L crossing over broad, expansive, grassy slopes, the open views from which are quite superb — these observed when you are not concentrating on avoiding patches of boggy ground!

A slight rise follows, before the progressive descent continues, still tracking E, down slightly steeper slopes to cross a rare stile, this encountered after having walked to the L of a wire fence for some distance. Near here, turn L along a faint, narrower path that leads NE slightly downhill through heather towards the more pointed, craggy spur ahead. This band of rock will connect you with the slopes of Derrybawn Mountain. The continuation way then climbs again to bisect

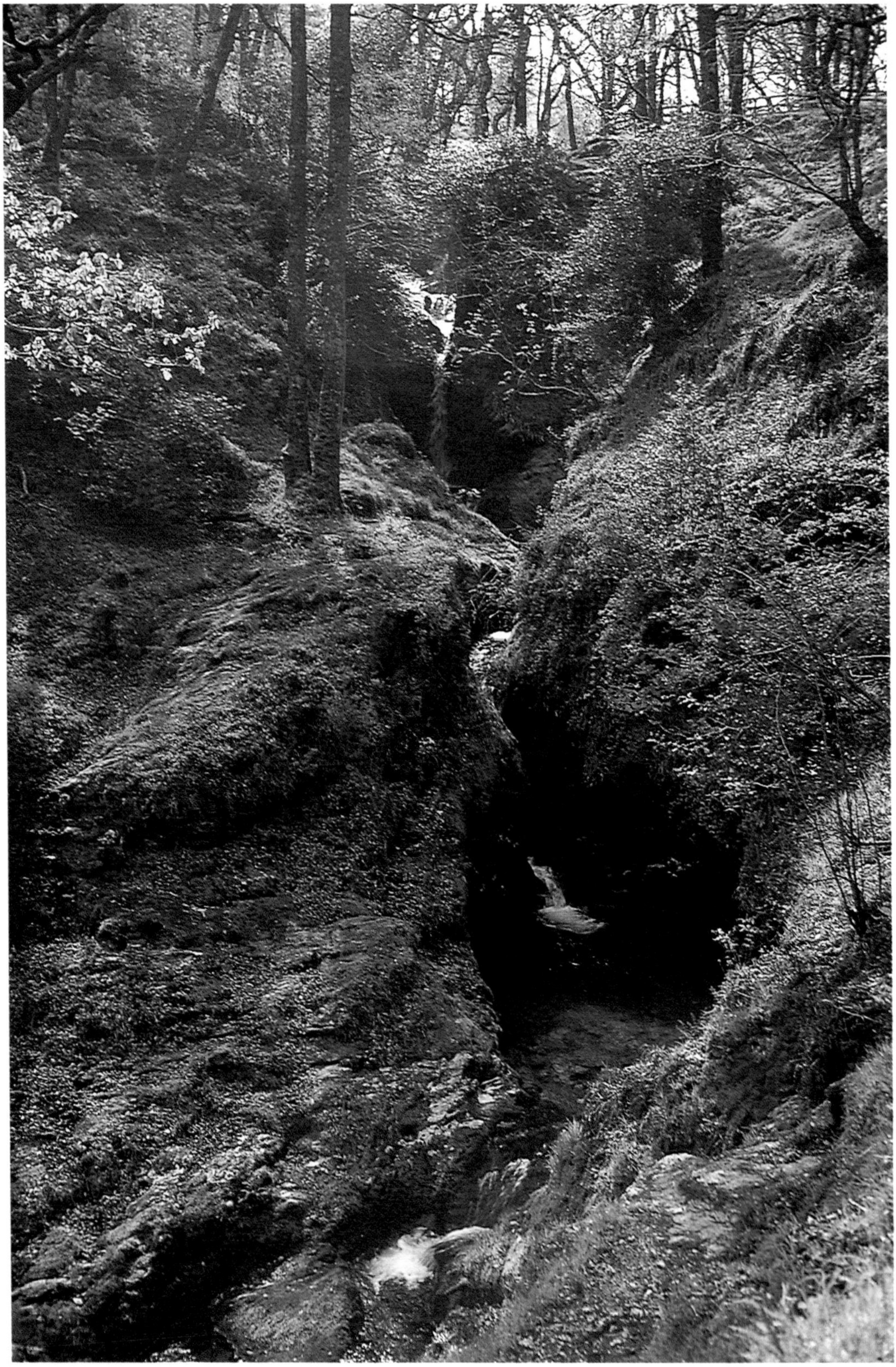

4:2 POLLANASS WATERFALL, GLENDALOUGH

a wider path at right angles and beyond this it leads you on to the hillock above. Progress remains to the NE veering NNE. From here, walk confidently along the crest of the undulating ridge to reach the summit of Derrybawn Mountain at 474 m (1555 ft). This mountain has a more pointed top, marked by a solitary cairn, than Mullacor, and although considerably lower, it still commands splendid views of the surrounding wild, desolate but magnificent mountain landscapes. Most of the sightings to be observed from here have already been positioned but in this vicinity, and previously along the ridge, part of Glendalough and the Upper Lake (An Loch Uachtair) are in view down to the NW.

THE WAY BACK TO THE CAR PARK — MR 111963 (Allow 1 hour)

Start your descent by initially continuing northwards along a clearly defined path. This will lead you around to your L following the spur of the mountain and change your direction of travel to NW. Then turn L below to head due W, descending along another narrow continuation path which threads through extensive areas of heather, dropping sharply down in this process. From here, just keep descending towards the extensive conifer forest directly below, crossing several fainter paths at right angles as you do so.

The correct way down will take you straight to a post stile, set into the perimeter fence of the forested area. Cross over this to continue downhill, now beneath a shady canopy of pine needles. This continuing steep descent will bring you to a wide forest road at a spot you passed through on your outward route. From here, cross over the track to continue walking downhill along the narrow path which is on the far side and which you used earlier on, then walking in the opposite direction uphill. At the bottom of the path, turn L along the wide forest road and retrace your outward steps back to the car park.

Alternative Ways

ESCAPES

Groups with youngsters may get no further than climbing up to the waterfalls and this is just fine. There are few other short cuts other than turning about at any stage before you reach a point of no return and either retracing your outward steps or selecting an alternative way down through the maze of interconnecting forest roads and tracks below.

EXTENSIONS

The obvious extension is to add the summit of Lugduff to your 'hit list', making this a quick there-and-back. From the summit of Derrybawn there are also longer, more circuitous descents back into Glendalough which entail approaching the car parking area from the NE along the forested hillsides.

Overleaf: Nire Church and surrounding wooded landscapes

Nire Valley Walks

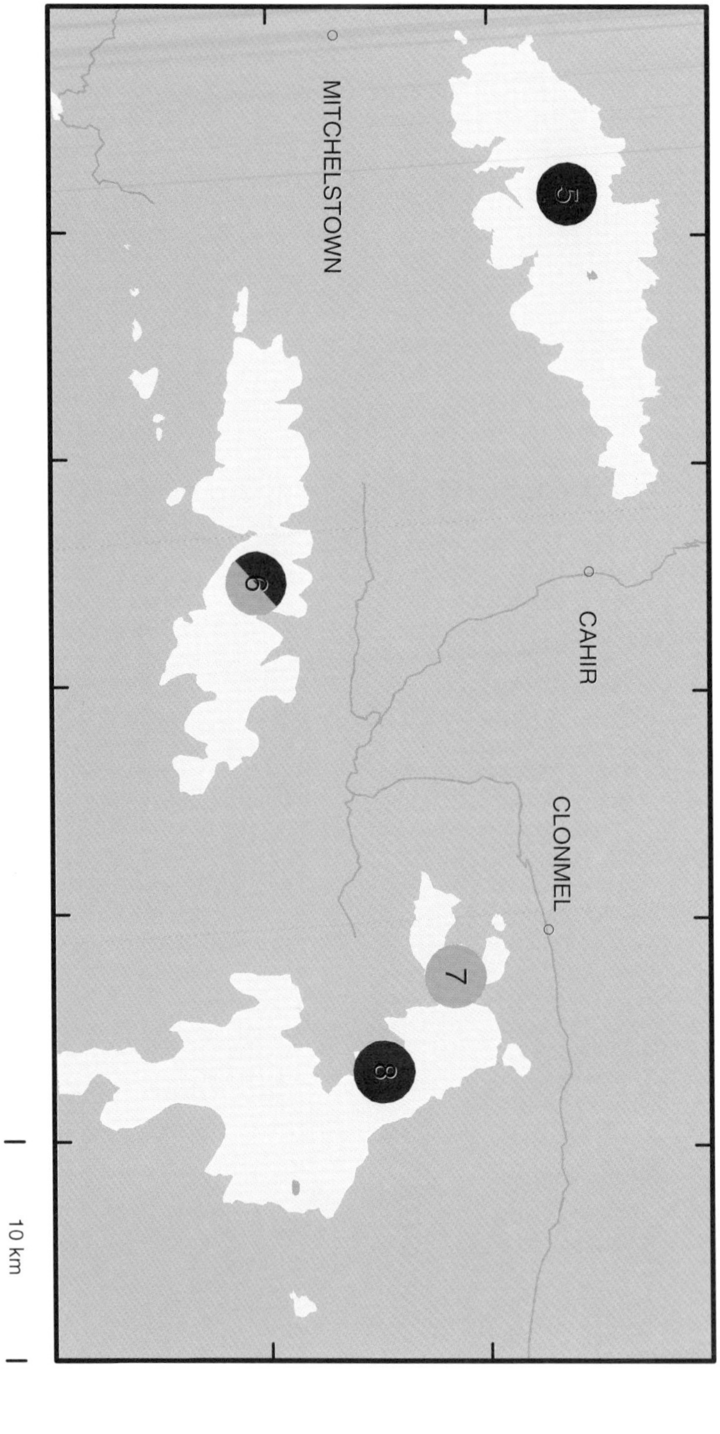
MITCHELSTOWN
CAHIR
CLONMEL
5
6
7
8
10 km

The Nire Valley and the Surrounding Comeragh, Knockmealdown and Galty Mountains

Getting There

The picturesque Nire Valley (Nier on OS map) is located just to the S of the historic town of Clonmel and it lies about 110 km (70 miles) SW of the southernmost part of the Wicklow Mountains, although the connecting roads between these two areas are not that direct.

There are two suggested ways of reaching Clonmel from the Wicklow Mountains, the 'fast' route and the 'scenic' route. The fast route commences down the main N81 road from Baltinglass, after which you turn off along the R726 road to Carlow. From here, use the major N9 and N10 roads to reach Kilkenny and then motor along the N76 road straight into Clonmel. Allowing for some traffic congestion in the towns, this journey should normally take less than half a day.

The scenic route is via Rathdrum and then using a combination of the R752, R753, R747, R748, R725 and R746 roads to reach Bunclody. You can visit Avondale Forest Park and stop at the 'Meeting of the Waters' *en route*. A continuation along the R746, R702 and R703 roads will take you through the attractive Blackstairs Mountains into Graiguenamanagh. This town, with its handsome, seven-arched, stone bridge spanning the River Barrow at a particularly peaceful riverside setting, is an ideal spot to have lunch and relax for a time. Continue along the R703 road across country into Thomastown and from here use part of the main N9 road travelling southwards before turning off westwards along the R699 road. The R701 and R697 roads will complete your journey into Carrick-on-Suir and from here a short distance westwards along the major N24 road will bring you into Clonmel. Allow a full day for this fascinating journey SW which is full of interest all the way.

There are two choices once you reach Clonmel. Either use the R671 road and turn eastwards into the Nire Valley at Ballymacarbry or alternatively leave Clonmel along the R678 road and, after passing by the immaculately manicured golf course, turn R along one of the mountain roads to then motor southwards into the Nire Valley. Allow between ½ and 1 hour for the drive from Clonmel, depending on exactly where you are staying.

Geological Perspective

A striking feature of the landscapes of this area is the general concordance of two shelves or benches, a higher one rising to heights between 180 and 240 m (600 and 800 ft) and a lower level, developed closer to the present coast, which rises to between 60 and 120 m

(200 and 400 ft). The higher mountains soar well above these surrounding platforms to over 900 m (3000 ft). There is agreement that the two concordant levels represent the remains of two erosional platforms. The higher level developed some tens of millions of years ago by erosion of the land down to the contemporary sea level. Subsequent uplift of the region then allowed the formation of the second erosional platform at a new sea level. Final uplift has elevated the land to its present altitude, and ongoing erosion by ice (during the Great Ice Age of the last two million years) and more recently by river action biting deeply into the two benches has shaped the topography observed today. The Comeragh, Knockmealdown, Galty and other mountains were highland areas, probably islands, at the time the higher platform was developed. The fine details of this fascinating history of uplift and erosion are currently matters of ongoing debate and continued research.

The rocks beneath the surface are mostly stratified and have been folded by powerful, crustal compression along WSW–ENE axes. The oldest (deepest lying) strata are composed of Old Red Sandstone (about 400 million years old) and have now been revealed by subsequent erosion as the cores of upfolds (anticlines). These rocks are generally the toughest rocks of the region and thus they form the higher ground between the river valleys. In many high places, such as along the Knockanaffrin Ridge, conglomerate rocks appear, revealing an intriguing assortment of pebbles and rock fragments embedded within the 'Old Red'.

The rock bands which lie above the 'Old Red' belong to the Carboniferous system and were laid down about 300 million years ago. They include limestone and other sedimentary rocks, all generally less resistant to erosion than the 'Old Red'. Accordingly, these newer rocks have been more completely worn away to form the lower ground of the present river valleys such as that of the River Nire. Over much of the area these valleys coincide with downfolds (synclines).

The higher mountains of the area, as would be expected, are generally composed of the 'Old Red' and they mostly lie along anticlinal fold axes. Their altitude ensured that they became extensively glaciated during the ice ages and there are many features such as corries and moraines which provide evidence of this. Walkers of today will find abundant, spectacular examples of these powerful glacial forces manifested by the numerous corries and their lakes secreted away within the precipitous cliffs which line the edges of the main mountainous areas. These include the magnificent Coumshingaun Lough which attracts geologists from many distant lands.

Present-Day Landscapes and Opportunities for Walking

The Nire Valley is truly a green and pleasant land! The lower reaches of the glen are pleasingly spacious and the River Nire meanders placidly through lush meadowlands, where gently sloping hillsides partly covered with mixed woodlands provide the sheltering horizons on either side. This area is popular with less energetic walkers, for there is a wide variety of connecting, quiet lanes, footpaths and forest trails that are ideal for short, leisurely strolls during which abundant wildlife may be observed and visits to sites of archaeological interest may be included in the explorations.

Surrounding and towering above the upper reaches of the Nire Valley are the nearby Comeragh Mountains, whilst to the S and W a short distance further away the Knockmealdown and Galty Mountains conspire to complete this fascinating encirclement. In total, these mountains provide almost endless challenges to strong, experienced and expert hillwalkers and they will allow your spirits to soar amongst a unique variety of high, mountain landscapes. Here, you may walk along craggy ridges, marvel at corrie lakes nestling below sheer cliff faces many hundreds of feet below, tramp across wild, remote heathlands, perfect your technique of crossing boggy ground including wading through peat hags, cool off by splashing about in the icy-cold, gushing waters of mountain streams and, on the summit of Galtymore, stand at over 3000 ft, one of only 12 places where you can achieve this in the whole of Ireland. Then, on your second day . . .!

Choice of Walking Routes

The selection of walking routes has been deliberately spread out over the area in order to provide a comprehensive taste of what is possible in this quite superb walking terrain which surprisingly is only just being discovered by the Irish themselves. Walk 5 presents a challenging ascent to the summit of Galtymore and serves as an introduction to the Galty Mountains, whilst Walk 6 is an enjoyable journey along an undulating ridge which will familiarise you with the Knockmealdown Mountains. Walks 7 and 8 represent two contrasting routes in the Comeragh Mountains, one a strenuous and the other a medium-graded exploration.

Local Walking Guides

Most of my more adventurous walking in this area has been completed in the enjoyable company of Michael Desmond, a local dairy farmer who is fast becoming acclaimed as a highly competent and professional walking guide. Michael, in addition to possessing a vast knowledge and experience of walking these valleys and mountains in all weathers, is also an authority on the flora, fauna, geology, archaeology and most other things of the area. This extensive know-how and his wide range of helpful contacts even extends, for instance, to the making and eating of the most delicious, local dairy products produced by the makers of the famed Bay Lough Irish Farmhouse Cheese at nearby Clogheen (Tel: 052 65275).

Michael works closely with a number of hotels and guest houses in and around the Nire Valley which specialise in offering walking holiday packages and in pampering independent walkers, and it is through one of these connections that I had the good fortune to meet and then walk with this expert and congenial young guide.

CONTACT DETAILS
Michael Desmond
Nire and Comeragh Guided Walks
Deerpark
Ballymacarbry
Via Clonmel
Co Waterford
Tel: 052 36238
Email: hiking@indigo.ie
Website: http://indigo.ie/~hiking/index.htm

Accommodation, Eating Out and Local Transport

ACCOMMODATION

The only accommodation we have used, and this on several occasions now, in the Nire Valley has been to stay with Mary and Seamus Wall at their attractively located and extremely comfortable guest house, Hanora's Cottage, located near to the old schoolhouse and Nire Church. The delicious fare served here will satisfy the taste buds of the most discerning gourmet and then the surrounding mountains are perfect for 'walking off' any unintended gluttony. Walkers in particular will receive a warm and friendly welcome here, and Seamus, the acclaimed local 'bog trotter', and his red setter dog will prove hard to keep up with if you persuade them to spend a day with you amongst the high hills.

As previously mentioned, there is a consortium of guest houses in and around the Nire Valley which cater especially for the needs of walkers and who work closely with each other and in conjunction with local walking guide, Michael Desmond. These are listed in the table below.

ACCOMMODATION REGISTER

Hotel/Guest House	Rooms en suite	Rooms other	Charge B&B	Open	Visited by Author
Seamus and Mary Wall Hanora's Cottage Guest House Nire Valley Via Clonmel Co Waterford Tel: 052 36134	F 0 D 5 T 3 S 0	F 0 D 0 T 0 S 0	£30–35	All year	Yes
Richard and Nora Hart Cnoc-na-Rí Country House Nire Valley Via Clonmel Co Waterford Tel: 052 36239	F 2 D 2 T 0 S 0	F 0 D 0 T 0 S 0	£20	All year	No

Hotel/Guest House	Rooms en suite	Rooms other	Charge B&B	Open	Visited by Author
Martin and Una Moore Bennett's Church Old School House Ballymacarbry Nire Valley Via Clonmel Co Waterford Tel: 052 36217	F 0 D 2 T 0 S 0	F 0 D 2 T 0 S 0	£15–17	? All year	No
Breeda Cullinan Sliabh gCua Farmhouse Touraneena Ballinamult Co Waterford Tel: 058 47120	F 2 D 0 T 2 S 0	F 0 D 0 T 0 S 0	£17	? All year	No
Paddy and Olive O'Gorman Glasha Farmhouse Four-Mile-Water Via Clonmel Co Waterford Tel: 052 36108	F 1 D 2 T 2 S 0	F 0 D 0 T 0 S 0	£20	All year	No
Laurence and Catherine McCarra Rivervalley Guest House Newcastle Via Clonmel Co Waterford Tel: 052 36105	F 1 D 1 T 2 S 0	F 1 D 0 T 1 S 1	? £16	All year	No

Rooms: F = Family; D = Double; T = Twin; S = Single

EATING OUT

With eating our evening fill, and quite often more, at Hanora's Cottage, our experiences of feasting out in this particular area are somewhat limited. We have dined as honoured guests at the Emperor's Palace Chinese restaurant at Clonmel (Tel: 052 24162), which, if you enjoy food served on a bed of rice as we do, is highly recommended. Also you may like to sample the value-for-money sandwiches and delicious bar snacks served at Melody's Inn at Ballymacarbry (Tel: 052 36147). This establishment also does good lines in horse riding and pony trekking should 'shanks's pony' not be entirely to your liking! However, the crowning pleasure at this popular pub is supping the 'black stuff' whilst listening to traditional Irish music and trying to make yourself heard above the lively din.

LOCAL TRANSPORT

The walk in the Knockmealdown Mountains and the Knockanaffrin walk in the Comeragh Mountains are linear routes and will probably necessitate you being supported by commercial transport. I have travelled with Laurence McCarra, who operates a coach, minibus and taxi service out of Newcastle (Tel: 052 36105), to rescue Michael and myself from the finish of the Knockmealdown walk. There are a number of other reliable taxi and minibus operators centred on Ballymacarbry/Clonmel and these include Ballymacarbry Hackney Service (Tel: 052 36477), Seán Condon, Clonmel (Tel: 052 22864) and Anthony Fennessy, Clonmel (Tel: 052 21765).

Galtymore Mountain

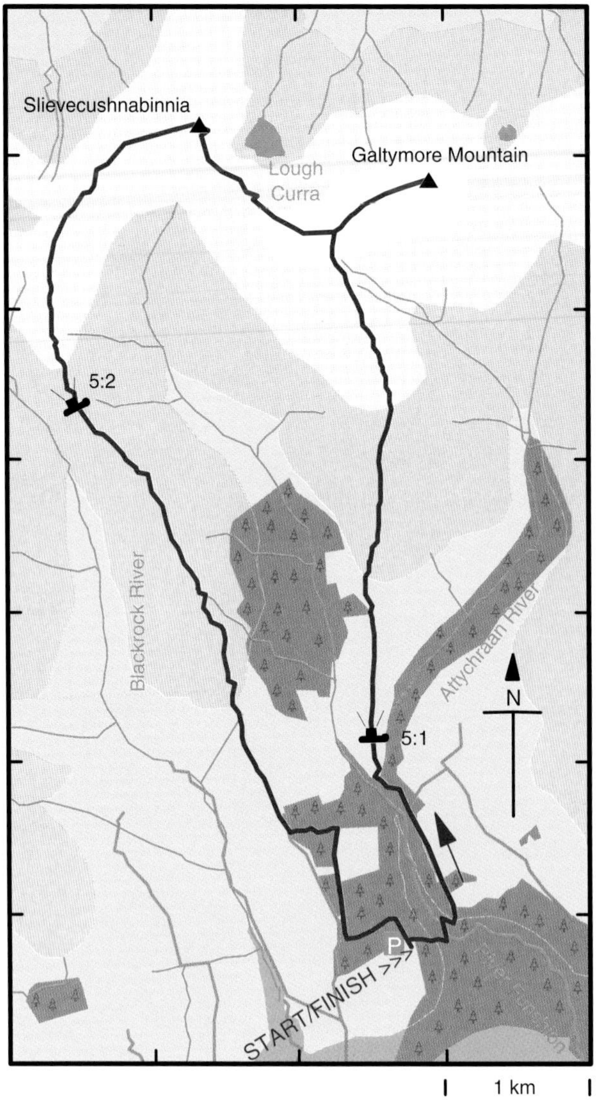

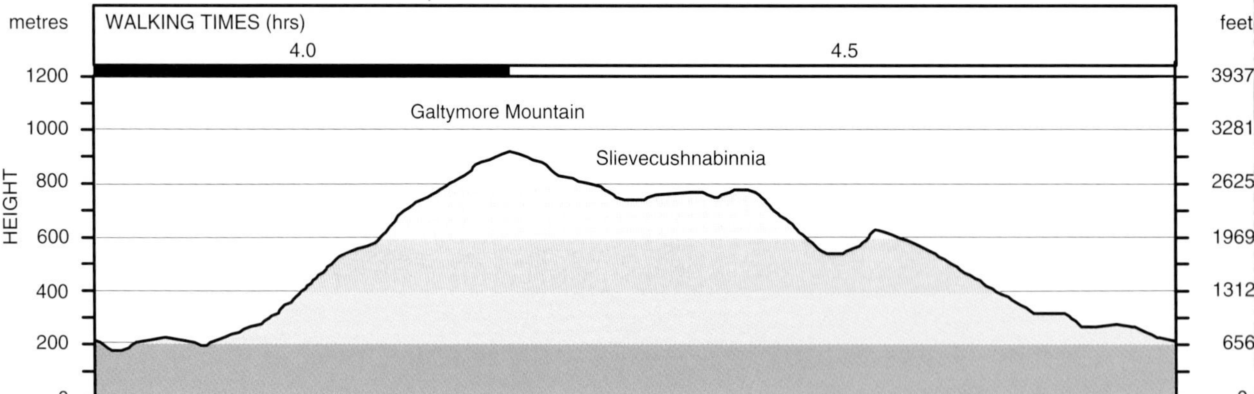

GALTYMORE MOUNTAIN

fact file

START/FINISH
Forest car park — MR 879188

DISTANCE
15.0 km (9.4 miles)

GRADING
Difficult/strenuous (colour-coded RED)

TOTAL HEIGHT GAINED
930 m (3050 ft)

WALKING TIME ALLOWANCE
8½ hours

PRINCIPAL HEIGHTS
- Galtymore Mountain 919 m (3015 ft)
- Slievecushnabinnia 766 m (2515 ft)

digest of walk

PARKING
Dedicated parking area in forest which holds about 20 to 25 cars.

OVERVIEW/INTEREST
- The route passes through a pleasing mixture of woodlands, farmlands and sweeping uplands to reach wild, wonderful, mountainous terrain far above.
- The vast slopes of Galtymore Mountain rise to over 3000 ft and there is much to see and explore when you reach the top.
- Bird's-eye view of Lough Curra, a spectacular corrie lake.
- Excellent vistas across the wide, flat valley of the River Suir towards the distant Knockmealdown Mountains.

GRADIENTS
There is a long, gradual and in places relatively steep climb from the starting-point to reach the summit of Galtymore Mountain. A high-level, undulating descent follows from this high spot, but this does contain some upward

sections, one of which is a short, sharp, rather unexpected climb.

MAPS, FOOTPATHS AND WAYSIGNS

OS Discovery Series 1:50 000 — Number 74 (Cork, Limerick, Tipperary and Waterford)

There is a clearly defined start along a mixture of forest trails and roads and then paths which lead upwards into the mountains. This cocktail of ways also accompanies the finish of the walk. In between there are extensive areas of rough, eroded ground to cover and in places this exposed terrain is waterlogged, with peat hags to add some spice to the challenge.

There are fairly adequate signs in the forested areas but passing through the open landscapes you will need to rely on your own, inbuilt navigational prowess.

GETTING STARTED

Travel down the section of the main N8 road between Cahir (Caher on OS map) and Mitchelstown and then turn northwards along a side road at MR 899173. This is at Skeheenaranky at the schoolhouse. Motor up the narrow road for just over 2 km ($1\frac{1}{2}$ miles), forking L and following the hairpin bends and car park signs to reach the secluded parking area.

Walk across the forest road below the car park and descend the steps which lead down to the wide track below.

Summary Description of Walk

THE WAY TO GALTYMORE MOUNTAIN — MR 879238 (Allow 4 hours)

The starting-point is from a really delightful spot hidden away amongst densely forested slopes. These, for the time being at least, restrict distant views. Turn L along the track, following the direction of the sign indicating Forest Walk No 1. The way loops downhill to connect with the approach road below and at this point the forest walk leads off to the L. Turn L along the road, continuing to descend, and then cross over a single-arched stone bridge which spans the Attychraan River, a fast-flowing stream which cuts through a deep, wooded valley.

The road then winds uphill and at the junction ahead, turn L still gaining height. Your direction of progress is northwards and this leads you past stone barns and farm buildings into more open country. At this point, the first clear views of the formidable Galty Mountains (Na Gaibhlte) appear, these vast slopes increasingly dominating the horizon ahead of you as you walk towards them. Cattle and sheep graze contentedly in the sheltered pastures to your R and a conifer-lined valley falls away on your L to complete a scene of relaxing tranquillity where walkers will feel at one with nature.

A virtually level section of path then passes under an avenue of trees, mostly beech, leading you towards the distant mountains rising directly ahead. Keep straight on towards the large farmstead, forsaking a track which leads uphill to the R. A gentle descent to cross a stream followed by tracking between the farm buildings (these are exited through double gates enclosing a sheep pen), a section of rougher, walled track and the negotiation of two more metal gates and you have reached open country. Walk further N into this exciting environment.

5:1 The gentle approach along green roads leading towards Galtymore Mountain

Pass through a series of bends and another metal gate to continue up a wide, grassy path, still progressing further N. Along here, the summit of Knockeenatoung pops up to the NE and, further on, the vast, higher slopes leading to Greenane (An Grianán) progressively reveal their features. Following a sharp bend to the L, ignore a rougher, banked, side path leading off on the R. Next, proceed through a high-level sheep pen and then select a steeper path leading off on the R. This way tracks up the broad, rising spur of the mountain, leading you away from a group of conifer trees below.

Height is now gained more quickly as the steepness of the slopes increases, and from this higher altitude additional, vast areas of the Galty Mountains over to your L and in the NW begin to appear. These include the expansive, eroded slopes leading towards the summits of Knockaterriff (Cnoc an Tairbh), Lyracappul (Ladhar an Chapaill) and Carrignabinnia (Carraig na Binne) — a massive, connected, mountainous wilderness. During your lengthy climb you will pass near to intermittent groups of stones and these are the remains of an ancient boundary wall.

Keep progressing uphill to the N across wide, expansive and for the most part reasonably well-drained slopes. Follow the crest of the rising spur as it subtly changes direction slightly towards NNE, where areas of boggier ground then have to be crossed as the gradient slackens off. Then, higher up still, revert you direction of travel to N. Eventually, the almost level summit platform of Galtymore Mountain (Cnoc Mór na nGaibhlte) appears above, with a series of craggy edges lining its flattish top. Head for the L-hand and most westerly point of this summit area which is marked with a substantial cairn. Nasty peat hags prevent a direct approach, so plan a way there with care in order to circumvent the worst of this difficult ground, working your way around to outflank them on the L.

Crossing this final, demanding section of ground to reach the inviting summit area and to plonk your feet on the highest point in the Galty Mountains will probably take longer than most walkers anticipate. So be patient and pace yourself accordingly, for the delights when you reach the top are well worth your present, concluding efforts! The final approach is to the NE, making use of a convenient, wide, eroded channel which leads through the surrounding peat bog. The twin summit area of Galtymore Mountain commands a height of 919 m (3015 ft). It is a massive area and in good weather you will probably want to spend some reasonable time walking across this interesting mini-plateau and exploring at your leisure the several features positioned there. These include, in sequence of discovery, a large cairn constructed of conglomerate and sandstone boulders, a white cross, another, more modestly sized cairn and a broken-off trigonometrical point. The views from along here in clear weather are fantastic and, in addition to those features already disclosed, there are riveting new disclosures of the northerly aspects and perspectives of the vast mountain range and of the landscapes tumbling down towards the flatness of Co Tipperary.

THE WAY BACK TO THE CAR PARK — MR 879188 (Allow 4½ hours)

Start your descent to the SW, this from the large, westerly cairn, keeping well clear of the steeper slopes to your R as you surrender height along a shallow channel in the lea of the falling ridge. This correct way down will lead you to the start of a long, winding, stone wall which denotes the boundary line between Co Limerick and Co Tipperary. There is adequate shelter in this vicinity and this provides a sensible place, out of the worst of the wind, to devour some refreshments when the weather is stormy!

After this, follow the line of the wall, keeping this on your R as you track westwards across stony and, quite often, waterlogged ground towards the pointed peaks of Lyracappul, Carrignabinnia and Slievecushnabinnia (Sliabh Chois na Binne), beyond which the distant Ballyhoura Mountains may be seen in good weather, these appearing in a gap between the nearer mountain peaks. The wall then swings around to the NW and you faithfully follow it as it continues to hug the crest of the ridge. An appreciable drop follows and then, after a relatively level stretch, the ground falls again, now towards the great shoulder of the ridge which leads towards Slievecushnabinnia.

Cross over the wall lower down to access and walk along easier ground. Keep descending but steer well clear of the edge and steep drop now developing to your R. Change over to the L of the dilapidated walling when the crumbling edge becomes more dangerous and only peep — with great caution and with firm footholds in position — down into the great void below, at the bottom of which the shimmering waters of Lough Curra fill the gouged-out basin. The view down is terrific, and the massive mountain spur stretching out to the NE from the central dome of the Galties far beyond the trapped lake is that of Knockastakeen (Cnoc an Stáicín).

Continue along beside the wall, now tracking uphill once again. Turn about along here to observe the superb views of the eroded slopes sweeping up towards the towering peak of

Galtymore. Then continue to keep faith with the remains of the wall as it turns sharply to the L. From here, the route continues across a wide, shallow hause and then mounts the broad hillside on the far side. Further up, the walling starts to swing away progressively to the R and this is the spot to abandon it by opting to walk straight ahead, following a compass bearing between SW and SSW. This continuation way is mainly across broad, grassy slopes but the occasional peat hag will have to be either taken in your stride or circumvented by evasive action.

5:2 Trekking across wide open spaces during the prolonged descent from Slievecushnabinnia

When the slope flattens off, change your direction to S and then, in misty conditions, be vigilant to locate and follow the broad spur which leads down across tufted grasses. In this vicinity you should be able to observe, given clear weather, lush, interlocking hillsides which form a V-shaped valley far below to the S. For very obvious reasons this has attracted the colloquial pseudonym of the 'Green Valley' but it is in fact called Blackrock. A relatively easy descent follows along a broad, grassy ridge which falls relatively gently towards the flatness below. Lower down, you have the luxury of a faint path as the rate of descent increases, this before you have to cross a broad saddle and again outwit a crop of peat hags and deepish trenches.

Climb over the rounded hillocks ahead which are part of the continuation of the descending spur, still heading S. For a welcome change, the steepish slopes of the final rise and fall are well drained and these support a mixture of heathers and bilberry. A small cairn marks the flattish top; this is located at MR 859219. From here, continue your descent to the SSE, crunching over the low-growing heathers and ensuring that an ever-enlarging watercourse remains well to your L. Then take care to find and use an important step stile in the wire fence below.

Continue your established descent to the SSE, heading towards a copse of conifer trees below, and this diagonal will connect you with a banked, grassy track which you then follow as it leads further downhill, crossing another track at right angles in the process. This descent route will then bring you to the interesting ruins of a hillside village. At this point, track to the R beside the wire fence which stretches below the stone rubble and then proceed through the gate on your L to continue, now to the SE, your descent towards the farm buildings below. Pass through more gate posts lower down, keeping to a bearing between SE and SSE, to then pass through a gap in the remains of a stone wall with sections of bushes forming a hedge. Beyond this, walk beside the wire fence, keeping this on your L before crossing over it at a streamlet below, having to scale a 3 ft high bank on the far side to achieve this manoeuvre.

Turn full R and then almost immediately fork L to continue walking S along the valley above the large and impressive farmstead you passed through on your way out. Initially, this section of the return route leads slightly uphill to pass through a gateway and this is followed by a long, gradual descent. Veer R at the junction ahead, thus avoiding the continuation way which bends around to the L, and follow the track as it leads uphill back into a wooded area. When this track bends to the R, be extra careful to spot and climb over a stile on your L (identified by blue and red arrowheads). The continuation path leads under the deciduous canopy by the edge of the trees; a section here requires some perseverance but the correct way becomes better defined and is again waysigned further on.

Locate the correct continuation path below which leads NE and turn L along this. Then, as directed by the blue and green arrows, turn R at the next T-junction to walk along a wide grassy path through forest land which has recently been harvested. Following this, turn L again along the signed way to descend further beside gorse hedging and after skirting around some fallen trees the way leads down to the car park, a short distance below.

Alternative Ways

ESCAPES

Apart from turning back either on the way up to Galtymore or from the summit area, there are no other practical escape routes on this walk. On no account be tempted to descend down the intervening Glounreagh valley, as this contains difficult ground at the bottom which is best avoided.

EXTENSIONS

Very strong and vastly experienced walkers could contemplate traversing across the higher ground as far as Temple Hill (Cnoc an Teampaill) in fair weather but there is a long, tedious descent from this far-away mountain with a less-than-straightforward, cross-country return, tracking E to get back to the car park. To only bite off the extra distance circling around from Slievecushnabinnia through Carrignabinnia, Lyracappul and Knockaterriff Beg to Knockaterriff is perhaps a much more practical and sensible proposition.

KNOCKMEALDOWN RIDGE

fact file

START/FINISH

Start from car park — MR 031100
Finish at minor road — MR 112081

GRADING

Moderate to difficult/strenuous, depending on weather (colour-coded BLUE/RED)

WALKING TIME ALLOWANCE

5½ hours

DISTANCE

9.6 km (6.0 miles)

TOTAL HEIGHT GAINED

720 m (2360 ft)

PRINCIPAL HEIGHTS

- Sugarloaf Hill 663 m (2175 ft)
- Knockmealdown 794 m (2605 ft)
- Knocknagnauv 655 m (2150 ft)

digest of walk

PARKING

Very adequate visitor car park at start; usually no problem parking for walkers who inevitably get there well before more general tourists and sightseers arrive! (Note: This is a linear walk and, therefore, ideally two vehicles should be used, the second one parked on the verge of the minor road at or near the finish of the walk where there is room for several cars in two or three convenient places. Otherwise, arrange transport to collect you from the end of the walk at your estimated time of arrival there.)

OVERVIEW/INTEREST

- A very enjoyable, undulating, ridge walk along the tops of several of the mountains in the Knockmealdown range.
- Expansive, fine views all day long, given clear weather.
- Sightings of secluded corrie lakes and eroded cliff faces.
- Airy route with the land falling away on both sides for much of the way.

KNOCKMEALDOWN RIDGE

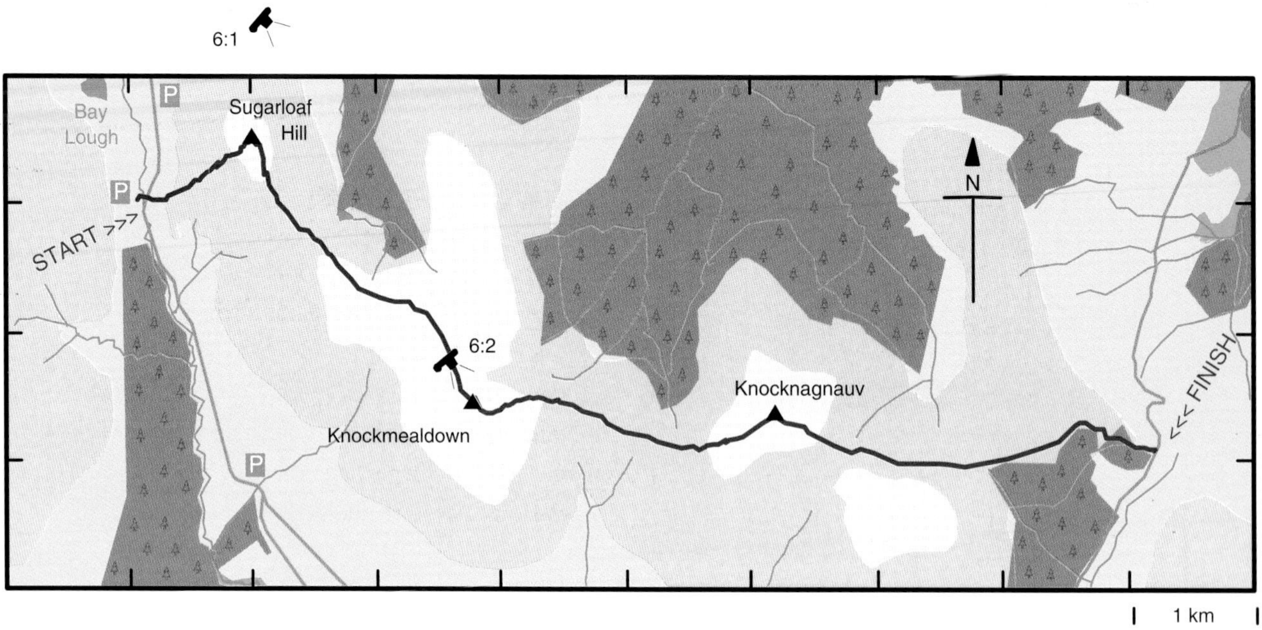

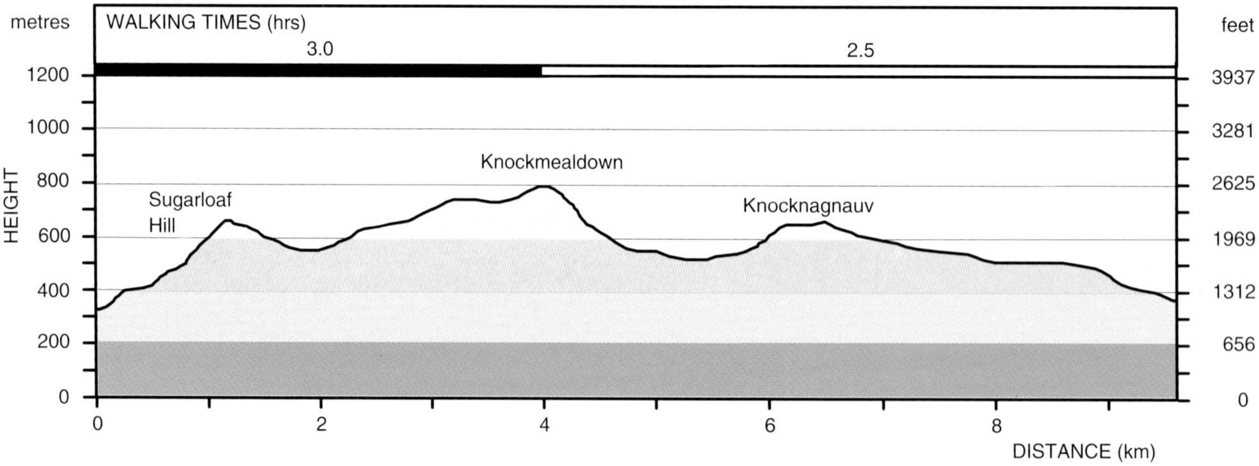

GRADIENTS

A steep, rough climb to the top of Sugarloaf Hill has to be tackled, straight from the parking area. After this, it is a switchback of a way with further steep ups and downs. These inclines include a long haul to reach the summit of Knockmealdown. Following further lengthy undulations and a traverse, the walk concludes with another steepish descent.

MAPS, FOOTPATHS AND WAYSIGNS

OS DISCOVERY SERIES 1:50 000 — NUMBER 74 (CORK, LIMERICK, TIPPERARY AND WATERFORD)

Although there are paths of sorts for much of the way, most of the going is either over rough, rocky ground or across heavy, waterlogged areas, and this combination tends to sap energy levels quite quickly.

There are no signs to help you find your way but this matters little, as with reasonably competent navigational skills and the help of a few strategically positioned cairns you should experience few, if any, serious route-finding problems.

GETTING STARTED

The starting-point may be reached from either N or S along the scenic R668 road. There is another access road, the R669, which tracks NW from Cappoquin.

From the parking area, cross over the road and tackle the well-used, wide, eroded track which climbs steeply up the rough, rocky slopes rising ahead to the NE.

SUMMARY DESCRIPTION OF WALK

THE WAY TO KNOCKMEALDOWN — MR 058084 (Allow 3 hours)

The going is tough at the start, so pace yourself accordingly and, in the flatter section between two steeper parts, allow yourself a breather should you feel you need or deserve this stop. (The author usually finds a good photographic excuse for this temporary delay when he is in the company of strong walkers who possess the abilities of mountain goats!) In clear weather, during this hectic climb you will be able to observe the distant outline of the Galty Mountains to the NNW with the distinctive, plateau-like summit of Galtymore, the highest point in this range, dominating the horizon in that direction over on your L. Higher up, turn about to observe the rounded summit of Knockshanahullion (Cnoc Seanchuillinn) rearing up to the W beyond the pass from which you commenced the walk. Down below is the rounded Bay Lough (Béal Locha), very popular with less energetic visitors to the area who enjoy the short, undemanding walk there and back from the strategically positioned parking area.

Suddenly, the steep slopes give way to ground up which more comfortable progress may be made, and this occurrence signifies that you are almost on the summit of Sugarloaf Hill (Cnoc na gCloch). There are two summit cairns to greet you when you get there, both of these over to the L of your approach. The lower one interestingly signifies the burial spot of a Major Ely who insisted on being put to rest 'standing up', with a shotgun and two dogs, in order that on

6:1 The distant profile of the Knockmealdown Mountains observed across the wide valley of the River Suir

the day of judgment he might conveniently just pop down into the woods once more to bag a few pheasants! (This really is a 'tall' story.) The observations in good weather from this elevated position at 663 m (2175 ft) include Galtymore to the NW, the isolated peak of Slievenamon to the NE, the Comeragh Mountains to the E and, much nearer, the summit of Knockmealdown (Cnoc Mhaoldomhnaigh) to the SE.

At Sugarloaf make a R-handed turn to then track beside the wall (boundary line between Co Waterford and Co Tipperary), descending along a path which leads southwards towards Knockmealdown. During the descent deviate for a short distance along a branch path which loops around to the L in order to avoid more difficult ground then directly ahead. The descent steepens before the continuation route crosses a broad saddle below. There is another serious climb up on the far side, although this is not nearly as steep or as rough as the first one up to Sugarloaf! Just continue upwards along the line of the wall and follow this as it swings to the R to then cross another shallow hause, tracking between E and S.

Higher up, cross over the wall and then keep this to your L in order to steer comfortably away from the edge and the steepening, precipitous slopes which begin to fall away on the far side of the stone barrier. After this, and above a craggy ledge, the summit of Knockmealdown is soon attained and your efforts for getting there are rewarded by locating a trigonometrical point and, in fine weather, observing distant Dungarvan to the SE, this located through a gap in the intervening mountains. You have now attained a height of 794 m (2605 ft) and are standing on the highest point in the Knockmealdown Mountains. Most of the other major observations to be made from here have previously been positioned, apart from further revealing views eastwards along the continuation of the high ridge towards Knocknagnauv (Cnoc na gCnámh), Knocknafallia (Cnoc na Faille) and Knockmeal (Seisceann na Maoile).

THE WAY TO THE FINISH AT THE MINOR ROAD — MR 112081 (Allow 2½ hours)

The summit of Knockmealdown is in fact narrow and wedge-shaped, like a huge piece of cheese. Leave it at its easterly edge and maintain this bearing as you tackle the very steep descent. Keep more or less in line with the wall, following an intermittent, narrow path. However, part way down divert to the R to avoid some of the steepest, roughest ground. Below, another expansive hause is crossed, this by heading SE. Along here, look out for the fine, spired building of a Cistercian monastery, Mount Melleray Abbey, visible in clear weather over to your R in the SSE.

As you traverse across the expansive hause, the rounded slopes of Knocknagnauv (meaning 'mountain of the bones'!) beckon you towards them directly ahead, and when you manage to escape from the magnetism of looking with mounting anticipation at this, glance around your feet to discover red-headed lichen thriving hereabouts. In crossing the bottom of the saddle (Bottle Pass) you will also reach St Declan's Way, a path which descends southwards to connect with the R669 road far below.

Then it is up again, and towards the top of this next slope you will come across another section of walling which then bears off to your L. Follow this helpful feature to the top of the rounded hilltop ahead, crossing recently burnt heathland to get there. Locate the area, for obvious reasons known as the 'Pile of Stones', just to the R of the walling across the burnt ground (recovery time about three years) and you are now standing just below the summit of Knocknagnauv at a height of 655 m (2150 ft). From this certain landmark, head off SE across the vast, open mountainside, walking gradually downhill in line with an area of conifer trees in the mid-distance. Then, when you reach rising ground again, traverse around to the L, maintaining a more or less constant height. You should now be aiming for the narrow ridge ahead and, therefore, avoid a track which leads uphill to the R, this as you cross another path at right angles.

Keep heading ESE across open terrain and, following the level traverse, you then surrender some height to arrive at another path below. The walking surface hereabouts, along a rough path, is a somewhat demanding concoction of fixed boulders, loose stones, wet, slithery peat and grass! The huge mountains now appearing in ever more detail ahead of you are Crohan West (Cruachán) to the NNE and Knockmeal to the ENE. Complete that part of the way which circles to the N around the lower slopes of Knocknafallia, still heading eastwards, and this will connect you with an intersection of ways at the corner of a forestry plantation directly ahead. Choose the middle path to progress ENE above the top edge of the densely packed pines.

There is now a marker line in the form of wooden posts which are the remains of a dilapidated fence. The continuation way then zigzags marginally uphill before straightening out into a more gentle, upward traverse. A diagonal descent follows and, after a sharp turn to the R, a steepening downward slope leads to the minor road below, the grassy path down hugging the perimeter of the forested area to your R. Ideally, you should have a vehicle in position to use at this point or transport, arranged in advance, should be well on its way to collect you. Incidentally, this collection point happens to be just on the Waterford–Tipperary boundary line. Otherwise, if you cannot quickly cadge a lift, there is little alternative but for you to grit your

6:2 LOCAL WALKING GUIDE MICHAEL DESMOND SILHOUETTED ON A CRAG NEAR THE TOP OF KNOCKMEALDOWN

teeth, turn L and walk down into Newcastle, some 5 km (3 miles) away to the N and about another hour's fast walking!

ALTERNATIVE WAYS

ESCAPES

Linear ridge walks are usually not the easiest types of mountain explorations for which to devise practical short cuts, and this particular walk conforms to this general rule. The most obvious escape in bad weather, apart from turning back, is when you reach MR 072081 to turn S along St Declan's Way. However, if you anticipate having to do this, take the precaution of parking a vehicle in the vicinity of where this descent connects with the R669 road (MR 065052), as otherwise you might have a long, tedious climb along the road to return to the starting-point of the walk. On no account be tempted to leave the ridge to the N because all descents in that direction are difficult, pathless ones, many with potential hazards. There is also the additional problem of getting through the densely forested areas at the base of these mountains which, in most places, is quite formidable. (Accept this advice from one who has tried to do just this!)

EXTENSIONS

Assuming you do not have the forced extension of the road walk into Newcastle, more exciting and interesting additions are to scale either Knocknafallia or Knockmeal — or both. These two summits are located towards the end of the route as described and, therefore, your options concerning climbing these may be kept open until you reach them later in the day.

KNOCKANAFFRIN RIDGE

fact file

START/FINISH
Start from verge of minor road — MR 255175
Finish at car park — MR 277129

GRADING
Moderate (colour-coded BLUE)

WALKING TIME ALLOWANCE
5 hours

DISTANCE
8.4 km (5.2 miles)

TOTAL HEIGHT GAINED
400 m (1310 ft)

PRINCIPAL HEIGHTS
- Shauneenabreaga 547 m (1795 ft)
- Knocksheegowna 678 m (2225 ft)
- Knockanaffrin 755 m (2475 ft)

digest of walk

PARKING
Limited parking at the start along a grassy verge near to the minor road; room for only about six cars at the most. (Note: This is a linear walk and, therefore, ideally two vehicles should be used, the second one positioned in the car park at the end of the walk where there is space for about 20 cars. Otherwise, arrange transport to collect you from the end of the walk at your estimated time of arrival there (see Alternative Ways below).)

OVERVIEW/INTEREST
- Craggy ridge route with ups and downs all the way, these leading across seven distinctive high spots.
- The way passes by an unusual high-level glider runway and then commercial turf-harvesting operations.
- Good, long-distance views during most of the route, given clear weather. Those of the nearby eastern Comeragh mountain plateau and the ones down on to several superb

KNOCKANAFFRIN RIDGE

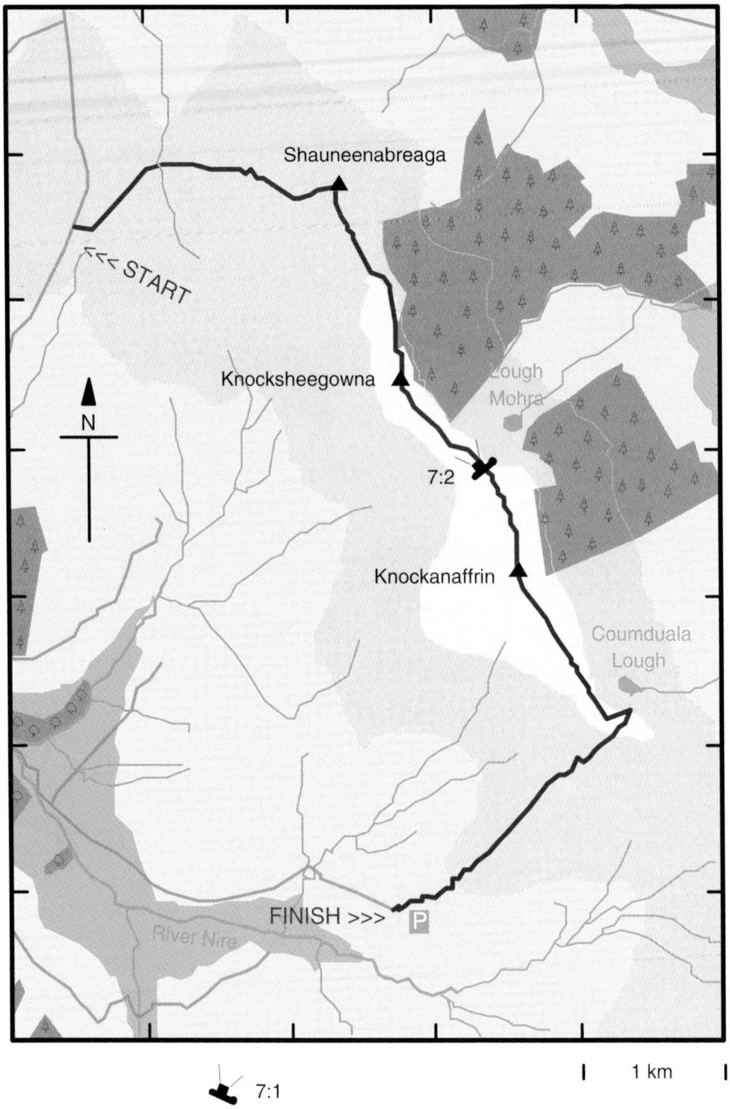

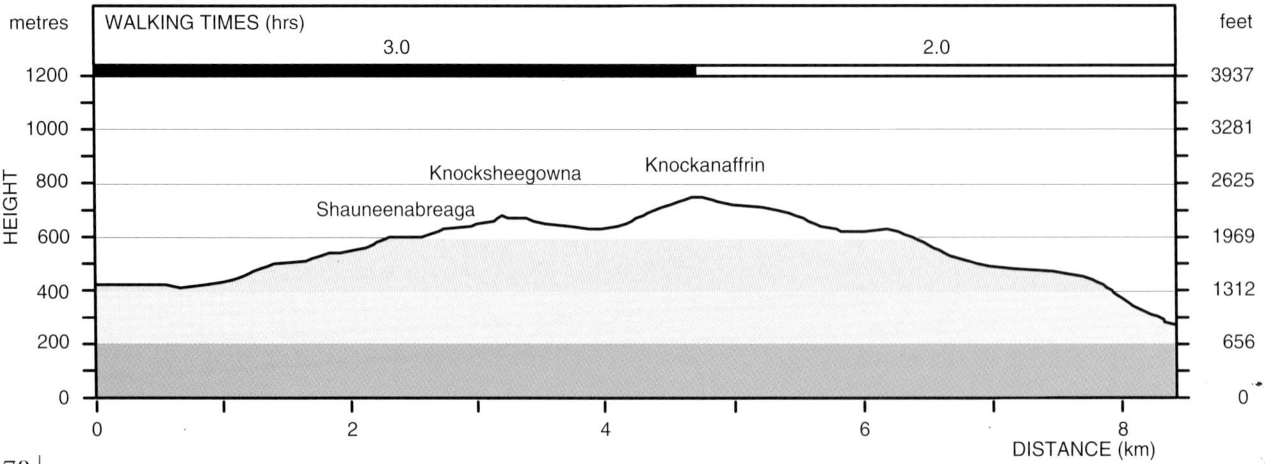

corrie lakes and beyond these across the green, open plains of Co Tipperary rank amongst the very best.

- Occasional bog pools, brimming with plant and animal life, are passed during the final descent.

GRADIENTS

The walk commences with a gradual, fairly lengthy climb on to the ridge, and there follows a succession of ups and downs, some of which are steep and rocky. There is a long, final descent with some rough slopes and quite demanding ground vegetation to cross near the top. The exacting going progressively eases off lower down.

MAPS, FOOTPATHS AND WAYSIGNS

OS Discovery Series 1:50 000 — Number 75 (Kilkenny, Tipperary and Waterford)

There are intermittent lanes, tracks and paths for part of the way but these easily navigable sections are interspersed in turn with both high, sweeping, pathless moorlands and then narrow, craggy outcrops of jumbled rocks.

Signs are non-existent and the only man-made directional aids are a few cairns scattered about, some marker posts and, in places, the lines of fencing.

GETTING STARTED

The starting-point lies about $2\frac{1}{2}$ km ($1\frac{1}{2}$ miles) to the S of the R678 road along a minor road leading there. The R678 connects, via the R677, Clonmel to the NW with Kilmacthomas. The start may also be accessed by travelling eastwards along the Nire Valley from Ballymacarbry.

The start of the walk is very straightforward — just commence striding E down the gravel lane and you are on your way.

Summary Description of Walk

THE WAY TO KNOCKANAFFRIN — MR 285153 (Allow 3 hours)

Just as soon as you get out of your vehicle you are surrounded by wild, remote and appealing landscapes, particularly so the scenery transfixed in your vision to the E which contains the craggy Knockanaffrin (Cnoc an Aifrinn) ridge towards which you immediately start walking, this by traversing wide, expansive slopes that rise gently ahead of you. Fork L ahead, skirting the bog and the commercial turf areas which are continuously being harvested. These fuels are extracted from blanket bogs which were most probably laid down about 10 000 years ago in a shallow lake and were formed from decayed grasses and sedges.

The route passes by a derelict stone building in which gliders were previously stored. There is still a launching pad here. An isolated peak then comes into view to the NNE over on your L; this is Slievenamon (Sliabh na mBan), which translates as 'woman's mountain'. There is a good story, much too long to repeat here, as to how it acquired its femininity; but to lift the skirts just a little on this, it did involve some young ladies of the district racing each other to the summit for a very masculine prize! When the wide track literally terminates, continue straight ahead, following a less well-defined, grassy way which narrows as it tracks further to the NE.

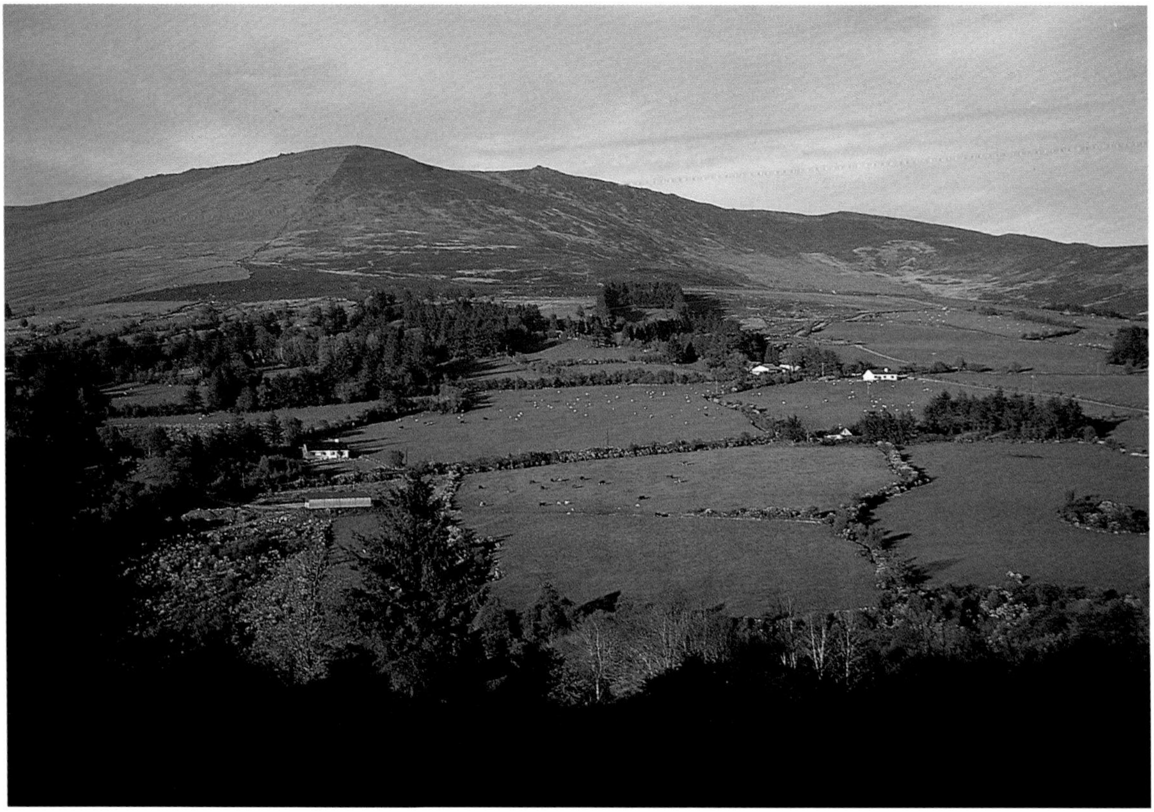

7:1 The Knockanaffrin Ridge observed beyond the upper reaches of the Nire Valley

Then bear R along the path to cross a shallow, boggy watercourse by means of an improvised wooden bridge. Insect-eating butterworts, red-feathered sphagnum mosses and tormentil (yellow flowers) thrive in the surrounding damp environment.

Waterlogged areas and wet, boggy ground lie in ambush ahead, and you will need to weave about and pick your way with care through this morass if you are keen on keeping your feet reasonably dry for when you reach the sanctity of the higher ground above. The main consolations here are sundews and wild orchids which flower in July. Keep to a predominant bearing of between ESE and SE now, as the slopes ahead begin to steepen. Then work your way around to the R and, as you gain further height, look behind you to take in the fine view of Lachtnafrankee, the rounded mountain in the W to your rear.

Rougher, steeper ground now has to be climbed, further progress being achieved between rocky outcrops and over bilberry and heathers. Another about-turn higher up will give you an opportunity to observe the Knockmealdown Mountains in clear weather, these rising some distance away to the WSW. Then follow a narrow path or sheep track around the brow to your R in order to outflank the more difficult ground of a boulder field directly above. After this, a sharp turn to the L will lead you E up a grassy strip which ascends steeper ground. This climb then passes an outcrop of conglomerate rocks away to your L, and beyond this the apex of the spur is reached.

From this higher elevation, providing the visibility is good, you can identify the Galty Mountains rising majestically to the WNW. Then you will arrive at a cairn and stone shelter positioned at the start of the ridge. These features also identify the summit area of Shauneenabreaga which rises to 547 m (1795 ft). New vistas open up from this peak, including vast, flat, cultivated landscapes punctuated by forested hillsides to the N, these extending in a wide semi-circle from W to E. These lands form part of the counties of Tipperary and Kilkenny. The major town of Clonmel lies to the NW, its loftiest buildings just peeping into view from here.

The route continues SSE along the rising ridge, and initially you should head for a rocky outcrop which appears ahead on the E horizon. There are seven discrete pinnacles or rocky outcrops located along this undulating spur of Knockanaffrin and these are known locally and affectionately as the 'Seven Sisters'. Skirt around the next outcrop to the R and then head towards the higher and more pronounced craggy rocks directly ahead, approaching these towards SSE. Again, pass by these to the R, making use of a rocky path or sheep track which traverses the slope at a fairly constant height.

Further on, veer more to the L to tackle the steeper slopes, thereby proceeding further SSE and walking through clumps of clinging heathers towards more craggy pinnacles now directly ahead. The way then passes below a wire fence before it continues along the crest of the ridge towards further rocky outcrops ahead. Then bear L again to cross a shallow saddle as a preliminary to making contact with the steeply falling, easterly edge of the ridge once more. Spectacular rocky buttresses now appear below, forming near vertical slopes which plunge precipitously towards the vast tracts of conifer forests sweeping up the more gentle slopes towards the impenetrable, rocky barrier.

After taking in these superb vistas, turn R along a faint path and follow this as it leads uphill to the S along a grassier part of the spur. Ahead and down below on your L the isolated, rounded peak of Croughaun Hill rises dramatically to present an elevated landmark for miles around. More impressive rock features are passed as you walk along the ridge and then the first of two major corrie loughs comes into view down below. This is Lough Mohra and is to the SE of you. Then climb up to the pointed peak ahead, crossing steep, grassy slopes to get to an elevation of 678 m (2225 ft) and the summit area of Knocksheegowna where an unusual trigonometrical point has been located.

Continue further southwards along the knobbly ridge composed of secure conglomerate rock to reach, after crossing the gap of Béal Mhuca, the summit of Knockanaffrin. This rises to 755 m (2475 ft) and is the highest elevation of the route. You will have to thread a planned course through rocks to get there but there is a choice of ways in the final approach, all along a SSE bearing. A peaty track which threads through the more difficult large slabs of rock is a definite help. There is a tiny cairn perched precariously on the jumble of rocks at the top of Knockanaffrin. In clear weather, the panoramic mountain views from this lofty place are majestic and most of the highlights in these have previously been identified. However, new and more revealing vistas do open up from here southwards towards the southern reaches of the Comeragh Mountains. Three small corrie lakes may also be seen from here, these filling basins in the steep, rocky slopes below.

7:2 Clearing mist reveals the craggy protrusions located along the Knockanaffrin Ridge

THE WAY TO THE CAR PARK AT THE FINISH — MR 277129 (Allow 2 hours)

Descend through the jumble of rocks along the continuation of the peaty path which winds SE towards more outcrops lower down. Then cross a wire fence with the aid of a wooden beam positioned near a marker post. On the way down, keep over to the L in order to spot the waters of Coumduala Lough, the second major corrie lough seen during the walk; it is hidden away far below beneath near vertical rock faces, hence its colloquial name of 'Lake with the Black Cliff'. The next rocky tor is passed on your R as the now ungraded, peaty track snakes around below this. Then branch L when you come to a fork ahead in order to continue along or near to the crest of the continuously dropping ridge.

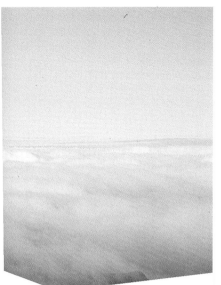

Two more wire fences then have to be crossed, again with the aid of improvised plank stiles. Be particularly careful of the barbed wire at the second of these! After negotiating these minor hurdles, turn full R to continue downhill, now heading SW along the line of a fence. The way is straight down the broad slopes, crossing over clumps of high-growing heathers where necessary. However, do be mindful of the occasional nasty bog hole hereabouts and do be prepared to take evasive action in advance of these when vigilantly spotted ahead!

Lower down, an isolated cairn is passed and, following this, bear L towards them when you spot a line of white marker posts. Afterwards, follow the line of these posts, walking along the relative luxury of a clearly defined path. This way leads through a metal gate and directly into the parking area.

Alternative Ways

ESCAPES

The exposed ridge is prone to sudden high winds and when necessary any obvious short circuit to the R, westwards, will lead you down to lower, safer ground and towards the Nire Road.

EXTENSIONS

There are problems in trying to extend the walk in the vicinity of the ridge. However, there are two possibilities for walking further. First, you could continue down the minor road from the finish of the prescribed route to reach Nire Church and Hanora's Cottage. (The cottage is in fact an upmarket guest house catering specially for walkers and you will receive a warm welcome there from the congenial proprietors, Mary and Seamus Wall; you may also have the pleasure of sampling their delicious refreshments if these have been ordered in advance. They also have arrangements with Michael Desmond, the local walking guide whose invaluable local knowledge has been incorporated into the above route description.) Second, if time permits, you could visit the famous Sgilloge Loughs below Curraghduff. These lie about $2\frac{1}{2}$ km ($1\frac{1}{2}$ miles) from the car park and, as there is a good path there once you have successfully crossed the River Nire, they make both an interesting and a not-too-strenuous addendum to this moderately graded walk.

THE GAP, CROTTY'S ROCK AND FAUS COUM

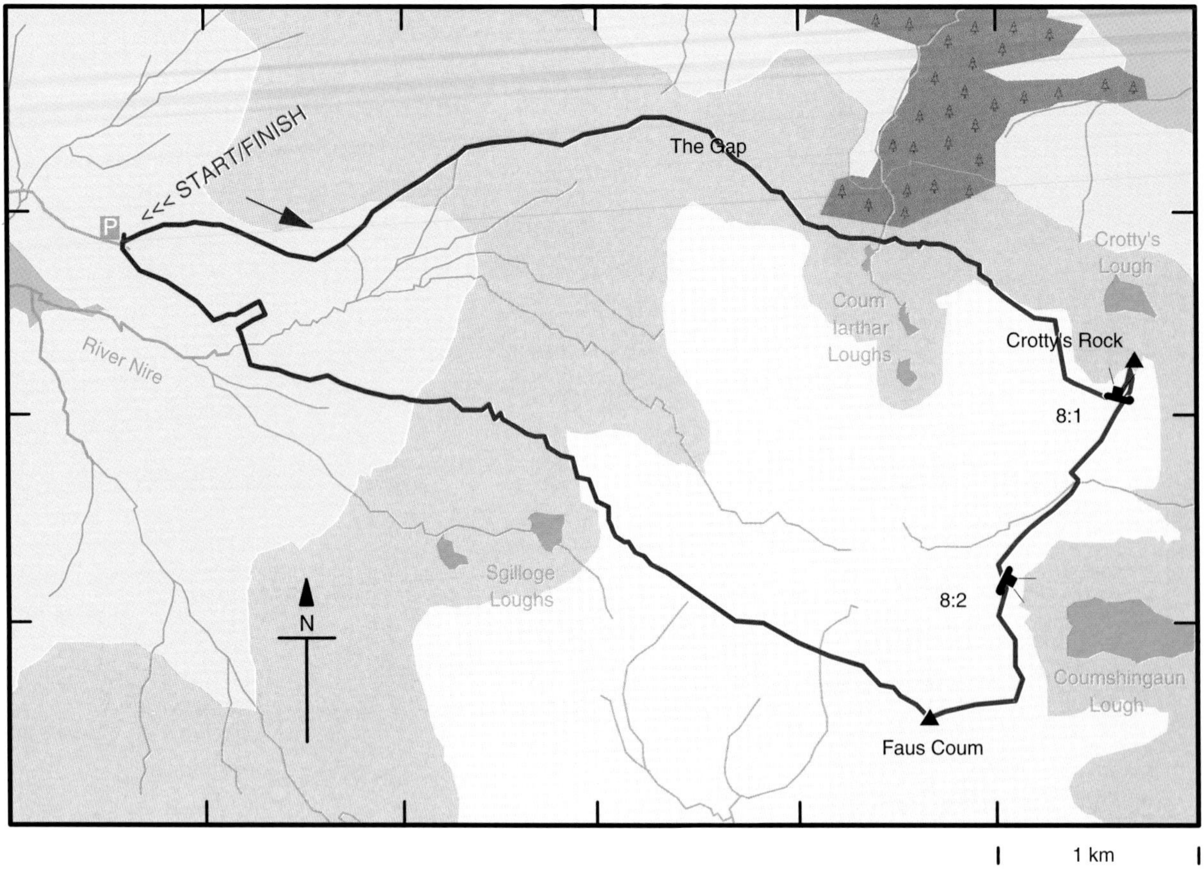

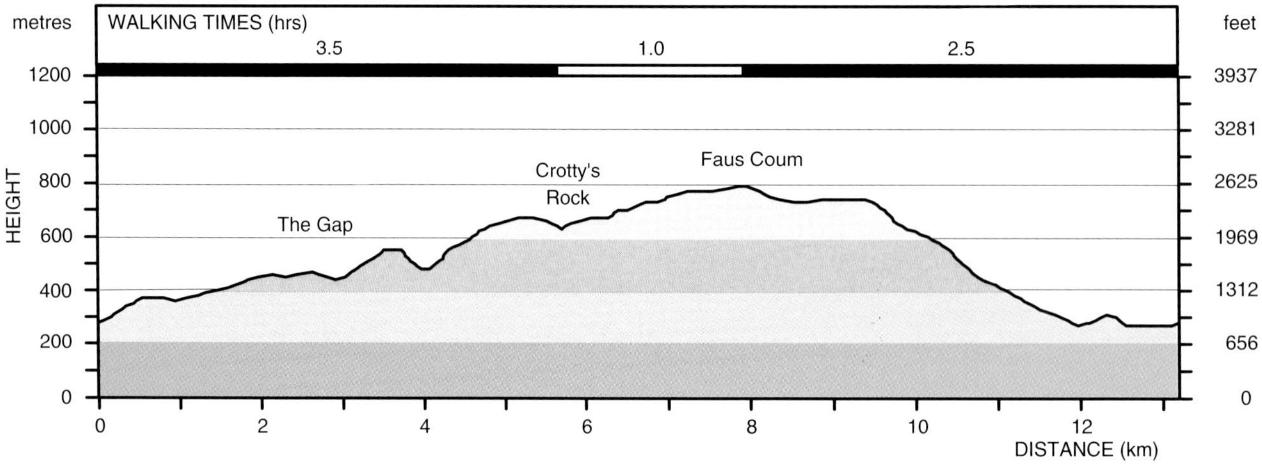

THE GAP, CROTTY'S ROCK AND FAUS COUM

fact file

START/FINISH
Car park — MR 277129

GRADING
Difficult/strenuous (colour-coded RED)

WALKING TIME ALLOWANCE
7 hours

DISTANCE
13.2 km (8.2 miles)

TOTAL HEIGHT GAINED
730 m (2400 ft)

PRINCIPAL HEIGHTS

• The Gap	466 m (1530 ft)
• Crotty's Rock	650 m (2130 ft)
• Faus Coum	792 m (2600 ft)

digest of walk

PARKING
Compact car park above minor road holds about 20 cars.

OVERVIEW/INTEREST

- The route threads through wild, remote, expansive and challenging terrain.
- Superb bird's-eye views of corrie loughs, of which Coumshingaun reigns supreme.
- Traverse through jumbles of rocks forming spectacular cliff faces, followed by section across sweeping, high moorlands which contain blanket bogs.
- Magnificent, rugged, mountainous scenery throughout entire route with riveting views of distant landscapes.
- A final gentle descent along a rounded ridge.

GRADIENTS

A modest climb to reach The Gap is followed by steeper sections across rougher, rocky ground containing undulations. These rise progressively to the heights of Crotty's Rock. More gentle slopes then lead to the summit of Faus Coum. From here it is downhill, mostly across spacious slopes which are never too severely angled.

MAPS, FOOTPATHS AND WAYSIGNS

OS Discovery Series 1:50 000 — Number 75 (Kilkenny, Tipperary and Waterford)

The walk commences along a waysigned path. Beyond The Gap much of the route is across open terrain with only intermittent tracks which do not always meander in the required direction! Rocky sections have to be crossed, as do high moorlands which contain peaty, boggy ground and eroded areas. The descent is along much better defined ways.

Signs away from the vicinity of the parking area are non-existent and there is only the occasional marker post and cairn to confirm the correct route.

GETTING STARTED

The starting-point may be reached either from Clonmel to the NW, using the R678 and then the minor roads leading S and then E, or alternatively from Ballymacarbry to the W, motoring up through the delightfully wooded, lower Nire Valley.

To commence the walk leave the car park walking E along the path signed 'An Bhearna — The Gap'.

Summary Description of Walk

THE WAY TO CROTTY'S ROCK — MR 327122 (Allow $3\frac{1}{2}$ hours)

The ascent to the higher ground of The Gap is straightforward, initially along a grassy path, the surface of which soon gives way to a mixture of stones as height is gradually gained along a section of the way helpfully defined by white-painted, wooden marker posts. Use an iron gate and then a double stile to cross fences *en route* to The Gap. When you reach The Gap, which stands at a height of 466 m (1530 ft), the surrounding panorama of the Comeragh Mountains becomes increasingly impressive, with the rugged, pointed ridge of Knockanaffrin rising on your L to the NW and the higher, more expansive, rounded slopes of Carrigshaneun in view in the opposite direction to the SE. It is towards the latter that you will next be heading. To approach these, turn R to continue SE along an indistinct path which initially follows the direction of a wire fence before veering L away from this barrier. Look to your L now to observe the vast, rounded cone of Slievenamon which dominates the distant view far away to the N.

The slopes progressively steepen as one of the spurs forming the northern flank of Carrignagower is gradually rounded to your L, reverting your continuation direction more towards E again. Wilder, rougher ground is then penetrated as your narrow path (sheep track) threads across a basin of rocks and boulders beneath spectacular, overhanging buttresses and rocky pinnacles as your steady climb continues. Then even more spectacular scenery comes into view, this a gigantic, awesome, gouged-out combe. This void is lined with near vertical rock faces sprinkled with an assortment of towering pinnacles and buttresses. Bear R along here, allowing the contours of the slopes to lead you first towards this compelling combe and then down to the first of several corrie loughs, known collectively as Coum Iarthar Loughs. This is a haven of peace and tranquillity and the perfect, sheltered spot to allow yourself a short coffee-break.

Then walk around to the L of the lough, fording the exit stream which bars your way. From here you have to tackle the steep, formidable slopes rising directly ahead! Do this on a traverse to the L, selecting a less severe rate of climb over heathers and boulders and setting a pace which you find comfortable to thread a way of your own choice through the fixed rock forms. Your heading here is still to the E. Keep climbing towards the higher ground which forms the rim of the extensive plateau above to your R, now walking towards a pointed pinnacle which you keep to your R as you track SSE along a still upward diagonal. This course will lead you to the dividing line between the steep, rocky slopes on your L and the gentler, more rounded inclines still above on your R. These vast, expansive, ranging hillsides higher up are now soon reached, and from here a final stretch to the SE, at a more or less constant height along the rim of the steeper ground falling away on your L, will lead you to the rocky pinnacle of Crotty's Rock.

This exciting rock feature comes into view ahead on your L. Carefully, thread your way across the intervening ground to gain the shelter of Crotty's Rock, being mindful, especially in blustery conditions, of the steep, and potentially dangerous, near vertical fall-aways on your L as you approach this sanctuary. The views from the meagre but sheltered perch — on which, with some modest effort, you can make yourself relatively comfortable — beneath this rocky sentinel are quite supreme. Down, many hundreds of feet below nestles Crotty's Lough (otherwise known as Lough Coumgaurha), its placid waters tightly cuddled within a cradle of loose, rock debris. Way beyond, to the N and E, the flat lands of Co Tipperary and Co Kilkenny disclose most of their topographical secrets. These, quite naturally, lead your inquisitive focus of vision across the many miles separating you from the distant coastline of Co Waterford.

THE WAY TO FAUS COUM — MR 317105 (Allow 1 hour)

Head S, veering SSW, from the rock, once again threading a route between the ground falling away steeply to your L and the more benign, rounded slopes ahead to your R. Further on, the correct way is confirmed by a more distinct path which traverses around the slopes at a fairly constant level, bearing R in doing so. Then the stream named Iske Sullas is crossed by hopping over white boulders. Following this,

8:1 LOOKING DOWN FROM CROTTY'S ROCK TO THE LOUGH FAR BELOW

first turn R to climb westwards up the heather-clad slopes and then bear L, changing your direction to SSW, to reach the edge above.

The reward for this climb are the first sightings of Coumshingaun Lough (Loch Chom Seangán), its blue waters shimmering over a thousand feet below in the embrace of one of the finest endemic corries to be discovered anywhere in Europe. The majestic setting of this gouged-out crater, together with its fascinating rock formations, attracts visits by geologists from many countries. The plummeting, sheer cliff faces of the vast combe are a breathtaking mixture of near vertical rock pitches and almost perpendicular grass slopes, these interspersed with exposed ridges, buttresses and ledges of every conceivable shape and size. Rock falls and shattered debris line the lower slopes and disappear beneath the still waters of the lake.

8:2 THE SPLENDOUR OF COUMSHINGAUN LOUGH OBSERVED FROM THE DIZZY HEIGHTS ABOVE

When you have feasted sufficiently on this magnificent setting, make your way along the airy rim of the corrie, following a faint path heading S to attain the rounded summit ahead. Along here, always be mindful of the precipitous fall-away, never more than a few feet away to your L! In clear weather you can sight Dungarvan Harbour from here, this towards SSW. Now turn to your R to head due W away from the cliff faces and walk across the high, gently sloping moorlands to reach the isolated cairn (a rarity in these parts!) directly ahead. Some patches of boggy ground have to be crossed and the occasional pool of water avoided in getting there, but higher up these minor challenges give way to drier ground. The cairn is positioned at 792 m (2600 ft) and marks the highest point in the Comeragh Mountains. Somewhat surprisingly it is not named on the OS map but is known by Irish walkers as Faus Coum, although there is some dispute about this description. In the clearest of weathers there is a quite superb 360 degree panorama from here which unmasks the spaciousness of this vast range of mountains now spreadeagled around and below you.

THE WAY BACK TO THE CAR PARK — MR 277129 (Allow $2\frac{1}{2}$ hours)

Start your long descent from the cairn to the WNW, then bearing NW, following a gentle, downhill slope of rough, peaty ground. The infant River Mahon is then crossed, this a mere oozy, brown-coloured trickle carving neatly through the peaty hags at this point. Keep descending between W and NW, following a course of your own choosing across the demanding terrain to reach another rare, but reassuring, marker cairn. The continuation way then progressively tracks around to the R to lead you to the edge of steeper slopes which fall away directly ahead of your approach. This connection is in the vicinity of a small rivulet which falls precipitously down a rocky gully to feed the trapped waters of Sgilloge Loughs, hundreds of feet below. (My expert local guides informed me that there was an adventurous scramble down this watery chute and this I readily accepted, declining their offer to test personally the validity of their contention!)

Pass by this arresting feature, keeping the fall-away to your L by circling around the massive mountainside, now heading NNW to reach a less demanding continuation way down along a broad ridge leading NW ahead. From here, an established path, circling above the corrie lakes, leads down in the direction of the car park. Continue descending to the NW, making use of the better-defined, grassy path which snakes through boulder fields and around wetter, boggy patches. The correct route here is identified by cairns followed by a line of wooden marker posts. An obvious way leads down towards the course of the River Nire, which you follow downstream for a short distance. When you reach another marker post, turn R to pass through dense bracken and drop down to cross the river.

Climb up the opposite bank, again passing through bracken, following a grassy path which strikes an upward diagonal to your L. Near the top of the brow, backtrack for a short distance to your R to reach another marker post positioned along the grassy way. Turn full L when you reach the next post, this located at the corner of a stone wall, and then turn L again to pass through a wooden gate ahead. Walk westwards downhill heading towards the conifers below along a narrow path which widens. This leads to a better-defined track which you bear R along, walking slightly uphill and ignoring another way off to the R signed 'Locha na hUidrire — Nire Lakes'. Pass through the metal gates ahead and beyond these the lane leads gently downhill back to the car park.

Alternative Ways

ESCAPES

At any point before you reach Crotty's Rock simply turn about and retrace your outward steps back to the car park. This should be done if either you are finding the route too strenuous for your liking or, in adverse weather, you are not sufficiently experienced in navigating across wild, exposed terrain where there are few identifiable landmarks. Additionally, from above Coumshingaun Lough the higher ground of Faus Coum may be avoided by striking off due W, heading straight for the ridge leading down NW past Sgilloge Loughs.

EXTENSIONS

The route as described is a challenging one and extensions are not generally recommended. In good weather conditions, strong and fit walkers could perhaps venture some distance into the spectacular corrie cradling Coum Iarthar Loughs or walk further around the exposed edges above Coumshingaun Lough.

Overleaf: Reflections on Cloonee Lough

Beara Peninsula Walks

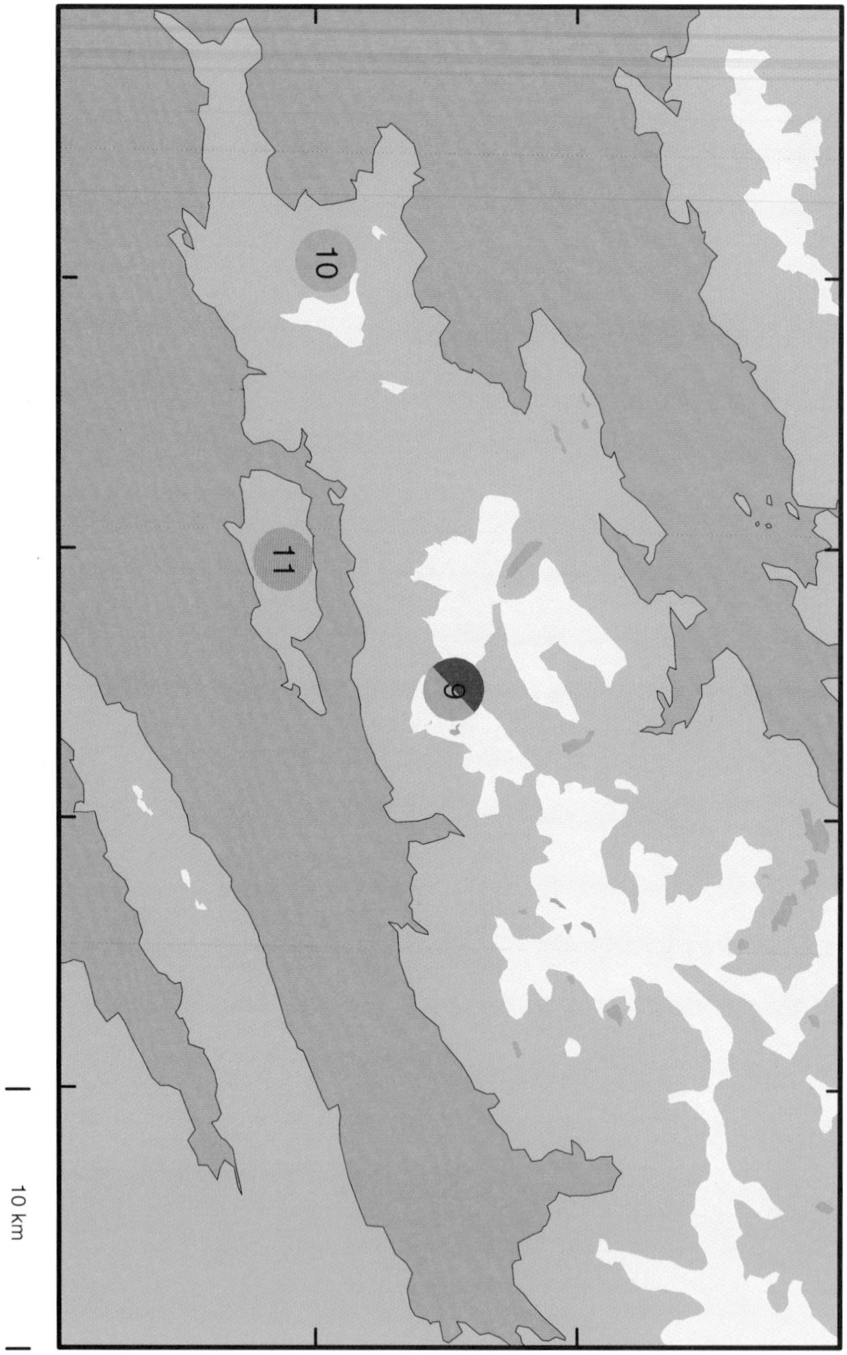
10
11
9
10 km

The Mountains of the Beara Peninsula

Getting There

As the crow flies, Castletown Bearhaven, an attractive harbour and fishing village located towards the end of the Beara Peninsula, is about 170 km (105 miles) WSW of Clonmel. The direct route by road, which is somewhat longer than the flight of the crow, commences westwards along the main N24 and N8 roads through Cahir (Caher on OS map) to Mitchelstown. From here, continue along the N73 road to reach Mallow and then the N72 road will take you through Rathmore towards Killarney. At Barraduff, turn southwards along the R570 road, use a short section of the N22 road to connect with the R569 road and travel along this through the mountains westwards towards Kenmare, the northern gateway to the Beara Peninsula.

Assuming you are journeying into the peninsula, you have a choice of routes from the Kenmare district, both of which could involve exciting crossings of high mountains. You can take the N71 road which threads southwards to Glengarriff, where you can turn off westwards along the R572 road which runs along the southern coastal fringe of Beara. Alternatively, you can travel westwards along the R571 road just S of Kenmare and then either use the R574 road which tortuously snakes over Healy Pass to reach the southern shoreline or follow the R571 road into Castletown Bearhaven. If you take the latter route you have the extra option of turning off along the R575 road to reach Allihies and the westernmost tip of the peninsula, finally arriving in Castletown Bearhaven by way of the R572 road.

There are opportunities for including interesting, more scenic interludes in this journey westwards. One of these is to motor SW from Clonmel, using the R668 road from Clogheen to pass through the Knockmealdown Mountains, perhaps visiting Mount Melleray Abbey near Cappoquin, before heading W through Fermoy along the N72 road to join the previously described direct route at Mallow. Between Mallow and Rathmore there are other possibilities for extending the route by travelling S through the picturesque Boggeragh and Derrynasaggart Mountains before heading W again towards either Kenmare along the N22 and R569 roads or Glengarriff via the R584 road. The latter choice will add winding through the Shehy Mountains to your itinerary. If you decide on one of the longer and slower variants, allow most of the day for the journey from Clonmel.

Geological Perspective

The scenery of this district is related directly to the nature of the rocks below. The mountainous high ground and the dominant headlands of the coastline are generally composed of tough Old Red Sandstone, whilst the lower ground and the coastal bays are formed from more readily eroded Carboniferous rocks. Normally layers of 'Old Red' have been overlain by the Carboniferous strata: the association of these two types of rock at the surface in this area is due to the presence of tight folds in the underlying layers. The 'Old Red' has been exposed by erosion in the cores of the upfolds (anticlines), whilst the Carboniferous rock is preserved in the troughs of the downfolds (synclines). Accordingly, the lofty spine of the Beara Peninsula with the Caha and Slieve Miskish Mountains rising to above 700 m (2300 ft) are formed by Old Red Sandstone some 400 million years in age, whilst inlets such as Bantry Bay and Kenmare River are floored by the less resistant Carboniferous strata which were laid down about 300 million years ago.

The Caha Mountains were glaciated during the Great (Pleistocene) Ice Age during the last two million years, and today impressive glaciated valleys may be observed, especially on the northern slopes of this high ground. Of special interest are the valley containing the string of Cloonee Loughs and the valley hosting Glenbeg Lough and its associated waterfalls. However, the glaciers of this area did not spread very far.

At lower levels, erosion has been mostly by rivers, and the major inlets — Bantry Bay and Kenmare River — are manifestly rias (flooded river valleys) rather than fjords (flooded glaciated valleys). Near to Bantry town there is a drumlin field, i.e. an area where debris dumped by glaciers has been moulded into conspicuous mounds. Some of these humps form islands at the head of Bantry Bay.

Most human activity — and the contribution this has made to shaping the landscapes of today — has been concentrated on the lower ground where the Carboniferous rocks have produced better and more fertile soils than those overlying the 'Old Red'. At the western end of the peninsula there is extensive evidence of the former workings of the Allihies copper mine, which together with other mines in the area was forced to close when the Zambian Copper Belt was developed to produce significantly more competitive ores.

Present-Day Landscapes and Opportunities for Walking

Beara is the most southerly and the most remote of the three major peninsulas jutting out into the Atlantic Ocean in the SW corner of Ireland. The Slieve Miskish Mountains and the higher Caha Mountains form the rocky spine of this peninsula, providing the kind of wild, rugged, adventurous terrain which strong, experienced hillwalkers dream about. Pointed peaks and flatter summit areas abound, and many of these can only be reached after walking or scrambling up and over formidable rocky terracing and ledges where boulder fields and cliff faces tumbling down on top of each other ensure that route planning and execution are real challenges. Many summits are also quite remote and often involve walking over lengthy and difficult approach routes.

Contrasting with this wild, rugged and awesome beauty is more gentle countryside, most of which is located along the coastal fringes and on Bear Island. Here, there are less demanding heights to climb, nature reserves to visit and the shores of loughs to explore. These more sheltered areas are ideal for casual walkers and family groups, and some of the shorter walks could also involve spending time relaxing on a beach or enjoying a trip on a ferry crossing.

Choice of Walking Routes

Standing on the top of Hungry Hill, the highest peak on the peninsula, had to be a must, and this is featured as Walk 9, following a rarely used route to the top which was disclosed to me by a local sheep farmer, Connie Doyle. Walk 10 from Allihies up a craggy ridge on to a mountain named Knockoura, explores the western tip of the peninsula, whilst a boat trip to Bear Island and a leisurely stroll to its modest high point features as Walk 11 and completes the trio of contrasting routes all centred on staying in or around Castletown Bearhaven.

Local Walking Guides

Beara was the one area where I did not complete any walks with local professional guides. However, as previously mentioned, Connie Doyle provided a worthy and most agreeable substitute for the most challenging route undertaken, namely to the top of Hungry Hill. You will be able to get in touch with Connie via the proprietors of either of the first two guest houses listed in the Accommodation Register.

Accommodation, Eating Out and Local Transport

ACCOMMODATION

Through our local farmer friend we had the good fortune to meet and stay with Ann and Teddy Black at their delightful bungalow-cum-guest house, 'Seapoint'. This is situated near to Castletown Bearhaven, just a short distance to the E off the R572 road, and is a perfect location for the three walks selected. Ann, who expertly runs this homely guest house, is keen on walking and on the great outdoors in general, and both she and her husband will prove a great source of knowledge on both local walking opportunities and the contacts you need to take full advantage of these possibilities during your stay with them. We also stayed with Helga Savage at the nearby 'Island's End' guest house, and the home comforts — including the odd tipple or two — which were bestowed on us here are also highly recommended.

These guest houses, together with a selection of other accommodation establishments which have been suggested to the author and which have a special empathy towards the needs of walkers, are listed in the table below.

ACCOMMODATION REGISTER

Hotel/Guest House	Rooms en suite	Rooms other	Charge B&B	Open	Visited by Author
Ann Black 'Seapoint' Castletownbere Beara Co Cork Tel: 027 70292	F 0 D 2 T 2 S 0	F 0 D 0 T 0 S 0	£16	March to Oct	Yes
Helga Savage 'Island's End' Rossmackowen Beara Co Cork Tel: 027 60040	F 0 D 0 T 0 S 0	F 0 D 2 T 2 S 1	£15	All year	Yes

Hotel/Guest House	Rooms en suite	Rooms other	Charge B&B	Open	Visited by Author
Eileen and Seamus Irwin Sea Haven Lodge Allihies Beara Co Cork Tel: 027 73225	F 2 D 2 T 0 S 0	F 0 D 2 T 1 S 0	£17	All year	No
Ford Rí Hotel Castletownbere Beara Co Cork Tel: 027 70379	F 0 D 0 T 17 S 0	F 0 D 0 T 0 S 0	£35	All year	No
Sea Front B&B Glengarriff Co Cork Tel: 027 63079	F 0 D 0 T 0 S 0	F 0 D 0 T 3 S 0	£14.50	May to Oct	No
Downing's 'Avelow House' Killarney Road Kenmare Co Kerry Tel: 064 41473	F 0 D 2 T 2 S 0	F 0 D 0 T 0 S 0	£16	Easter to Oct	No
Fern Height B&B Lohart Castletownbere Road Kenmare Co Kerry Tel: 064 84248	F 0 D 2 T 1 S 0	F 0 D 1 T 0 S 0	£14–16	May to Sept	No

Rooms: F = Family; D = Double; T = Twin; S = Single

EATING OUT

By arrangement you can have dinner at either Seapoint or Island's End and thus our experiences of dining out in Beara are somewhat limited. Castletown Bearhaven and the larger town of Kenmare have a range of restaurants, pubs, cafés and hotels to suit all tastes and purses, while the renowned Lawrence Cove Seafood Restaurant (Tel: 027 75063) on Bear Island not only specialises in delicious fish dishes but operates an inclusive ferry service from the mainland as part of the evening out.

LOCAL TRANSPORT

Being based close to Castletown Bearhaven, the only commercial transport we used was the ferry crossing to Bear Island. However, O'Donoghue's (Tel: 027 70007) and Shanahan's (Tel: 027 70116) provide taxi services throughout the peninsula should you need them. In addition, most of the guest houses listed will be able to arrange taxi or minibus services for you.

Hungry Hill

fact file

START/FINISH
Parking space adjacent to R572 road — MR 745474

GRADING
Moderate (difficult/strenuous in bad weather) (colour-coded BLUE/RED)

WALKING TIME ALLOWANCE
$5\frac{1}{2}$ hours

DISTANCE
9.5 km (5.9 miles)

TOTAL HEIGHT GAINED
660 m (2160 ft)

PRINCIPAL HEIGHTS
- Hungry Hill 685 m (2245 ft)

digest of walk

PARKING
Tiny parking area, holding no more than four or five cars. Additional private parking further up the lane; seek permission to use this if necessary.

OVERVIEW/INTEREST
- Magnificent mountain walk with challenging slopes as well as rock buttresses and ledges that in places call for skilful manoeuvring and some elementary scrambling.
- The route passes by the delightful reeded waters of tiny Park Lough.
- Superb views — both near and far — of dramatic mountain scenery and sweeping coastal landscapes, including Bear Island.
- A peep down the vertical cliff faces to observe Coomarkane Lake far below.
- Peat harvesting and an abundance of wild plants.

HUNGRY HILL

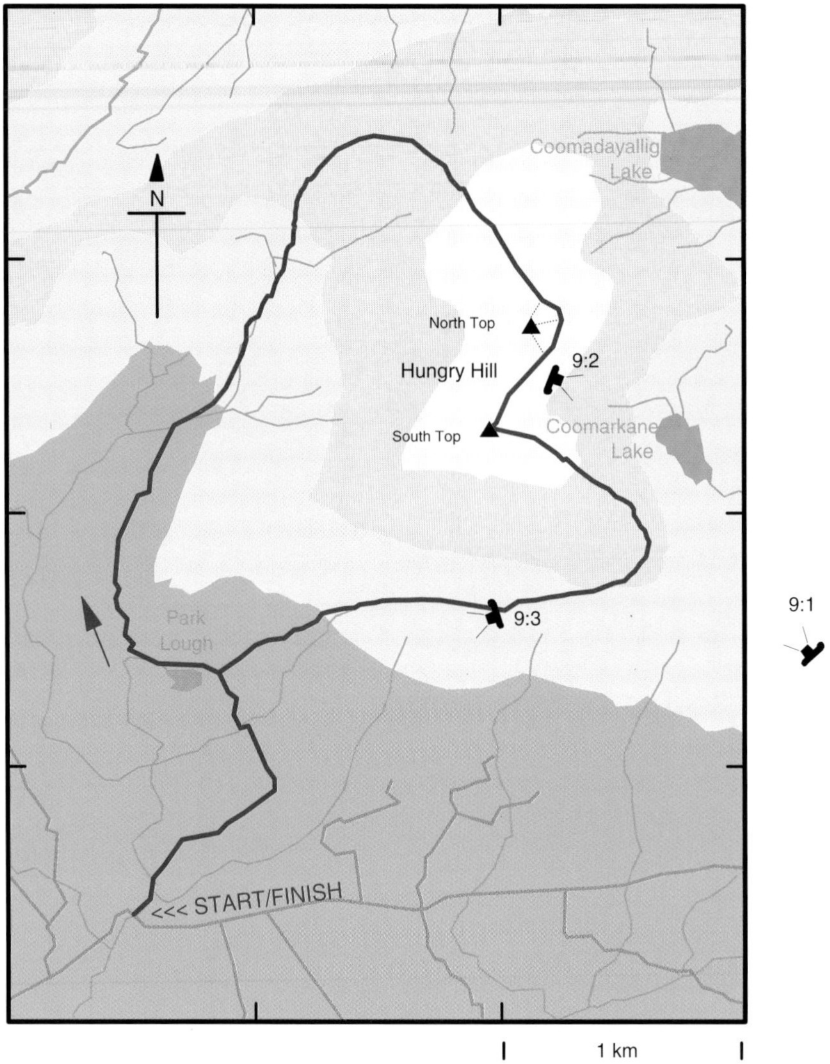

N
Coomadayallig Lake
North Top
Hungry Hill
9:2
South Top
Coomarkane Lake
Park Lough
9:3
9:1
<<< START/FINISH
1 km

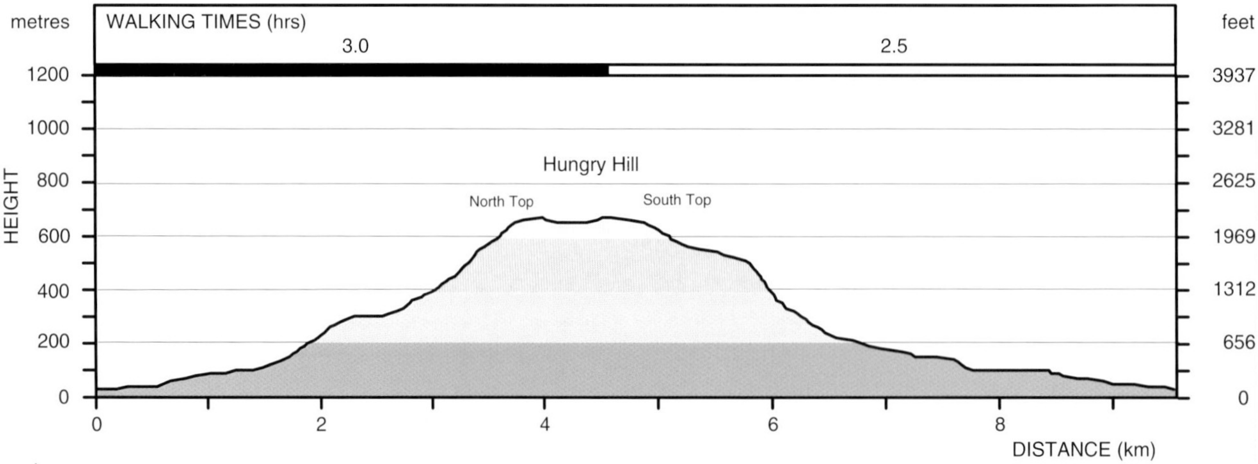

metres
WALKING TIMES (hrs)
3.0
2.5
feet
1200
1000
800
600
400
200
0
HEIGHT
3937
3281
2625
1969
1312
656
0
Hungry Hill
North Top
South Top
0
2
4
6
8
DISTANCE (km)

GRADIENTS

Following a modest initial approach, there is a steep climb up a severe grass and rock gully to reach the flatter ground leading to the summit of Hungry Hill. Most of the descent is also extremely steep, this down a craggy spur which contains rock ledges and pitches that demand caution and the careful planning of your way down.

MAPS, FOOTPATHS AND WAYSIGNS

OS Discovery Series 1:50 000 — Number 84 (Cork and Kerry)

The start and finish of the route are along minor lanes and wide tracks. The major part of the climb and subsequent descent do make use of some intermittent narrow paths and sheep tracks but there are prolonged sections where you have to walk across rough, open, uncharted ground. The flattish top area of the mountain has similar characteristics.

The lower parts of the walk use sections of the Beara Way and these are well waysigned. Elsewhere, you will have to rely on cairns to provide guiding markers.

GETTING STARTED

Travel along the scenic R572 road which winds around the southern coastline of the Beara Peninsula and the parking area lies about midway between Castletown Bearhaven to the W and Adrigole to the E. The parking area is just off the road at Rossmackowen Bridge where there is a hairpin bend.

The walk commences by striding up the side lane, heading NE away from the R572 road.

Summary Description of Walk

THE WAY TO HUNGRY HILL — MR 761497 (Allow 3 hours)

Even from the parking area and along the lane, the jagged, craggy westerly spurs rising steeply above provide a good idea of what lies ahead. Many walkers seeing these formidable, rocky slopes for the first time will experience mixed emotions of excited anticipation diluted by a twinge of apprehension: this is as it should be, for this challenging mountain does need to be respected and climbed with due diligence.

A sign near the start indicates that you are heading towards 'Cnoc Daod — Hungry Hill', so all is well thus far! Pass by an imposing residence named Hillbrook Park and follow the lane as it winds pleasantly uphill between high hedgerows containing a bountiful assortment of flora, including trees, bushes, flowers and grasses; in the summer flowering season, the honeysuckle and fuchsia in particular provide a blaze of rich colour. The lane then swings around to the L gaining further height and from here the hilly, elongated shape of Bear Island appears across Bear Haven, down below to your rear.

Your direction of progress changes to NW, and beyond a metal gate you reach the placid waters of Park Lough, these down to the L of the continuation track which provides a section of the long-distance walking route, the Beara Way. The tiny, reeded lough attracts plenty of bird-life and a collection of marginal plants thrive along its boggy shores, whilst water lilies do

9:1 The massive bulk of Hungry Hill rising beyond Adrigole Harbour

their best to cover its limited surface area. The wide, grassed-over cart-track then winds into an increasingly remote, wild and mysterious landscape. This is a huge bowl sandwiched between rising ridges of layered, folded rocks of awesome dimensions which contain formidable, steep, craggy rock pitches, buttresses and shelving. These rise impressively ahead on your R and some distance away over to the L also. Quite often jackdaws swoop overhead, their screeching adding to the mystical atmosphere of the enclosing, brooding amphitheatre which is now your stage.

Meanwhile, your comfortable, broad path tracks further into this remote and seemingly hostile wilderness, winding about and rising slightly in the process. You may be fortunate enough along here to spot the rare plant Holy Furze, which also grows on the top of Hungry Hill. (Note: I had the pleasure of walking this way with a local sheep farmer, Connie Doyle, who appears to be aware of the location of every rare plant on this mountainside. So if you do want to see a particular specimen up here, he is definitely the person to be with!)

This easy part of the way continues to zigzag upwards, and further on watch out for a tiny hut located to your L on the far side of the valley. This remote accommodation was enterprisingly built by a historian as a retreat for writing books. The long, knobbly ridge rising above this modest dwelling marks the border between Cork and Kerry. Around the next bend to the R there are better views of your continuation route, and you will be able to observe that the route steepens very appreciably as it scales the seemingly near vertical rocky slopes leading towards the vast summit area of Hungry Hill. Your still wide path leads directly into the gouged-out basin at the foot of these impressive rocky slopes. The direction towards these features remains northwards along Comnagapple Glen, which on most occasions you will have all to yourselves.

You keep company with the Beara Way until you reach the most northeasterly point of the section you are walking along. At this point, branch off to the R, keeping to the course of the stream and walking further NE towards a grassy strip ahead which threads into the rock faces high above. Initially, you still have a wide but somewhat rockier track beneath your boots. This continuation way is in fact a bog road which is now seldom used but you will pass evidence of recent turf cutting further on. This general area is soon reached as rougher, more open slopes lead across the peat-harvesting area, over ground that is often boggy and waterlogged.

Beyond this wetter area, you need to cross an infant watercourse and on the far side of this, much steeper, grassy slopes will lead you further NE between craggy, rocky outcrops and cliff faces which appear on either side as the way funnels into a narrower gully. This more exacting part of the climb roughly follows the course of the trickling stream to your L which flows down the hillside in a series of miniature waterfalls. Pause on the way up to look around and admire, given favourable weather, the excellent views behind you which now reveal the complete positioning of Bear Island together with its main features, that part of the mainland which curls around its W and N shoreline and the waters of Bantry Bay which lap around it.

Keep pushing upwards with a ground cover of intermingled grass and rocks to support your footsteps and watch out for more rare mountain plants which, hereabouts, will only survive in nooks and crevices beyond the reach of roaming, ravenous sheep. Maintain your established NE bearing as you climb higher, now penetrating the domain of grouse, kestrels and sparrowhawks. Higher up still, a faint path becomes established as several, separate, seldom-used ways consolidate along a narrowing strip of land between the rock faces. This way degrades into a steep funnel which it is best to climb on the R side beside the rock slabs, carefully threading a tight, zigzag way up through the rocks and loose stones.

Further on, the ground fans out again and when you reach this, veer to the L in order to access easier, less steep, grassy slopes which lead further to the NNE. Up here you will have to cross several tiny watercourses on a diagonal line of approach. From here on, further progress becomes appreciably easier as three tiny corrie lakes come into view to the WNW. These are Glas Loughs which straddle the border between Cork and Kerry, with this line actually bisecting one of the lakes.

A gently sloping band leads higher up the broad mountainside and usually you will have to avoid some boggy patches crossing these shallow slopes. When you reach the wide ridge ahead, you can see — in the clearest of weather — much of the mountainous backbone of the Iveragh Peninsula to the N, with the pointed peak of Carrauntoohil discernible to the NNE. The much nearer Glanmore Lake is also visible from here. Then circle around the rising spur before bearing

R, seeking out the higher ground by walking SSE across a mixture of grass and rock bands, with peat, sand and shale also forming part of the footing.

Zigzag through the rock benches, pausing in fine weather to absorb the superb mountain vistas all round before continuing to the SE across relatively featureless terrain which becomes progressively less steep. Bear slightly to the R along here and then select a final approach to the north summit along a faint path which will lead you S to the flat-topped summit area. Some partly concealed peat hags will need to be avoided in getting there. There is a massive cairn and a trigonometrical point at the top, these features standing 685 m (2245 ft) above sea level. This and the surrounding area provide a superb, safe viewing platform in good, clear weather. Wander around the place to observe much of the mountainous Beara Peninsula, together with more distant seascape panoramas across the wide sweep of Bantry Bay towards the deeply indented southernmost tip of Ireland — quite magnificent scenery! However, in doing this be ever mindful of the treacherous, sheer drops to the E of this otherwise benign summit area.

Afterwards, head to the south summit where there are more extensive views out to sea towards Sherkin and Clear Islands, both flat strips of land just visible above the waves. On clear, windless days venture over to the L to observe, from safe and secure vantage points, the spectacular views from the crumbling E edge of the mountain, down hundreds of feet of sheer rock face, towards the trapped waters of Coomarkane Lake. There is a large, round, stone castle at the south summit and the tale goes that this was built here when it was believed this was the highest point of the mountain!

THE WAY BACK TO THE PARKING AREA — MR 745474 (Allow $2\frac{1}{2}$ hours)

Commence your descent along the rocky ridge which drops to the SE. At the start there is a path but this soon becomes intermittent, being fairly clear and obvious across softer ground but quite often lost amongst the rock benches. You therefore need to consider carefully each discrete section of the way down and avoid getting stuck on any of the more difficult rock pitches by simply outflanking these. In general, try to keep towards the crest of the falling ridge and avoid the temptation to get down more quickly along the steeper grooves and gullies on either side, because most of these lead, lower down, to places where you will most probably need the expertise and skill of a rock climber!

Use the easier grassy channels which thread between a succession of rock bands and where you are most likely to have a path to follow. Work your way down with continuous care, planning your route ahead with skill. Although in places you will need to zigzag to either side to avoid rocky buttresses and steep protrusions, do maintain a dominant descent line to the SE. Fortunately the surface of the rock hereabouts provides an excellent purchase underfoot and you can tread on sloping rock surfaces of up to about 40 degrees with no great difficulty or danger of falling, providing these outcrops are dry.

Lower down, your descent route should bring you to a rock pool and in the vicinity of this, start to gradually change your direction from SE to SW, seeking out the easier, grassy slopes along the side of the rocky band and below the severe rock faces which now lie above your continued line of descent as you bend around to the R. This important manoeuvre needs to be made before you reach a shallow hause which lies along a continuation of the craggy spur. The changed direction will also lead you to significantly less steep slopes and, following a short, fairly level traverse further around to the R across peaty ground, easier, grassy slopes are reached, which change your continued descent towards W.

Keep descending on this diagonal to the W in line with distant Castletown Bearhaven, surrendering height gradually. Lower down, Park Lough comes back into view and when you sight this, trim your direction of approach to walk directly towards it. This continued direction of travel will lead you down to connect with the Beara Way again. When you reach this signed route, turn R along it and follow this better defined pathway further W. The connection is made near marker post 47 and you will pass posts 48, 49 and 50 before you reach a point which you passed much earlier in the day on your outward journey. At this place, turn L along the wide track below and retrace your previous steps back to where you have parked your vehicle.

9:2 A bird's-eye view of Coomarkane Lake from near the summit of Hungry Hill

Alternative Ways

ESCAPES

Should the weather turn nasty or should you for any other reason not wish to continue, at any point before you reach the north summit, the best way of curtailing the route is to simply turn about and retrace your steps from that point.

EXTENSIONS

It is feasible for strong walkers to return from the north summit by a longer, more circuitous route which leads around on the higher ground. This is initially NW, then W along the descending ridge which forms the county boundary, then S along a track which connects with the Beara Way and then along part of this way walking E to reach the NE tip of this section of the way where you left it earlier in the day, before finally retracing your outward steps from here back to the parking area.

Another possibility in good weather, again from the north summit and for strong, adventurous walkers only, is to traverse NE along the undulating ridge over Coombane to Healy Pass where you will need to either have a vehicle positioned or have transport arranged to pick you up.

On no account be tempted to depart from the summit of Hungry Hill either to the E or along the crest of the spur leading SW.

9:3 The view south-west towards Castletown Bearhaven observed during the final diagonal descent from Hungry Hill

KNOCKOURA AND KNOCKGOUR

fact file

START/FINISH

Village of Allihies — MR 584449

DISTANCE

11.6 km (7.2 miles)

GRADING

Moderate (colour-coded BLUE)

TOTAL HEIGHT GAINED

530 m (1740 ft)

WALKING TIME ALLOWANCE

6 hours

PRINCIPAL HEIGHTS

- Knockoura 490 m (1610 ft)
- Knockgour 481 m (1580 ft)

digest of walk

PARKING

Ample, tidy parking within village with space for several cars outside the church.

OVERVIEW/INTEREST

- The walk entails scaling a craggy ridge with some adventurous sections.
- Excellent views along the Beara Peninsula and across Kenmare River towards Iveragh and the MacGillycuddy's Reeks.
- The route passes an area of peat harvesting and a telecommunications complex.
- Open, airy terrain all the way.
- Wide range of flora and plenty of wildlife.

GRADIENTS

Following a moderate climb through the disused Bearhaven Copper Mines, a craggy, undulating ridge has to be tackled; this ridge gradually rises, with some steep sections, to the summit of Knockoura. There is a virtually level section to Knockgour, from where tracks and lanes lead downhill, winding across further moderate slopes back towards the village.

Knockoura and Knockgour

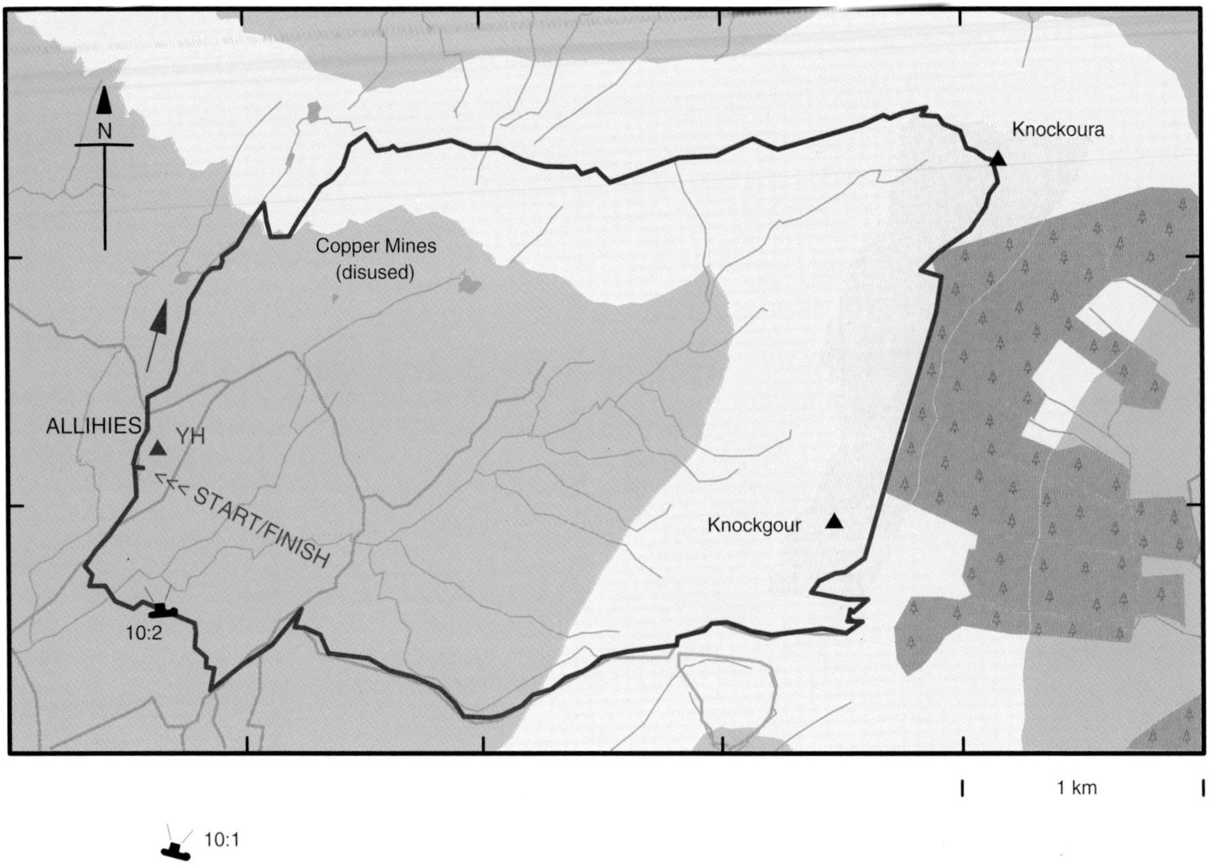

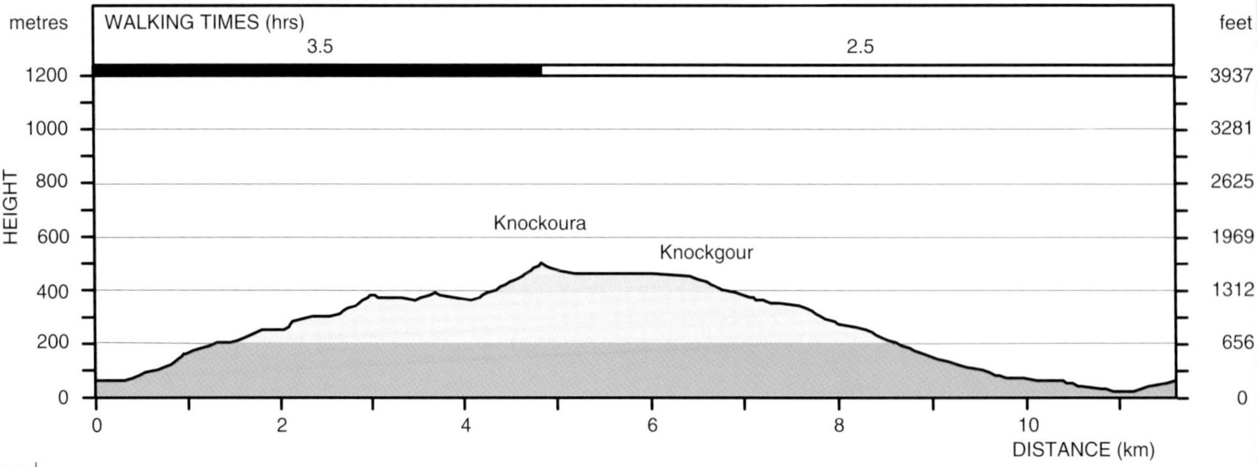

MAPS, FOOTPATHS AND WAYSIGNS

OS Discovery Series 1:50 000 — Number 84 (Cork and Kerry)

The way starts and finishes along a combination of roads, tracks and good paths. The rising approach towards Knockoura is across rough, rocky ground which undulates upwards and is devoid of any clear paths until you are almost at the top.

The route begins and finishes along clearly signed sections of the Beara Way. There are also warning notices in a disused mining area. In between, there are no guiding markers whatsoever!

GETTING STARTED

The tiny village of Allihies lies near the westerly tip of the Beara Peninsula and may be reached by travelling along the R575 road.

Walk northwards out of the village and you are on your way.

Summary Description of Walk

THE WAY TO KNOCKOURA — MR 621462 (Allow $3\frac{1}{2}$ hours)

The attractive village of Allihies lies just inland from the rugged coastline at the westerly tip of the Beara Peninsula. There is an excellent sandy beach near Allihies Point to the SW of the village and the area is very popular with both walkers and general holiday-makers. The land on which the village and the surrounding farms have developed slopes gently down to the coast, and, looking westwards from this vicinity, there are magnificent seascapes out towards Dursey Island which projects into the Atlantic Ocean. In the opposite direction, high craggy mountains form the skyline to the N and E, and standing on top of some of these is the principal objective of the walk.

Make your way to the upper end of the single-street village, passing by John Terry O'Sullivan's supermarket and petrol pumps and then O'Neill's bar and restaurant, both really 'colourful' establishments. As you walk along, look to your L to place, for future reference, the lovely view of the white, sandy beach below with the attractive, sheltering promontory jutting out to sea beyond it. A youth hostel is then passed and there are toilets on your L. Continue northwards, heading towards the craggy, jagged-edged mountain spur which rises directly ahead.

Just past a row of houses at the far end of the village, fork R along the wide lane signed 'Baile Chaisleáin Bhéarra — Castletownbere — 16 km — and Copper Mines'. This is also part of the long-distance walking route, the Beara Way. Within another 75 paces, branch off to the L along a signed way to follow a grassed-over cart-track which leads further uphill to the NE. There are often muddy patches along here. Proceed through the gate and keep to the obvious way as it winds upwards to provide extensive views down on your R of attractive, rolling, hilly landscapes which contain farmsteads with their surrounding walled pasture enclosures. Beyond, the flattish summit area of Knockgour commands the skyline to the E.

10:1 A scattering of homesteads protected by the craggy ridge leading eastwards to Knockoura

Climb over an awkward stile, and beyond this a grassy path threads through clumps of gorse to lead you through disused copper mine workings. The path then connects with the abandoned, former access road to these mines which you bear L along, still gaining height up the surfaced roadway. There are fine views from along here of Allihies which may now be properly positioned in its attractive, seascape environs. The narrow road twists around rocky outcrops and spoil heaps from the mines, and further up its surface deteriorates into one of compacted stones and shale. Here you are separately cautioned 'Old mineshaft ground — liable to subsidence' and on the R 'No go area'.

The steady climb continues zigzagging along the track towards the rocky spur above, and higher up there is a fascinating example of folded rocks exposed on your L which was caused millions of years ago by the combined effects of intense heat and pressure. Just before the wide track reaches its highest elevation and immediately prior to passing below a line of electricity cables, branch off to the R to follow a grassy cleft along a faint path. This takes you between rocky protrusions rising, somewhat intimidatingly, above as the shallow slope leads NE. Branch to the R ahead to then skirt around boggy ground, walking away from and to the L of the rising rocky ledges and pinnacles.

A steeper section of climbing then follows. Sticking studiously to a faint path which winds through more grassy chinks in the formidable rock faces, you again make contact with more open slopes towards the crest of the rising ridge, and in fine weather there are the most wonderful 180 degree panoramas from along here. These superb views not only display your ascent route but also reveal fascinating perspectives of the Iveragh Peninsula and the high places of the MacGillycuddy's Reeks. After absorbing these fine vistas, cross over another wet area and then veer slightly to the R to attain the rocky apex of the craggy, undulating spur.

From this higher ground, follow the contours of the rising ridge, progressing further eastwards and threading a delicate way of your own choice: there are several to choose from, of varying degrees of excitement, through a succession of rock benches and intervening hollows. Magnificent views are now your constant companion, providing the weather is reasonably fine, and as you gain additional height and the long-distance vistas become more complete you may be able to identify individual peaks in the MacGillycuddy's Reeks, including Carrauntoohil, the highest peak in all Ireland. Further on, follow the grassy continuation way which keeps just below and to the L of the apex of the ridge to avoid the tedium of a succession of unnecessary ups and downs, and this route has the added advantage of also providing the best continuing views northwards towards the Reeks.

Ever upwards, the way winds through a bewildering assortment of rocks, stones, rough grassy slopes, sedges and boglands with their tiny, muddy pools. Then to provide something new, the long, slim shape of hilly Bear Island with its round look-out towers comes into view on the R to the SSE. Higher up, the undulations become steeper and deeper; when tackling these, always take care to plan a safe way across the rocky depressions, progressing in the lea of any strong winds blowing across the ridge, as they often do, whenever this is possible. Further on, a succession of grassy hillocks signifies that the end of the long approach is nearing completion and that the most challenging ground now lies behind and below you.

Another faint track then leads across easier terrain, an area of virtually flat grassy ground. Beyond this, the wide spur bends around to your R above a wire fence, to lead you towards the massive summit area of Knockoura, above to the SE. In misty conditions along here, as you progressively swing around to the R, be particularly careful not to surrender any height, always keeping towards the crest of the continuously rising spur. Otherwise you will only have to climb back up again further on! When the weather is clear you will be able to observe some of the detail of Scariff Island and Deenish Island breaking through the seas to the WNW.

The final, moderately steep section of the ascent is through eroded, peaty ground and then up a shallow channel composed of shales. This approach will lead you directly to the summit on which a trigonometrical point has been positioned. You are now at a height of 490 m (1610 ft), and in good weather conditions, further glorious mountain panoramas may be observed from here: those eastwards along the peninsula taking in the massive bulk of Hungry Hill and those southwards across the indented coastline of the southernmost tip of Ireland are amongst the very finest.

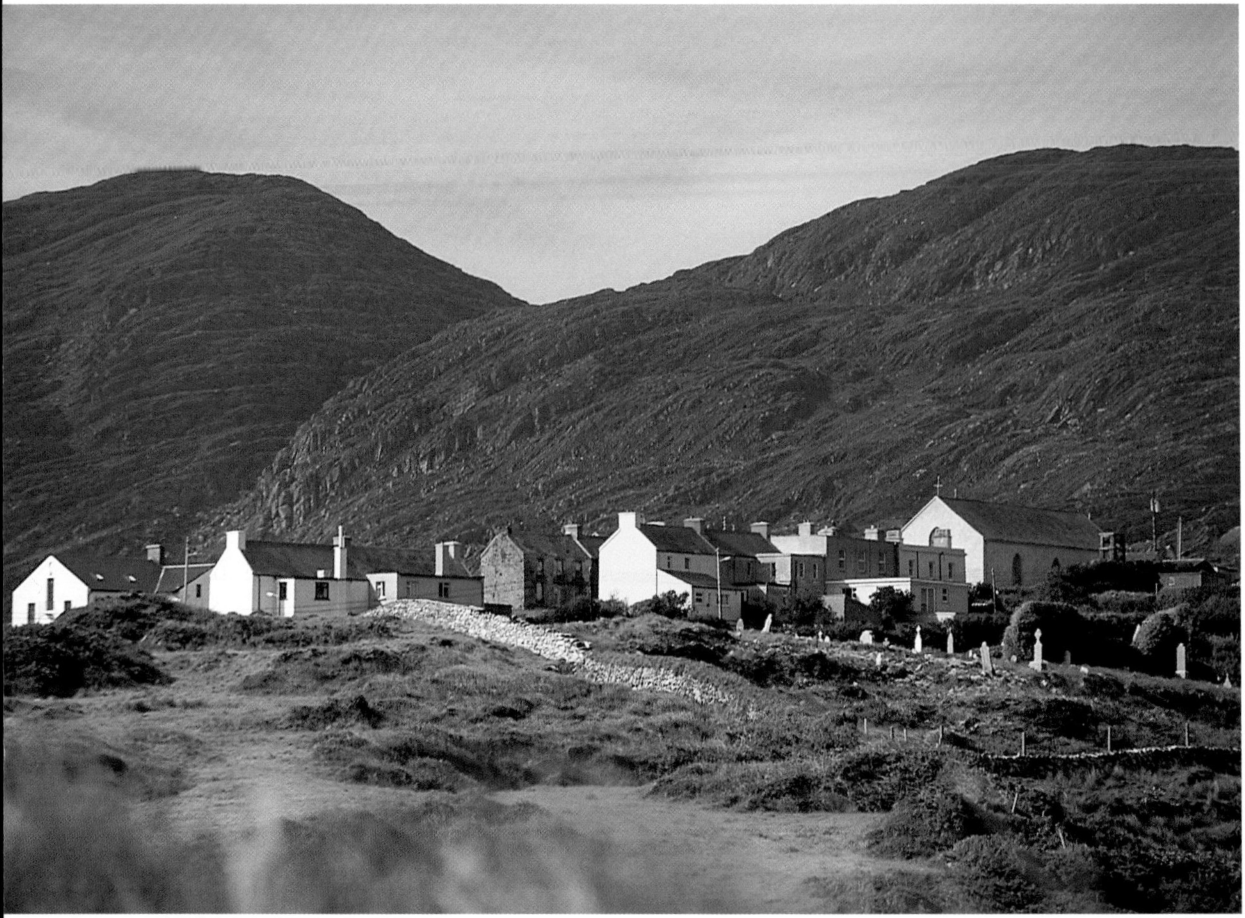

10:2 Approaching the village of Allihies near the end of the walk

THE WAY BACK TO ALLIHIES — MR 584449 (Allow $2\frac{1}{2}$ hours)

Continue the walk by striding southwards along the ridge heading towards the ground on which the concentrated battery of communications aerials is located. Extensive peat-harvesting operations are passed in walking towards these high masts. Locate the broad, stony track which winds along the top of the mountain and follow this through the peat hags across a relatively desolate, enclosing landscape. However, fast progress can be achieved through this less interesting section of the way along a virtually flat surface.

Keep L along the major track when you reach a fork ahead and, beyond this turning, quality, revealing views begin to appear again, now down towards the town and port of Castletown Bearhaven and Bear Island. Great tracks of conifer forests sweep down the hillsides on your L, leading the eye towards the coastline beyond and out across the hilly island. Proceed through a gate and follow the track as it skirts below the enclosed area of steel pylons and man-made technology which is located around the summit of Knockgour at a height of 481 m (1580 ft).

You now commence a gentle descent, passing beneath electricity cables which serve the communications centre. The continuation way then bends around to the R, heading down towards the coastal fringe and the village of Allihies away to the W. Pass beneath more power lines and then through a series of contorting, hairpin bends where more height is surrendered at a much faster rate and the views of the fascinating, indented coastline below just get better and better. Beyond another metal gate your stony track descends to connect with another one which joins from the L. This incoming track also serves as part of the Beara Way. Bear R along the merged way and follow this as it leads more directly towards the coast, still some considerable distance below.

Turn L when you reach the T-junction below as indicated by the yellow waymarker. Within a short distance, fork R to continue further downhill along the signed route. At the next junction follow the narrow road around to the R and then keep bending R in compliance with the directional arrow placed there. This will allow you to continue along a walled track which has a rougher surface. The final part of the descent will lead you across a sheltered valley back into the outskirts of Allihies, passing by dense thickets of gorse along the way. Turn R up the R575 coastal road to cover the short distance back into the village, where refreshment facilities await the chance to quench your thirst and hunger.

Alternative Ways

ESCAPES

Once committed to climbing the ridge, apart from turning back lower down, there are no practical or convenient ways of curtailing this route and it is best to continue along the way described as this provides an easy and clear descent route.

EXTENSIONS

Practical and sensible opportunities for extending the high-level part of this walk are also strictly limited. Strong walkers, with time to spare, could walk W and then NW along the ridge to stand on the top of Knocknagallaun, before returning the way they came to then tackle the main spur rising to the E as described in the main route. From Knockgour there are two spurs leading off further S but descending along either of these will involve greater distances, additional sections of road walking and complicated route finding. Such extensions, for the reasons cited, are not recommended!

Bear Island

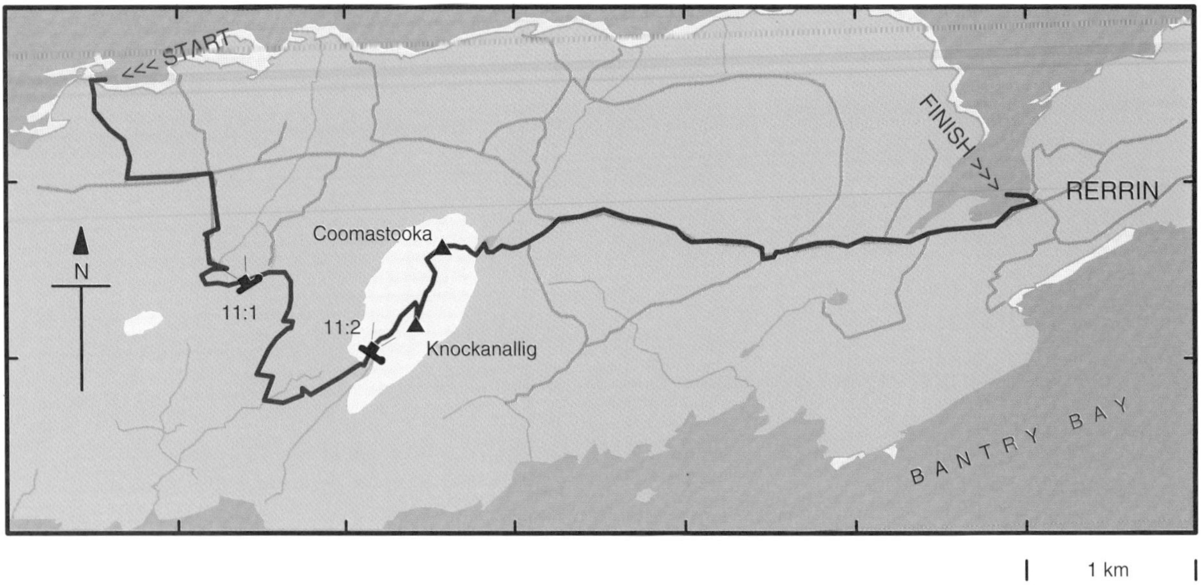

<<< START
FINISH >>>
RERRIN
N
Coomastooka
11:1
11:2
Knockanallig
BANTRY BAY
1 km

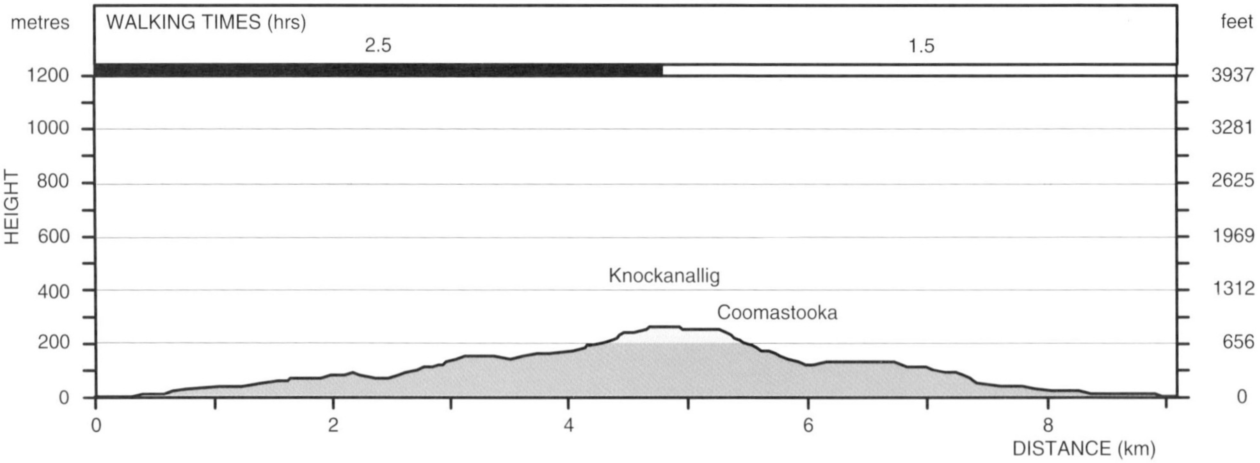

metres
feet
WALKING TIMES (hrs)
2.5
1.5
HEIGHT
1200
1000
800
600
400
200
0
3937
3281
2625
1969
1312
656
0
Knockanallig
Coomastooka
0
2
4
6
8
DISTANCE (km)

BEAR ISLAND

fact file

START/FINISH
Start at ferry pier — MR 686446
Finish at quay — MR 739439

GRADING
Easy/straightforward (colour-coded GREEN)

WALKING TIME ALLOWANCE
4 hours

DISTANCE
9.1 km (5.6 miles)

TOTAL HEIGHT GAINED
300 m (980 ft)

PRINCIPAL HEIGHTS
- Knockanallig 258 m (845 ft)
- Coomastooka 248 m (815 ft)

digest of walk

PARKING
Leave your vehicle at the port of Castletown Bearhaven on the mainland. Plenty of parking space near to the docks and ferry pier. (Note: Depending on route of return ferry crossing, it may be necessary to arrange transport back to Castletown Bearhaven.)

OVERVIEW/INTEREST
- Delightful, short walk to the highest points of Bear Island.
- Children will love the two contrasting ferry crossings.
- Good views out to sea and back across the mainland towards both Hungry Hill and Knockgour.
- Varied scenery on the hilly island with both sheltered, lowland slopes and more exposed, higher, craggy terrain.
- Fascinating bays, inlets and harbours with the waters of Bear Haven sound lapping around the northern shoreline.

GRADIENTS
The walk is a varied up-and-down, with most of the way across fairly gentle slopes. There are

some steeper parts — both ascending and descending — near to the summits of the two mountains.

MAPS, FOOTPATHS AND WAYSIGNS

OS Discovery Series 1:50 000 — Number 84 (Cork and Kerry)

Most of the route is along a series of connecting narrow roads, tracks and paths. There are a few areas of open ground where the way forward is temporarily less clear but these can be assimilated easily into your stride. There is virtually no boggy or badly eroded ground to cross.

The minor roads are well signed, and indeed much of the route coincides with the Beara Way which is marked with numerous waysigns. However, do not be confused if you come across the occasional sign which has been turned around, this perhaps deliberately intended to confuse less experienced navigators than yourselves!

GETTING STARTED

Take the ferry from Castletown Bearhaven and disembark at the pier protected by tiny Sheep Islands.

From the pier, walk around to the L along the narrow continuation road, then heading S and walking slightly uphill.

11:1 The view back towards the ferry crossing and Castletown Bearhaven

Summary Description of Walk

THE WAY TO KNOCKANALLIG — MR 705432 (Allow $2\frac{1}{2}$ hours)

In fine, sunny weather, the views across Bear Haven from the vicinity of your disembarkation point are supreme. The massive bulk of Hungry Hill reaches up into the blue skies to the NE, whilst the flat-topped summit of Knockgour assumes supremacy to the W. All is peace and tranquillity on the island as you move away from the hustle and bustle of the pier, walking southwards towards the mountain peaks directly ahead which contain a signal tower. The craggier, higher profile of Knockanallig, the highest point on the island and one of the main objectives of the walk, rises to the SE, to the L of the slopes supporting the tower.

Follow the narrow road around to the L in the direction signed to 'Rerrin', to almost immediately pass by a simple grotto on your R. This way will lead you E into spacious countryside that contains open views of pleasing landscapes ahead. These cover, to the L, the sloping ground falling to Bear Haven sound which separates the island from the mainland and, to the R, gently rising, rounded hillsides, the lower slopes of which are liberally covered with rhododendron bushes seen in flower during late May and June. Dense clumps of gorse also proliferate on these inclines.

Turn R at the crossroads ahead to change your direction of travel towards S once more. This also involves walking uphill again! An attractive, walled lane now determines your onward progress, its hedgerows filled with a wide assortment of well-known wild plants including buttercups, dandelions, ferns, foxgloves, fuchsias, gorse and lilies. A group of isolated buildings are then passed and beyond a metal gate a much rougher, surfaced track continues to wind uphill, bending L and R in a graceful curve.

Above these twists, be careful to turn L off the wide track in order to continue E along part of the signed Beara Way. This is at marker post No 25. From here, a narrower, rougher, stony path traverses the grassy slopes, more or less on the level. However, there are some wet, waterlogged patches along this section of the route. The continuation path is also somewhat less than obvious in places as it bends around to the L maintaining its easterly bearing. The correct way then rises to the R, sheering away from a metal gate straight ahead which you do not use. From here, contour around the slopes beside a wire fence and stone wall. This rougher part of the way then falls slightly to connect with a more distinct and wider track ahead where waysign post No 27 has been positioned. (Obviously, when the author walked this way, waysign post No 26 had gone missing!)

Turn R, as directed, up the better-defined way to continue gently uphill but now with stones and shale crunching beneath your boots. The open Atlantic Ocean to the S is visible from the top of the next rise, shimmering beyond the rugged coastline below. The track bends full L near this vantage point to continue slightly downhill before you are directed, at marker post No 28, to branch off further to the L up more rising ground. The obvious continuation route snakes further upwards towards the summit area of Knockanallig and the next marker post, No 29, is reassuringly positioned as you approach some formidable cliffs and rock overhangs which line the westerly faces of the hill ahead.

Keep faith with the wide track until you spot a narrower, more adventurous way which you can use to short circuit part of the continuation way, this achieved by walking NE through the gap above after skirting around some boggy ground. This indistinct side path, a minor diversion, will lead you back to the wide track higher up, where you turn R along it to continue towards the craggy summit. This now lies just above you on the R. To get there, branch off once again to the R just a few paces further on (be careful here crossing the partly hidden ditch) and then thread your way through the rocks and bracken above to gain the higher ground.

Turn R when you reach the flatter slopes ahead (this is in fact a broad ridge), and climb the remaining short distance across heathers to reach the cairn positioned on the summit of Knockanallig. This is at 258 m (845 ft) and marks the highest point on Bear Island. Walk around the extensive summit area, absorbing the fine views in all directions which may be observed from here when the weather is clear and visibility is good. The precise shape of the island is fully displayed below you and, further away, many of the mountainous highlights of the Beara Peninsula are also revealed from here.

THE WAY TO THE QUAY AT RERRIN — MR 739439 (Allow 1½ hours)

A walk to the NE will take you across the short distance to the dominating cross positioned on the neighbouring hill of Coomastooka. To get there, start descending to the NNE, initially along a well-defined track which then crosses a continuation of your approach route. From here, a veritable maze of tiny paths may be used to track NE across the undulating, open ground to the cross, positioned at 248 m (815 ft) on the top of Coomastooka. This white cross is really massive, in both height and bulk, and it carries the simple inscription: AMDG — HOLY YEAR 1950 — ERECTED BY THE PEOPLE OF BERE ISLAND AT HOME AND ABROAD.

After perhaps standing in awe under its towering frame for some time, continue your descent eastwards, using a rough, grassy path to reconnect with the better-defined track running below and weaving about the hillside to achieve this. The connection may be made at any convenient high point in the vicinity of marker post No 31 and this signifies that you are back on a continuation of the Beara Way once again. From here, a less exacting way winds further downhill in a series of graceful curves to deposit you at a brightly painted, yellow ladder stile. Another round watch-tower positioned on the hillock ahead comes into view as you make this part of the descent.

Cross the stile with care as it is a bit wobbly, or use the metal gate as an alternative, and then turn L along the surfaced lane as waysign No 32 indicates you should. There is an impressive Standing Stone over to your R here. The continuation lane winds further E, following an undulating course below the watch-tower, to merge with a wider road which you veer R along. Waysign No 33 is positioned at this junction. From here, continue eastwards along the road, ignoring all side turnings which lead off to either L or R.

The continuation way descends progressively towards the sheltered anchorage of Rerrin passing through pleasant, green landscapes and attractive inlets. From here, the view along the tiny creek of Lawrence's Cove towards Hungry Hill across the separating straits is supreme. The way then descends into the picturesque village of Rerrin where the quay may be located around to the L. However, your forward plans may include having a meal at Lawrence Cove Seafood Restaurant, which is featured in Egon Ronay's 1997 Guide. (The inclusive price of the meal could include your return ferry trip back to the mainland later on.) If this is the case, you have another climb ahead of you; however, this is one of the very shortest duration, just up to the restaurant which is located on the R-hand side of the cove.

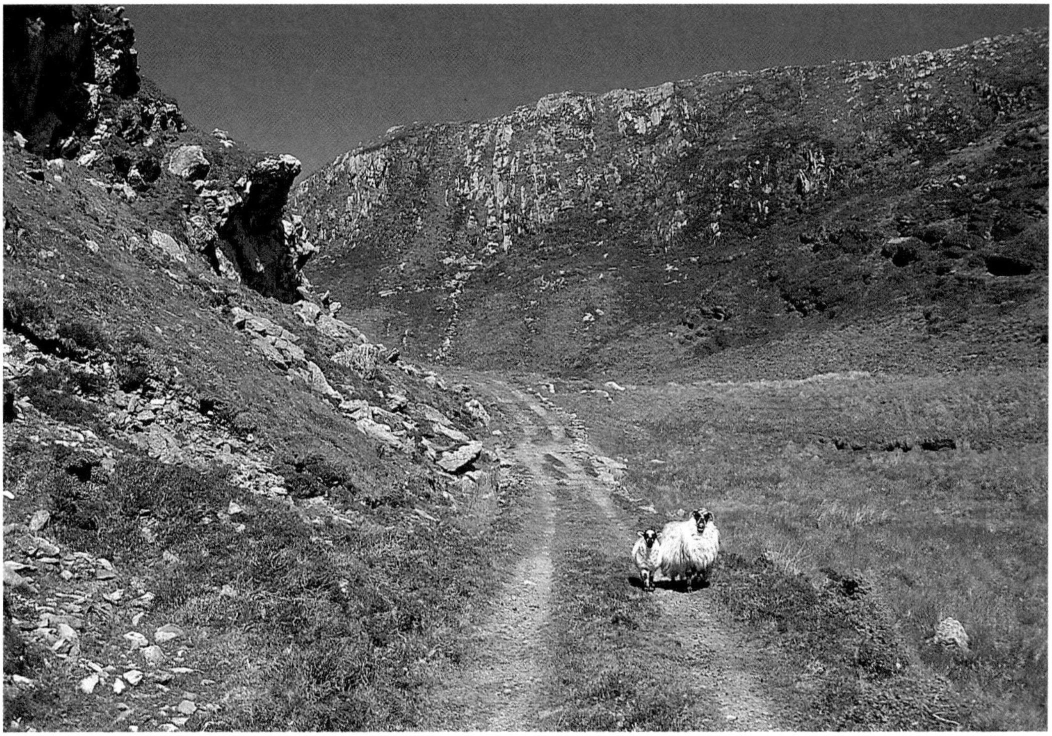

11:2 Two shaggy inhabitants of the upper slopes of Knockanallig

Alternative Ways

ESCAPES

In walking from one ferry point to the other, you have no need to do much climbing at all if you decide to keep to the minor roads which run W to E below the hills along the northern side of the island.

EXTENSIONS

There are several possibilities for extending the walk using more sections of the Beara Way. These include the more westerly loop or the sections which fan out into the most easterly parts of the elongated island. However, do be mindful of the time and your scheduled crossing back to the mainland; otherwise either take a tent with you or be prepared to negotiate bed and breakfast terms and arrangements for a night spent surrounded by the sea.

Overleaf: Looking down on the rugged approach to Devil's Ladder, Carrauntoohil

Iveragh Peninsula Walks

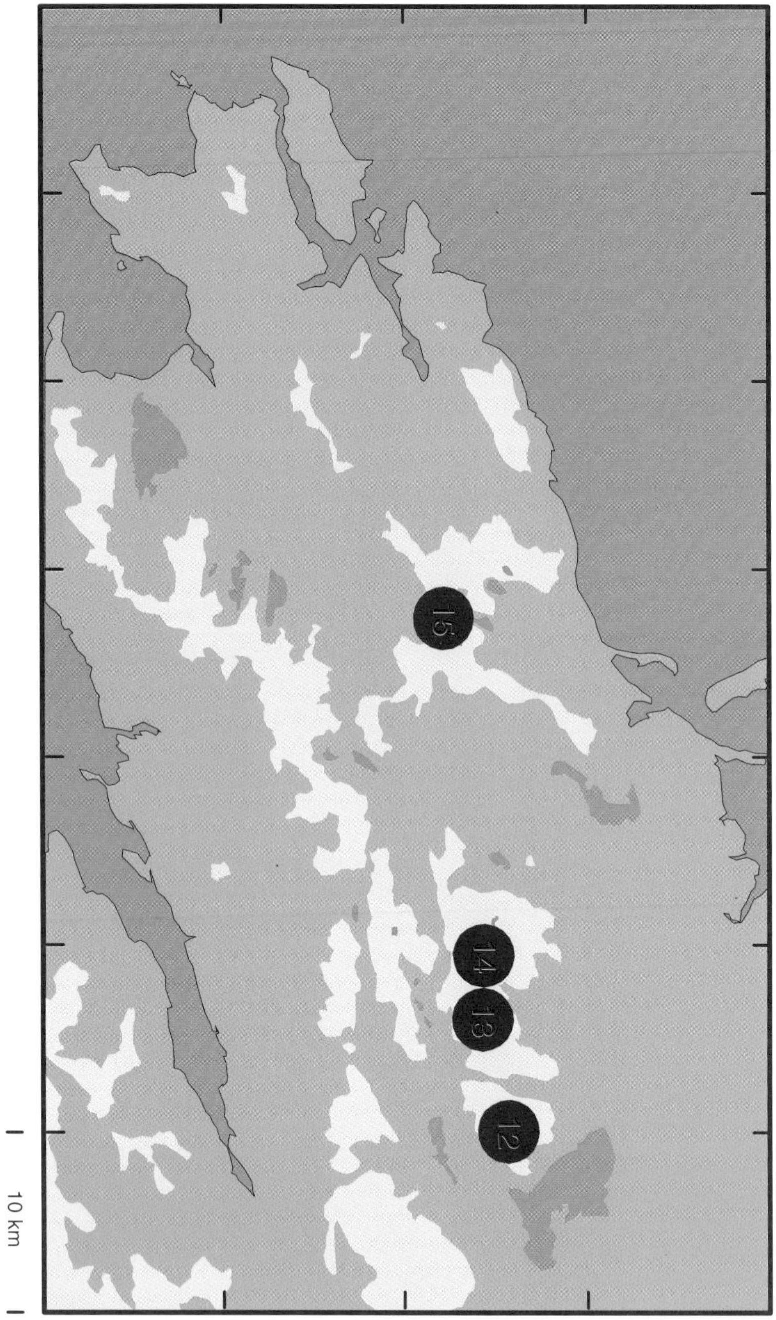
15
14
13
12
10 km

THE MOUNTAINS OF THE IVERAGH PENINSULA (RING OF KERRY)

GETTING THERE

The various routes from Castletown Bearhaven to Kenmare may by now be familiar to you and if there is one which you have not yet used, this is an opportunity to do so. Kenmare provides a convenient base for exploring on foot the eastern parts of both the Beara and Iveragh Peninsulas. Alternatively, it is less than a pleasant half-day's motoring to travel from Castletown Bearhaven to most locations on the Iveragh Peninsula, providing the superb, ever-changing scenery all around you *en route* does not delay you too often with stops to appreciate this and to permanently capture it on film.

From Kenmare you have the choice of travelling directly westwards into Iveragh, heading for the Waterville area around sheltered Ballinskelligs Bay along the N70 road (Ring of Kerry), or motoring northwards up the N71 road through the magnificent Killarney National Park. And if the latter does not play havoc with your envisaged timetable, then it must be assumed it is bucketing down and you are shrouded in low mist! When you reach Killarney town, turn W along the R562 road towards Killorglin. This busy town and the nearby village of Glenbeigh provide excellent bases for your walking explorations within this mountainous peninsula and are particularly convenient for climbing amongst the MacGillycuddy's Reeks.

GEOLOGICAL PERSPECTIVE

The scenery of the Iveragh Peninsula, like that of the area immediately to the S, is determined by the rocks below. The succession of the Old Red Sandstone beds beneath and the Carboniferous strata above was folded some 250 million years ago during the Hercynian fold system into tight E–W anticlines (upfolds) and synclines (downfolds). Subsequent uplift of the region has resulted in erosion of these rocks to expose the 'Old Red' rocks which form the cores of the anticlines and the Carboniferous rocks which are present in the troughs of the synclines. The more resilient 'Old Red' rocks form the highest ground including the MacGillycuddy's Reeks, which in turn contain Carrauntoohil, at 1039 m (3410 ft) the highest mountain in Ireland. The 'Old Red' rocks also resist marine erosion along the coast and thus shape the prominent headlands such as Bolus Head located at the western tip of the peninsula.

The more easily eroded Carboniferous rocks form much of the lower ground, as is well evidenced, for instance, along the shore of Lough Leane, the largest of the Killarney Lakes. The lower levels of the valleys which have been cut into the Carboniferous rocks have been flooded in more recent geological times to form the present-day rias which are so characteristic of this part of the Irish coastline. Dingle Bay is a good example of this action.

The extensive mountain mass of the MacGillycuddy's Reeks with its soaring peaks contains some of the finest and wildest scenery in Ireland. The 'Old Red' rocks which form these formidable slopes are made up of coarse-grained sandstones, as seen on Carrauntoohil, and finer-grained sediments. The latter have been largely converted, by the same pressures that produced the rock folds, to purple slates and these appear on Purple Mountain.

As might be expected from the relatively high altitudes of the Reeks, the area was heavily glaciated during the Pleistocene (the most recent period of geological time). This has resulted in numerous glaciated valleys and corries, well evidenced for example below Devil's Ladder on Carrauntoohil and also further W in the precipitously steep walls around Coomasaharn Lake. The U-shaped valleys such as the Gap of Dunloe, Moll's Gap and Windy Gap are all of glacial origin and their location indicates the forces of glaciers draining a large ice sheet to the S. The present-day lakes of the region, too, owe their origin in large measure to the Great Ice Age. Lough Leane, for example, is dammed by moraine dumped by a glacier and it also occupies a glacially eroded hollow. When the ice last retreated from this district, some 10 000 years ago, there would have been vast quantities of melt water and such fast-flowing energy is believed to be responsible for the excavation of the Colleen Bawn Caves.

Present-Day Landscapes and Opportunities for Walking

The Iveragh Peninsula contains the famed MacGillycuddy's Reeks which soar to above 3000 ft. This mountain range is uniquely spectacular, consisting of pointed peaks linked together by a series of rocky spurs which range from broad bands to narrower ridges to knife-edged arêtes. The last-mentioned are the province of experienced hillwalkers who have a head for heights and have no problems with some limited exposure. Lord of all these high places is Carrauntoohil, which has both a shape and a location befitting its distinction as the highest mountain in the whole of Ireland.

There are numerous other lofty peaks in this mountainous peninsula and these provide an almost endless variety of challenging walking routes for practised and fit hillwalkers. Many of these heights cradle spectacular corrie lakes with precipitous cliff faces falling down many hundreds of feet towards the trapped waters below. However, there are also elevated areas of almost flat ground which provide suitable horseshoe routes for walkers around and above some of this awesome and spectacular glaciated topography.

A series of sheltered valleys and gaps criss-cross the peninsula dividing the mountains into discrete groupings, and these valleys and gaps — together with the beautiful lower landscapes towards the western extremity of the peninsula and also around the famed Killarney Lakes to the E — provide an abundance of routes which are more suitable for less energetic walkers. This countryside, with its many other outdoor attractions, is also ideal for family groups, and the children will have some difficulty in deciding what delights to try next! The walks hereabouts include climbing up modestly sized hills, strolling around lakes and by the side of fast-flowing streams, visiting impressively high waterfalls and exploring sheltered woodland and forest trails.

Choice of Walking Routes

I believe that all walkers capable of undertaking the physical effort might aspire to stand on the summit of Carrauntoohil. Two routes, Walks 13 and 14, have, therefore, been described for getting there. The first of these, a there-and-back walk via adventurous Devil's Ladder, is the easiest way to navigate with certainty to the highest place in the land, whilst the second walk is a more challenging route suitable for experienced walkers who relish some modest exposure amongst these high, craggy, precipitous peaks. A walk through the Gap of Dunloe followed by a climb onto Purple Mountain and Tomies Mountain features as Walk 12, and this will provide a feel of the easterly mountains and the perspectives down over Killarney National Park. Walk 15, an adventurous horseshoe route above Coomasaharn Lake with its fantastic, gouged-out combes of immense size, together with walking along a friendly arête towards the end of the walk, will give you a further taste of exposure in high places.

Local Walking Guides

Go Ireland, a well-established and enterprising walking organisation based in Killorglin with whom I have contact through Countrywide (a nationally known United Kingdom walking organisation who arrange walking holidays in Ireland in partnership with Go Ireland), provided expert local guides to accompany me on some of the more ambitious routes up Carrauntoohil and around Coomasaharn Lake. These very experienced, enthusiastic and most congenial walking companions included Mary-Frances Thompson, Catherine McMullin and Noel Doyle. The principal walking guide for Go Ireland is Seán Ó Súilleabháin, who also writes with great authority on walks in the SW of Ireland, and I have also tapped into his vast experience, which was conceded most generously.

CONTACT DETAILS
Go Ireland
Old Orchard House
Killorglin
Co Kerry
Tel: 066 62094
Freephone from UK: 0800 371203
Fax: 066 62098

ACCOMMODATION, EATING OUT AND LOCAL TRANSPORT

ACCOMMODATION

My wife and I have had the pleasure of staying at several friendly hotels and guest houses around the Iveragh Peninsula, some of which we were introduced to by either Go Ireland or Countryside Tours (another organisation specialising in walking holidays and activities) who use them for their walking holidays. All these places serve the needs of walkers well, are clean and comfortable, provide hearty breakfasts and appear interested and genuinely pleased to have walkers staying with them.

These hotels and guest houses are listed in the table below.

ACCOMMODATION REGISTER

Hotel/Guest House	Rooms en suite	Rooms other	Charge B&B	Open	Visited by Author
Tommy and Kay Woods Park House Laharn Killorglin Co Kerry Tel: 066 61665	F 2 D 0 T 0 S 0	F 1 D 1 T 1 S 0	£14–16	March to Oct	Yes
Teresa Clery Slieve Bloom Manor Guesthouse Muckross Road Killarney Co Kerry Tel: 064 35055/34237	F 10 D 3 T 0 S 0	F 0 D 0 T 0 S 1	£16–20	All year	Yes
Angela O'Grady O'Grady's Waterville Co Kerry Tel: 066 74350	F 1 D 2 T 4 S 0	F 0 D 0 T 0 S 0	£16–20	March to Oct	Yes
Rosie Garde Glencar House Hotel Glencar Co Kerry Tel: 066 60102	F 2 D 4 T 9 S 3	F 0 D 0 T 0 S 0	£32–42	All year	Yes
Johnny and Anne Walsh Climbers' Inn* Glencar Co Kerry Tel: 066 60101 Fax: 066 60104	F 3 D 9 T 0 S 0	F 0 D 0 T 0 S 0	£13–23	March to Nov plus Christmas/ New Year	Yes

ROOMS: F = Family; D = Double; T = Twin; S = Single

* A village under one roof containing accommodation, bar and refreshment facilities, foodstore, post office and information point.

EATING OUT

The Iveragh Peninsula is a Mecca for walkers and tourists alike and there are consequently numerous hotels, restaurants, cafés and pubs which cater for a wide range of tastes and budgets. Delicious evening meals that we have particularly enjoyed after a strenuous day spent amongst the mountains include those provided by the Bianconi Traditional Pub and Restaurant in Killorglin (Tel: 066 61146), Kate Kearney's Cottage near the Gap of Dunloe (Tel: 064 44146), the Red Fox Inn and Restaurant adjacent to Kerry Bog Village Museum near Glenbeigh (Tel: 066 69184/69288) and, in Waterville, the Huntsman Hotel and Restaurant (Tel: 066 74124) and the Sheilin Seafood Restaurant and Wine Bar (Tel: 066 74231).

LOCAL TRANSPORT

Supporting transport will almost certainly be needed for Walk 14, the linear route over Carrauntoohil and Caher. Tom Melia, Killorglin (Tel: 066 61226) and Michael Moriarty, Glencar (Tel: 066 60108) provide reliable taxi and minibus services throughout Iveragh.

The dramatic amphitheatre of precipitous peaks cradling the head of Coomasaharn Lake

Purple Mountain and Tomies Mountain

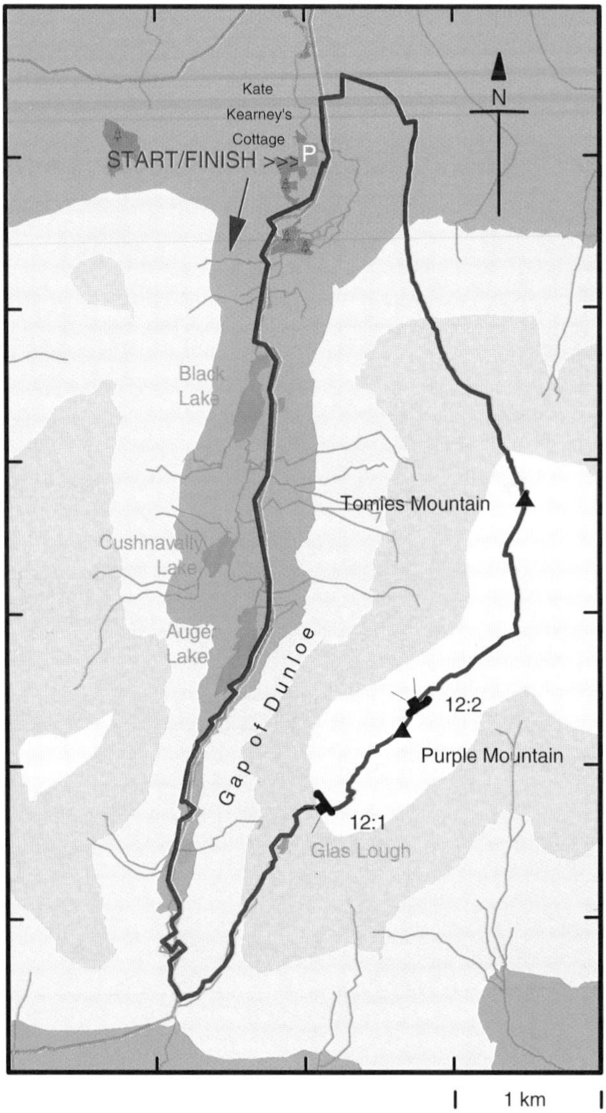

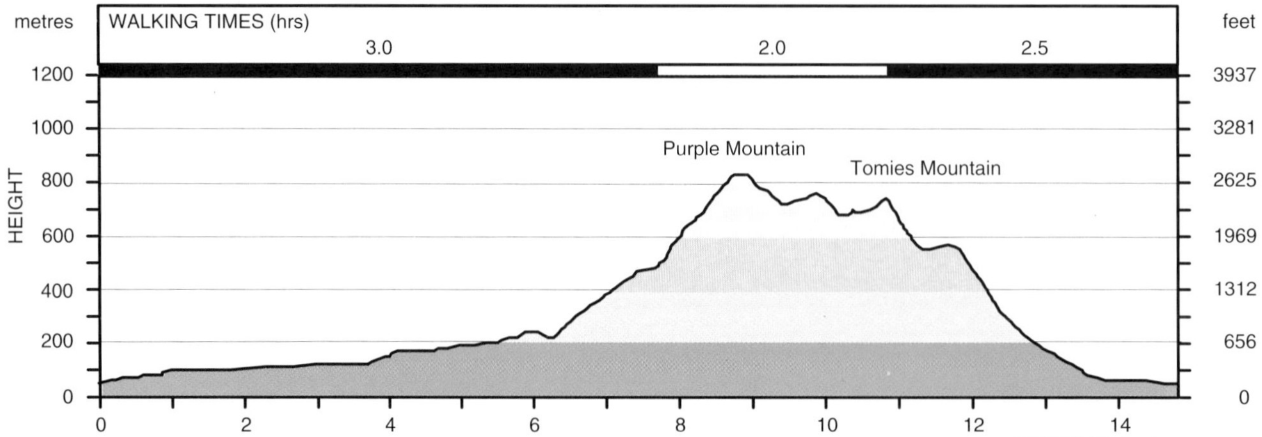

PURPLE MOUNTAIN AND TOMIES MOUNTAIN

fact file

START/FINISH

Car park near Kate Kearney's Cottage — MR 881890

GRADING

Difficult/strenuous (colour-coded RED)

WALKING TIME ALLOWANCE

7½ hours

DISTANCE

14.8 km (9.2 miles)

TOTAL HEIGHT GAINED

930 m (3050 ft)

PRINCIPAL HEIGHTS

- Purple Mountain 832 m (2730 ft)
- Tomies Mountain 735 m (2410 ft)

digest of walk

PARKING

Large, public car park; however, this is very popular with climbers, walkers and tourists alike and becomes full early on, both at weekends and during peak holiday periods.

Toilets are situated at the car park and there is a choice of refreshment facilities and gift shops nearby.

OVERVIEW/INTEREST

- Delightful start to the walk through the Gap of Dunloe (see how many pony traps you can race on the way up!).
- A number of fascinating corrie lakes are passed or visited along the route.
- Precipitous cliff faces, rock buttresses, ledges and pinnacles may be observed at close quarters.

- Spectacular distant scenery, including the arêtes of the MacGillycuddy's Reeks and the Lakes of Killarney.
- Plenty of bird-life, both in flight and resting on the ground.

GRADIENTS

The walk commences with a gradual climb to the top of the Gap of Dunloe. Following this, there is a much steeper ascent to the top of Purple Mountain across significantly rougher, exposed ground. A prolonged descent follows and then it is up again across barren, open slopes with more challenging gradients to conquer before reaching the summit of Tomies Mountain. It is all downhill from here but much of this descent is very steep, walking through clinging high heathers which render the going down burdensome and prolonged.

MAPS, FOOTPATHS AND WAYSIGNS

OS Discovery Series 1:50 000 — Number 78 (Kerry)
OS MacGillycuddy's Reeks 1:25 000
OS Killarney National Park 1:25 000
A good, wide, partly surfaced lane threads through the Gap of Dunloe, snaking to its top. The rest of the way is probably about equally divided between following rough, narrow paths and tracks and crossing open ground without this assistance.

Once you climb out of the Gap of Dunloe there are no waysigns to help your progress and, therefore, you will have to rely on your own navigational skills and the strategic positioning of a few cairns.

GETTING STARTED

The parking area is located along a minor road, to the N of the Gap of Dunloe. It is situated just less than 4 km ($2\frac{1}{2}$ miles) S of the main N72 road which connects Killorglin and Killarney. There are several approaches from the N72 but the most straightforward is to turn off at Beaufort Bridge, cross over the River Laune and follow the fairly direct route southwards, through the hamlet of Beaufort, to reach the parking area.

Turn R out of the main car park, heading SSW into the Gap of Dunloe and you are on your way.

Summary Description of Walk

THE WAY TO GLAS LOUGH — MR 878844 (Allow 3 hours)

The walk starts virtually on the flat but with high mountains rearing up on either side of the gap towards which you are heading. The steep slopes on your L rise to the summit of Tomies Mountain (Na Tóimí) and you will be standing on the top of this later in the day. Those on your R eventually culminate in the formidable, narrow summit ridges of the MacGillycuddy's Reeks (Na Cruacha Dubha) far away to the SW, but standing on these is for another day! Walk on past the pony trap assembly area, which you will be able to locate by smell even if visibility is down to only a few feet! The wide lane, surfaced with a mixture of stones and compacted shale, then passes between mature hedgerows and, climbing slightly, enters the gap.

12:1 The rugged mountainous landscapes around tiny Glas Lough

The route quickly penetrates more open country, tracking through clumps of gorse, and then a sign reading 'Going Climbing?' — which provides sensible precautions for those who are, together with a summary of 'The Country Code' — is passed. After this, most of the hustle and bustle of the starting area is quickly left behind as you gradually walk into a different environment of apparent remoteness and increasing stillness where the high mountains, corrie loughs and overall grandeur of the scenery encapsulate you in a bubble of tranquillity where all is peace, quiet and utter contentment.

Tiny Coosaun Lough is the first of several lakes lining the gouged-out floor of the gap which you pass by. Its silent, reeded waters are very pretty with, on windless, sunny days, the peaks of the mountains above faithfully mirrored on its becalmed surface. A refurbished, arched, stone bridge spanning the River Loe is crossed and this manoeuvre will be repeated several times higher up the gap. The larger Black Lake is then passed down to your R, and at Colleen Bawn Cottage you are informed that tea, coffee and scones are available for purchase.

The next waters trapped in the gap belong to Cushnavally Lake, some distance away to the R. These fill a deep basin below craggy, precipitous slopes which disappear into the inky depths of the corrie lough. Following more river crossings, the narrow road skirts around Auger Lake, the penultimate stretch of water lining the gap. Beyond this, the mountainous jaws of the gap squeeze the rising valley into a tighter cavity and the road has to climb more steeply up the rising slopes ahead. The way now snakes upwards in a series of tight twists and turns as it passes through even wilder terrain containing shattered rock debris and boulder fields.

The final lake, tiny Black Lough, is then passed to your L, this resting snugly in the rock beds just below the top of the gap. After crossing two more venerable, arched bridges the upward slope, somewhat unexpectedly, slackens off and a section of fairly level ground is crossed. Soils have accumulated here and these support a sparse group of mixed bushes and trees including ash, hawthorn, holly, pine, sycamore and rhododendron; sheep graze here too on the relatively lush, flat pastures — quite a revelation! The top of the gap is just above and new vistas open up to the S from this elevated vantage point when you get there. These include Black Valley, a vast, wooded tract of country through which the Gearhameen River flows. This is the exit stream of Cummeenduff Lough, which lies to the WSW, higher up the valley, together with other stretches of elongated water that occupy the lower parts of this beautiful, remote basin.

Just below the crest on the far side of the gap after the initial twists and turns down and near to where the narrow road bends decisively to the R, be careful to swop the road for a more challenging way on your L. This is up steep, grassy slopes and along a faint path which follows the course of a tiny steam and the line of a wire fence. The changed direction is to the E, quite quickly veering NE where a rusty wire fence running at right angles across your approach has to be crossed. The steep ascent continues through long, tufted grasses and small boulders where continued upward progress is quite demanding.

The rate of climb varies as the faint path snakes higher and higher, tracking above the noise of the infant stream gurgling merrily below, and further on clumps of heathers and gorse are penetrated. Keep tracking upwards to the NE following the meanders of the tiny watercourse and, higher up, the line of a stone wall as well. Another dilapidated wire fence is then crossed, and following another lengthy traverse, partly through a shallow gully, the welcome sight of the cool, clear waters of diminutive Glas Lough appears over the brow ahead, these partly shaded by a protective cliff face. During your final approach to the lough, look above to your L to observe the serrated arêtes of the mountain range to the W. These alpine-like features are part

12:2 Looking down on the Gap of Dunloe from the heights of Purple Mountain

of the MacGillycuddy's Reeks, deservedly soaring up to the highest places in the whole of Ireland. On hot, sunny days to settle down for a short time by the side of the lough, perhaps have a cooling dip and partake of some refreshments, is sheer ecstasy!

THE WAY TO TOMIES MOUNTAIN — MR 895868 (Allow 2 hours)

The pointed, scree-covered peak piercing the sky further to the NE of Glas Lough is Purple Mountain (An Sliabh Corcra) and this lofty summit is your next major objective. Walk around the lough to the L to follow the narrow path which rises from the far northern tip of the water. This rough way leads further upwards beside a decrepit, rusty wire fence and it then bears around to the R, traversing eastwards up the steep, craggy slopes. Higher up, the narrow, adventurous way becomes better defined as a mixture of grass, fixed rocks and loose stones. Up here, redundant iron posts and the remnants of rusty wire confirm that you are continuing on course.

The track then twists NE, rising more steeply into heather-covered slopes. In gaining additional height, start to track around to your L when you approach the crest of the broad ridge above, progressively changing your direction of travel back towards the dominant one of NE. There are several different ways to the twin-peaked summit area of Purple Mountain, with one false horizon before you attain this. Avoid the steeper scree slopes to the L and continue walking up the interconnected paths leading NNE — some clearly defined in parts, others more obscure — until you can climb no higher. You will then be standing on the top of Purple Mountain at a height of 832 m (2730 ft). There are several cairns positioned at and near the wedge-shaped, flattish summit area, together with a stone shelter.

The views from up here in clear weather are stunning. In addition to the highlights previously positioned, the countryside containing Lough Leane and the many smaller lakes of Killarney stretches away, far below, for many miles between E and NE, whilst nearer to, both in distance and height, your continuation route towards Tomies Mountain and the spur extending to Shehy Mountain are revealed in fine detail. Additionally, part of the mountain structure of Beara is visible to the S and that of Dingle rises majestically to the NW. You can also observe where you started from, down below to the NNW!

Commence your descent to the NE, quickly locating a faint continuation path which leads that way. Lower down, the edge on your L becomes increasingly steep so keep a safe distance from this precipitous fall-away. Along here, the rough slopes continue to fall across a surface area covered with a mixture of rock, loose stones and peat. Then on the far side of a shallow hause, a wide, well-used, peaty path will lead you up a gentle, grassy incline taking you to an intermediate high point of 757 m (2485 ft) at Tomies South. Here, another broad, undulating, grassy ridge links in from the E in the direction of Shehy Mountain. Cairns also mark this summit area, a flattish, triangular dome.

Head N from here by turning slightly to the L to pass by a cairn which is positioned directly in line with Tomies Mountain. Another fairly lengthy descent follows, again across rough, rocky ground and then across another expansive, grassy hause below. More of this type of terrain, now sloping upwards, has to be climbed to gain the summit of Tomies Mountain, directly above.

This part of the way is well drained and consequently dry and easy to cover but the higher slopes do become increasingly barren, supporting mainly bilberry, lichen, mosses and St Patrick's Cabbage. The top commands a height of 735 m (2410 ft) and it is sobering to reflect that after all your most recent efforts, the net loss of height from standing on the summit of Purple Mountain is only some 100 m (just over 300 ft)! More cairns and a large shelter offer little consolation to this thought process.

THE WAY BACK TO THE CAR PARK — MR 881890 (Allow $2\frac{1}{2}$ hours)

From the L of the summit shelter, locate a faint path leading down to the NNW and diligently follow this across the steep, rough slopes. Locating the correct continuation line of this path is quite exasperating as it has a habit of disappearing and then turning up again lower down! Persevere with your exacting descent, always mindful of the extremely steep angle, and where necessary resort to a series of zigzags to negotiate the most difficult sections.

The best descent route then crosses the wide dip of a grassy hause followed by a rise which you veer up to the L to reach another guiding cairn positioned on a flattish hillock. Continue tracking NNW to reach this certain point. The descent continues on your established diagonal towards NNW to reach heather-covered ground. This adds to the venturesome descent, as lower down the heather grows taller and presents the problem of entanglement as you tread through it. Choose your way forward with some care, avoiding as much of the heather as is possible by working your way to the L and keeping towards the crest of the broad spur, heading down between NW and NNW.

Further down, on no account attempt to descend directly towards the parking area as there are steep, potentially dangerous slopes and cliff faces in that direction! Instead, continue northwards along the falling ridge following a clearly defined section of path. Lower down still, track along the line of a wire fence as the path enters an area covered with extensive bracken. Then a barbed wire fence ahead has to be surmounted in order to access a wide track immediately below. Turn L along this and follow it down to the road which is entered through a metal gate. Turn L again and cover the short remaining distance back to the car park.

Alternative Ways

ESCAPES

Curtailing this walk, apart from turning around and retracing your steps, is really not feasible. The about-turn might sensibly be undertaken at any point up to Glas Lough.

EXTENSIONS

Unless the weather is particularly fine it is not recommended that you add any extensions on to this route because the final descent from Tomies Mountain often takes much longer than most walkers, including strong ones, anticipate. One sensible addition in good conditions is to include Shehy Mountain, but this is a there-and-back addendum and may not be to everybody's liking.

WALK **THIRTEEN**

CARRAUNTOOHIL VIA DEVIL'S LADDER (TOURISTS' ROUTE)

fact file

START/FINISH

Parking area at Lisleibane — MR 826875

DISTANCE

10.9 km (6.8 miles)

GRADING

Difficult/strenuous (colour-coded RED)

TOTAL HEIGHT GAINED

870 m (2850 ft)

WALKING TIME ALLOWANCE

$6\frac{1}{2}$ hours

PRINCIPAL HEIGHTS

- Carrauntoohil 1039 m (3410 ft)

digest of walk

PARKING

Limited parking for up to about 10 cars on the grass verge at the end of the approach lane. (In wet conditions be mindful of the soft ground here.)

OVERVIEW/INTEREST

- Magnificent hike up to the highest point in Ireland.
- In mysterious Hags Glen the route threads between two enchanting corrie lakes where precipitously steep mountain slopes and high, rocky ridges surround you.
- The challenge of scrambling up Devil's Ladder with its rocky ledges, severe, almost vertical gradients and trickling watercourses.
- The thrill of looking down on the rest of Ireland from the summit of Carrauntoohil, with the most majestic, mountainous views below and around you.

CARRAUNTOOHIL VIA DEVIL'S LADDER

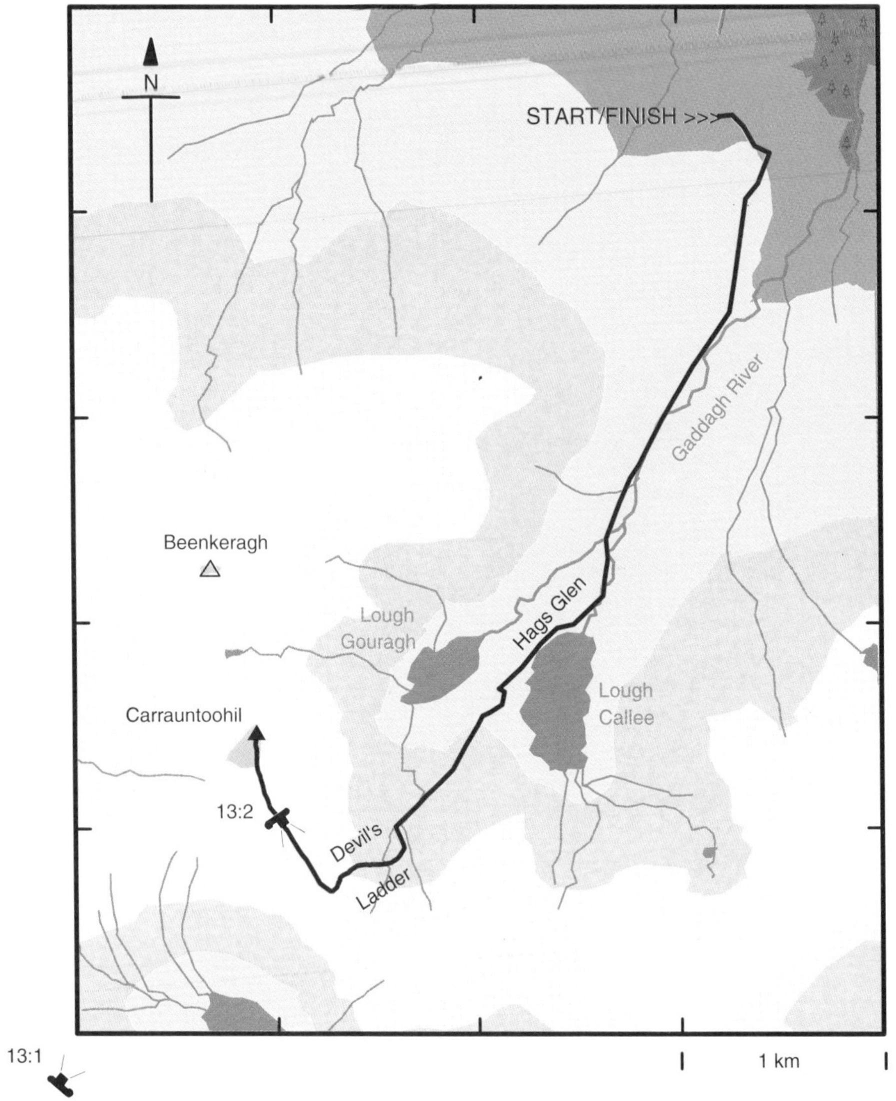

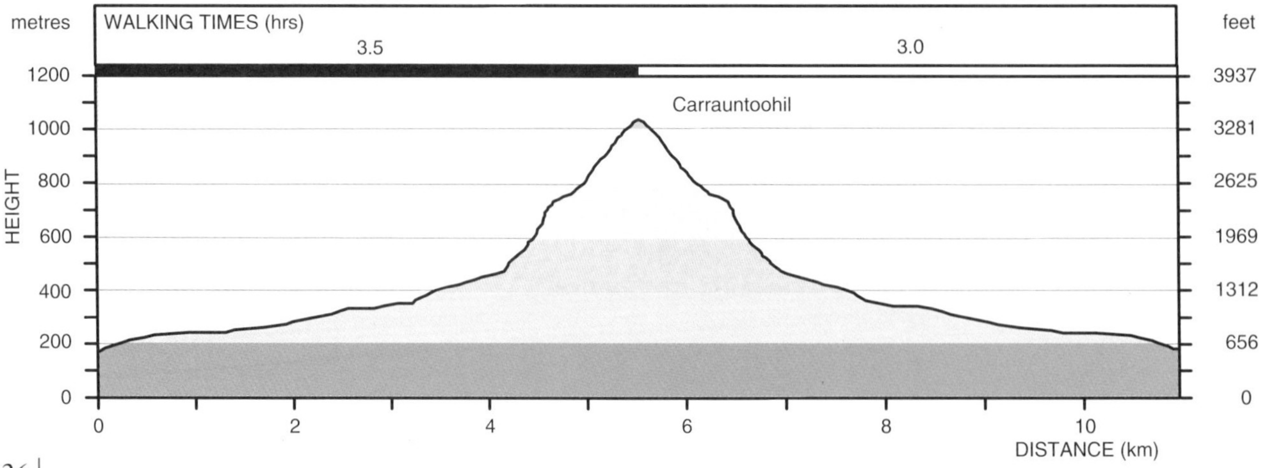

GRADIENTS

After a fairly level approach, you encounter steepening slopes which lead to the rocky gully of Devil's Ladder. This narrow crevice rises almost vertically in places to provide a challenging scramble up its rocky ledges and loose scree slopes. At the top, the ladder fans out on to a broad band of rock and from here a steep, scree-covered slope, which you have to zigzag up, leads to the summit. The descent is the reverse of the climb up.

MAPS, FOOTPATHS AND WAYSIGNS

OS DISCOVERY SERIES 1:50 000 — NUMBER 78 (KERRY)

OS MACGILLYCUDDY'S REEKS 1:25 000

The initial part of the walk is a lengthy stretch along a wide path of compacted gravel and loose stones. This surrenders to a narrower, rougher path which crosses boggier ground and watercourses higher up. A formidable scramble is then necessary up a challenging, rocky funnel where there are only limited sections of paths, these surfaced with loose stones and rock debris. Emerging from this ladder, there is a clearly defined, stony way which zigzags up formidable, steep, rock-covered slopes to reach the summit pinnacle of Carrauntoohil. The same mixture of paths is used, in reverse, going down.

There are no waysigns on this route but sections of it are well identified by cairns, particularly so the final high-level approach to the summit area. However, the correct way is still not always obvious in heavy mist or fog and in these conditions great care needs to be continuously exercised.

GETTING STARTED

The starting-point may be reached from Killorglin or Killarney by turning S off the N72 road at Beaufort Bridge and then motoring through the maze of minor roads to connect with the one running W to E along the northern fringe of the mountains. Turn S again off this at MR 830892 near to the bridge over the Gaddagh River and then after about another kilometre, turn L and follow the narrow lane to its terminus at Lisleibane.

Proceed through the middle one of three gates (the one with high wooden posts) just above the parking area and walk along the grassy track on the L which leads eastwards adjacent to a stone wall.

SUMMARY DESCRIPTION OF WALK

THE WAY TO CARRAUNTOOHIL — MR 804844 (Allow 3½ hours)

The views right from the start of this walk are superb and most walkers will be filled with both keen anticipation and a sense of awe for what they are about to experience. The jagged edges of the Reeks rise impressively to your R whilst the coastal plains of the Iveragh Peninsula fall gently in the opposite direction, leading your gaze northwards across the sea towards the far-away mountains of the Dingle Peninsula which rise to form the horizon beyond.

The wide track bends progressively to the R to lead you into the wide, glaciated valley now being further eroded by the waters of the Gaddagh River, tumbling down along a meandering

13:1 The distant MacGillycuddy's Reeks observed from Beara

rocky bed. High mountains of wild beauty and seductive attraction peer down on you, making you feel quite insignificant as you confidently stride along into their embraces. This awesome approach route leads you southwards up the valley and further into the enclosing amphitheatre of steeply rising slopes with their assortment of towering rock faces, pinnacles and buttresses. These views are a joy to behold, and with a keen anticipation of the challenges and delights which lie ahead of you, the long, fairly level trek towards the two loughs above which straddle Hags Glen is quickly accomplished.

On the way there and around a bend to the R, the first revelations of the scar of Devil's Ladder appear. This is observed as a band of lighter-coloured rock and stones tumbling down amongst the cliff faces to the SW. In good weather you will be able to observe the summit area of Carrauntoohil (Corrán Tuathail) — a pointed peak to the R of the ladder — from along here, with some of the arêtes leading to this lofty platform also visible. Walkers with good long-distance eyesight will also position the tall cross which stands on the summit. Have a guess here and now as to how high the cross is!

Your obvious way continues upstream and, ahead to the R, fantastic pinnacles of rock piercing the skies high above start to appear. Combes and small hanging valleys also appear beneath crumbling, concave faces, these fleeting features quite often partly shrouded in hanging, early morning mists which add to the allure and atmosphere of this mysterious place. This area contains the rock features known as Hags Teeth and Eagle's Nest, and Walk 14 will lead you up to these fascinating places! As you pass by these wondrous sights you will need to ford the river and then walk between Lough Gouragh (Loch Gabhrach) and Lough Callee

(Loch Caillí). There is a choice of ways to approach these waters: either continue along the rough, uneven, stony track or opt for a narrower, grassy path that leads off to the R skirting above the river. Both wind SW directly towards Devil's Ladder but the more interesting, grassy way does cover ground which is often soft and boggy and there are then some peat hags in the triangle ahead which you will need to avoid.

Further on, a wide, rocky path becomes established and this threads between the two remote lakes, rising gradually to provide clear views of the size and shape of both stretches of water cradled in the massive, mountain slopes which sweep down to them and then disappear beneath their placid surfaces. The ground and your continuation way rise appreciably more steeply beyond the loughs as your rocky path leads you ever nearer to the seemingly almost vertical rocky gully, where large boulders, scree and rocky steps and ledges tumble down one on top of another in a quite incredible, long, extension ladder. Hence the derivation of its name, which to all those walkers about to mount it appears uncomfortably appropriate!

Cairns mark the correct way into the recess and here the ground can become wet and boggy, whilst tumbling watercourses have to be crossed on several occasions, their number varying with the particular choice of ways you select. When you arrive at the bottom of Devil's Ladder you will become aware of just how massive and high the rocky chute is, although from here, several pitches further up are hidden from view! However, you will be able to see more clearly and in greater detail that much of the ladder is in fact composed of a mixture of fixed rock ledges, loose boulders, stones and scree, these intermingled with small areas of grass and compacted gravel, shales and peat. A rock face forms the R-hand side as you look up at it, whereas the other edge merges into wilder, and more formidable, tumbling-down rock pitches and ledges which are to be avoided. Watercourses trickle down amongst the rocks, their size and momentum determined by recent rains.

There are many acceptable ways of scaling Devil's Ladder and do not be put off by looking up at it. Make a start right away, scrambling up the ledges where you need to do this, walking up the steep connecting paths and weaving a way between the more difficult sections. If you were to climb this face a dozen times you would probably use twelve slightly different routes! In several places, the easiest, least exposed way up is near to the rock face on the R because the rocks and ground there are generally firmer. Sections of path do rise on the other side and the choice is really yours. In exercising this preference, do plan each discrete section with care and if you come to a pitch which causes you technical problems or necessitates unwelcome exposure, simply go back down for a short distance and then outflank the place you are not keen on, for there are always alternatives available to you.

The first sections of the ladder are characterised by a preponderance of fixed rock whilst the final funnel is mainly covered with a less secure mixture of loose stones and shifting scree. There are well-used and identifiable footholds on the rocks and there are sections of path beside and across the steep, looser pitches further up. Make good use of these aids and the main things to remember are always move with care from one secure footing to the next, retaining your balance at all times, and when you are climbing over rock debris avoid getting small loose stones caught beneath your boots. The exit from the ladder is up an eroded, muddy channel of quite often wet, clinging peat, which in these conditions can be slippery. Again, move with care, there is no desperate hurry, and you will emerge from your temporary confinement onto more open and appealing ground as Devil's Ladder fans out on to the broad shoulder of the spur above. A small cairn is positioned at this exit spot and you should memorise its location, for you will need to turn L here, down the ladder, on your return route.

In clear weather, the views which may be observed from this airy spot are breathtaking. Take time to look around and fully absorb these. First position your continuation route, which is upwards to the NW across steeply rising slopes covered mainly with shattered rock and stone fragments. You should be able to make out your cairned way, a well-walked, stony path zigzagging up these arresting slopes which for the time being effectively blot out any more distant views in that direction. Turning away from these, in the semicircle from E through S to W, there are vast panoramas of the interconnected mountain spurs and ridges which rise towards the highest place in Ireland, and beyond these fascinating features part of the mountainous backbone of the Beara Peninsula may be seen to the SW stretching out into the Atlantic Ocean.

Turn R to tackle the final steep slopes of the huge mountain. The cairned route will lead you ever upwards, initially NW and then NNW along a stony path, obviously trod by many walkers before you. After more endeavour and numerous twists and turns, including one definite fork to the R, the top of the cross appears quite suddenly and this welcome sighting signifies that within a few more paces you will be standing on the top of Ireland. This is at a height of 1039 m (3410 ft) and only those with wings will be able to soar above! The large, black-painted, metal cross is about 10 to 12 metres high and it bears the following simple inscription: MADE 1976 T O'SHEA (the T represents Tony).

13:2 TACKLING THE FINAL STEEP SLOPES LEADING TO THE SUMMIT OF CARRAUNTOOHIL

There is a large stone shelter on the summit but in clear, windless weather you will not need to use this protection and may concentrate your attention on marvelling at the gargantuan mountain scenery, spreadeagled below you in all directions, which surrounds this lofty viewing platform. Among the highlights are, firstly, looking northwards to take in the peak of Beenkeragh (Binn Chaorach) and to work out exactly how you would tackle walking along the knife-edged arête to get there, and secondly, peering westwards beyond multi-summited Caher (Cathair) along the mountainous spine of the Iveragh Peninsula out to sea. Fine views of parts of the parallel peninsulas of Dingle to the NW and Beara to the SW, with their competing high-level skylines, complete an epic picture as fine and as stunning as any you may have the pleasure of observing elsewhere.

THE WAY BACK TO THE PARKING AREA — MR 826875 (Allow 3 hours)

This is simply a question of retracing your outward steps! Leave the summit area to the SE and be very careful in misty conditions to immediately locate the approach path and the line of guiding cairns which marks this. If you miss this, quickly return to the top and try again! Descend along the way you came up to reach the top of Devil's Ladder, approaching this to the SSE. The entrance to the ladder is at the bottom of a wide hause, marked by a small cairn, the location of which you should have committed to memory earlier.

Turn L and descend NE along the rock slabs, boulders, stones and scree, retracing, though not quite step by step, your upward route earlier in the day. Go down with care at a pace which suits you, being diligent to always maintain your balance and be in full control of the way down and rate of descent, in both choice and execution. At the bottom, walk back down Hags Glen, again bisecting the two corrie loughs, and then retrace your steps along the valley back to where you parked your vehicle, almost certainly exhilarated — and rightly so — with what you have achieved.

ALTERNATIVE WAYS

ESCAPES

Apart from turning back and retracing your steps, at any point, before you reach the top of Carrauntoohil, there are no other obvious and sensible curtailments.

EXTENSIONS

In fine weather, strong walkers may choose an alternative, longer and more exciting descent to the W, either over Beenkeragh or along the summits of Caher, in either case finishing at the minor road at MR 771871 where you will need to have either a vehicle in position or arranged transport to collect you. If you decide to venture over Beenkeragh you will need to have a head for heights because you will have to traverse an arête to get there. The jumbled rocks which form this narrow ridge are awkward to get across rather than technically difficult, and most of the really exposed parts may be avoided by scrambling just below the crest of the rising arête. The alternative descent across the multi-pinnacled Caher is less adventurous but you do need to always keep away from the precipitous cliff faces to your R.

Carrauntoohil and Caher

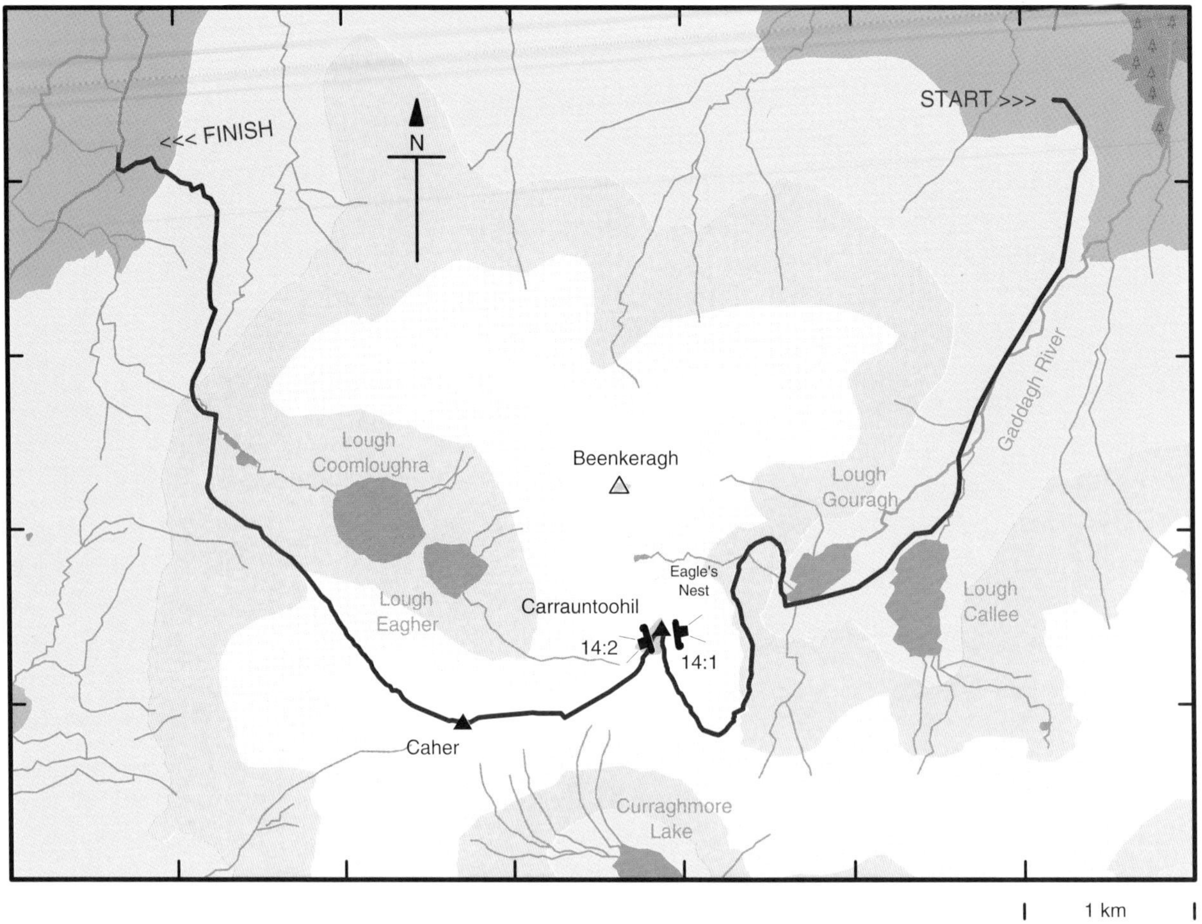

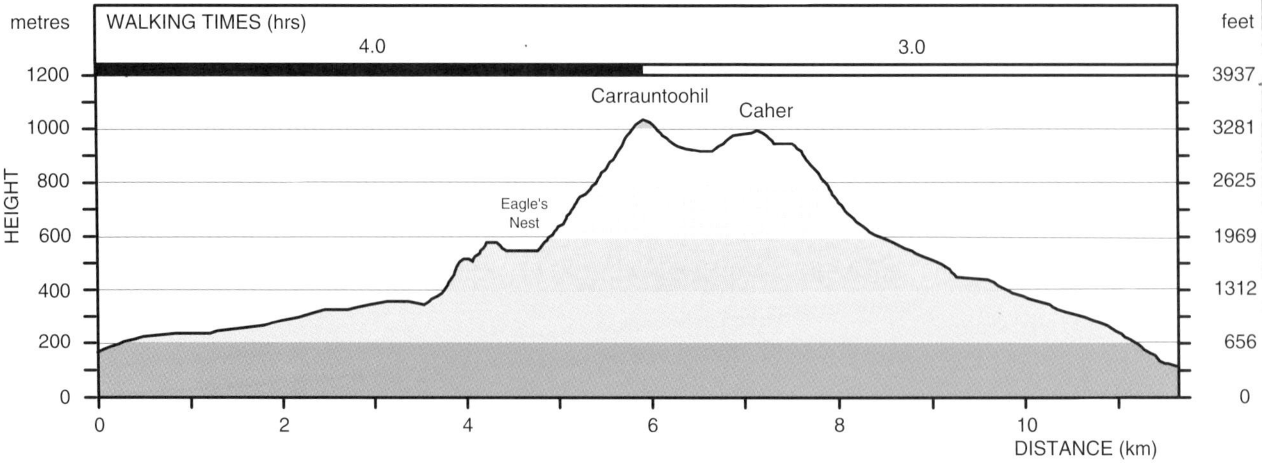

CARRAUNTOOHIL AND CAHER

factfile

START/FINISH
Start at Lisleibane — MR 826875
Finish at road — MR 771871

GRADING
Difficult/strenuous (colour-coded RED)

WALKING TIME ALLOWANCE
7 hours

DISTANCE
11.6 km (7.2 miles)

TOTAL HEIGHT GAINED
1000 m (3280 ft)

PRINCIPAL HEIGHTS
- Carrauntoohil 1039 m (3410 ft)
- Caher 1001 m (3285 ft)

digest of walk

PARKING
Same place as for Walk 13. Limited parking for up to about 10 cars on the grass verge at the end of the approach lane. In wet conditions be mindful of the soft ground here. (Note: This is a linear walk and, therefore, ideally two vehicles should be used, the second one positioned at the end of the route where there is limited parking for about six cars along road verges. Otherwise, arrange transport to collect you from the end of the walk at your estimated time of arrival there.)

OVERVIEW/INTEREST
- Like Walk 13, a magnificent hike up to the highest point in Ireland.
- Identical initial approach through Hags Glen and between two enchanting corrie lakes.
- More adventurous ascent route after this by way of Eagle's Nest and a severe climb up a rocky gully to rejoin the 'tourists' route' higher up.
- Thrills continue during the longer descent across the several peaks of Caher.

- Magnificent views throughout the walk, highlighted by the mountain panoramas visible in clear weather from the summits of Carrauntoohil and Caher.

GRADIENTS

After a fairly level approach identical to Walk 13, there is a series of very steep slopes, some covered with grass and stones and others necessitating some elementary scrambling up rock pitches and gullies. A traverse across rough ground leads to a final steepish climb to gain the summit of Carrauntoohil. An undulating descent follows across the several peaks of Caher with some steep sections both down and up. There is a long, gradual descent along a ridge from the summit of Caher, this composed of varying gradients, with some quite steep downward sections.

MAPS, FOOTPATHS AND WAYSIGNS

OS Discovery Series 1:50 000 — Number 78 (Kerry)

OS MacGillycuddy's Reeks 1:25 000

There are good approach paths and a wide track at the end of the walk. The difficult part in between these is served by a variety of paths and mountain tracks, some obvious and well defined such as the final climb to the summit of Carrauntoohil whilst others are less obvious and more difficult to follow. There are also sections across rough terrain and up and down rocky slopes where there are no paths.

There are no waysigns but a moderate number of cairns indicate the course of paths and strategic interchanges/choices of way.

GETTING STARTED

The starting-point is the same as that for Walk 13. This may be reached from Killorglin or Killarney by turning S off the N72 road at Beaufort Bridge and then motoring through the maze of minor roads to connect with the one running W to E along the northern fringe of the mountains. Turn S again off this at MR 830892 near to the bridge over the Gaddagh River and then after about another kilometre, turn L and follow the narrow lane to its terminus at Lisleibane.

Proceed through the middle one of three gates (the one with high wooden posts) just above the parking area and walk along the grassy track on the L which leads eastwards adjacent to a stone wall.

Summary Description of Walk

THE WAY TO CARRAUNTOOHIL — MR 804844 (Allow 4 hours)

The first part of this walk, as previously mentioned, is identical to Walk 13, this as far as bisecting the two corrie lakes located in Hags Glen. The two walks do not diverge until you reach MR 816846 and, therefore, refer to pages 127–9 for a more complete description of the scenery and route details up to that point. To recapitulate briefly on these, the starting landscapes are quite magnificent with rugged mountain slopes rising ahead seemingly beckoning you into their embraces, whilst more docile countryside in the form of coastal plains sweeps down gently to reach the coastline to the N. The obvious approach way leads southwards along the course of the Gaddagh River which you eventually ford. Beyond this, you track through Hags Glen along the stony path which leads between Lough Gouragh (Loch Gabhrach) and Lough Callee (Loch Caillí). Part way up the steeper section of path, towards the N end of Lough Callee, branch off to the R and head W across the grassy slopes aiming towards the SW tip of Lough Gouragh. This is where you bid a fond farewell to any walkers in your party who intend continuing up Devil's Ladder as detailed in Walk 13.

A pleasant, elevated traverse follows across sloping ground as you make your way towards the quite formidable, near vertical, rock faces straight ahead and down which a waterfall cascades. Cross the feeder stream above the lough to continue across more grassy slopes as you circle around the top end of the lake. You need to gain height at a faster rate, and you do this by maintaining an upward diagonal, heading towards the waterfall and threading your way through a boulder field just below the first, lower cliff faces of the steeply rising mountainside. You probably will experience absolute solitude working your way cautiously along here. Continue traversing upwards, selecting a steeper line by bearing L and heading NNW towards the formidable pinnacles and gouged-out combe that have been quite appropriately named Eagle's Nest.

Zigzag up the higher grassy slopes to connect with a faint path tracking at right angles to your direction of approach. Turn L along this and use it to scale the minor rock pitches ahead. More zigzagging up further steep, grassy slopes is then required to reach a drier, better-defined path above, which you again turn L along. This welcome respite quite quickly leads to an unexpected, flat, grass-covered hanging valley or combe which is surrounded on all sides, save the entrance you have accessed, by precipitous rock faces and towers — a quite magnificent and awesome place where you just could imagine eagles soaring, high above!

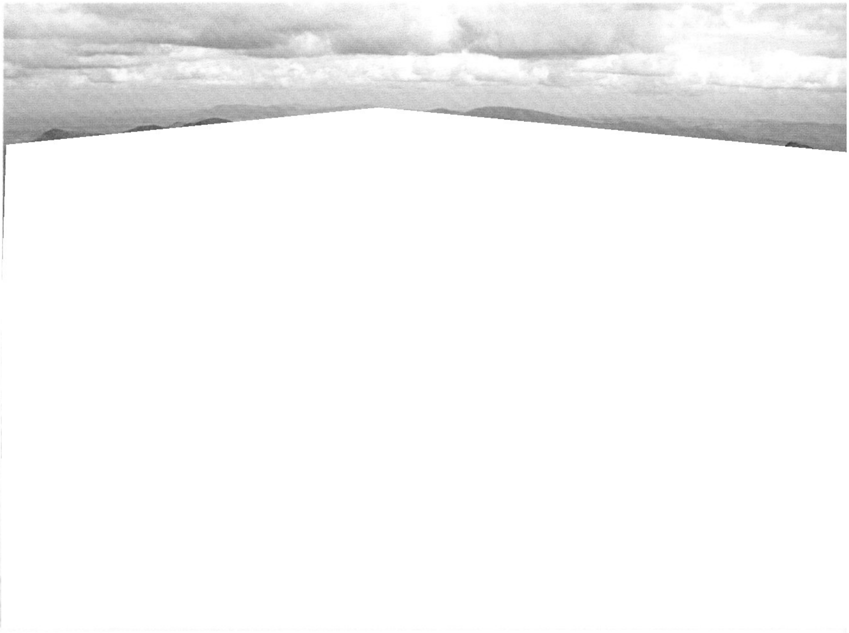

14:1 The eastern panorama beyond Lough Callee observed from the summit of Carrauntoohil

Turn L to scale the rising, rocky ground ahead, following a faint track and walking S. Then veer to the R up steeper ground to climb above the dangerous rock pitches ahead, resorting to more zigzags before crossing a section of wire fencing. There are revealing views from here back into the combe where you should be able to spot the trickling waterfall feeding into it. There is also a grand bird's-eye (or eagle's-eye) view of Lough Gouragh and Lough Callee, now some hundreds of feet below. The ground temporarily levels off further on and good use has been made of this flatter area to locate a stone hut which is used by climbers, some of whom actually built it.

Continue climbing up the rounded, rocky spur heading towards the intimidating rock faces looming up straight ahead. You have the relative luxury of a distinct, dry, stony path to encourage you to get there. Then cross over to the R to reach the walls of rock and to access a narrow gully which leads steeply upwards beneath their towering bulk. A well-defined, stony path zigzags beside the cliff faces and you will gain height rather rapidly up here by scrambling up a narrowing chute. This cleft is carpeted with a mixture of fixed rocks and loose stones and this surface will continuously remind you to be extra careful where you place each step! Progress is to the SSW whilst in the rocky chute and this route has been named 'The Heavenly Gates'.

The gully fans out on to wild, rugged but much more open terrain at the top. These mountainsides rise steeply towards the summit area of Carrauntoohil but your ascent route, fortunately, does not go straight up! Instead, the next section traverses across the steep, rocky pitches along a narrow, but in most places reasonably well-defined, stony path which circles around these vast, featureless slopes, climbing steadily and bending around through S in the process. The lengthy traverse will lead you around the massive, rock-strewn shoulder of the mountain to reach less steep slopes on which grass has become established, and in this vicinity your continued direction of travel will cause you to make contact with a cairned path which leads further upwards in a series of zigzags.

The way continues to the NW after you have either progressively veered or turned to the R, to then follow the stony, cairned path which after many more twists and turns will bring you to a vantage point from which you will be able to see the large cross which marks the summit of Carrauntoohil looming up above you. The final part of the climb is along the path which is also part of the way up via Devil's Ladder and so the big question is: are any members of your party who went that way already on the summit or are they still below you? This interesting conundrum will be resolved within a few more paces!

14:2 The continuation route westwards over pointed Caher revealed from the top of Carrauntoohil

The summit of Carrauntoohil commands a height of 1039 m (3410 ft) and when you get there you will be standing on the top of Ireland. The cross is large, black and made of metal and is about 10 to 12 metres high. It bears the modest inscription: Made 1976 T O'Shea (the T represents Tony). There is a large stone shelter nearby but in good, clear, windless conditions you will not need to huddle in this and you can spend the whole of your time up here absorbing the many-splendoured views to be observed from the roof of this fair land. In the clearest of weathers, much of the spectacular, mountainous countryside of SW Ireland may be studied from here and the rugged peninsulas of Dingle, Iveragh and Beara stretching out into the Atlantic Ocean reveal many of their secrets. You will have your own favourite views but those westwards towards and beyond Caher (Cathair), that northwards to survey Beenkeragh (Binn Chaorach) and the arêtes leading to it, and those to the E to absorb the many precipitous peaks forming the long, majestic ridges rising to Cnoc na Péiste must rank amongst the very finest.

THE WAY TO THE ROAD AND FINISH — MR 771871 (Allow 3 hours)

Start your descent to the SW across gently sloping, rocky ground which supports thrift (sea pink) and mosses in the many crevices amongst the rocks. Be careful to quickly locate a wide, stony path which leads down more steeply to reach an important cairn, this strategically positioned to identify a division of ways. The spurs and arêtes leading to the summit of Beenkeragh peel off to the R whilst your continuation route is along the L fork, heading SW to almost immediately pass by a second guiding cairn. An easy, gradual descent then follows along a stony and gravel-surfaced path which zigzags across the falling slopes.

These broad slopes gradually funnel into a narrow, rounded spur which you walk down along, maintaining your established diagonal of SW. Cliffs begin to develop on your R which plunge down towards the two corrie lakes, Lough Coomloughra (Loch Chom Luachra) and Lough Eagher (Loch Íochtair), many hundreds of feet below. By contrast, the rounded, grassy slopes to your L appear relatively benign. Keep going down as the well-trodden way just below the crest of the falling ridge subtly changes your forward direction to WSW.

Further on, progress is across more rugged, rockier ground and the ridge narrows to assume arête-like characteristics. However, a secure path tracks on the L-hand side and just below the jagged crest of the rocky spur. Then, for a short distance, the nature of the two sides reverses, and at this point the narrow path crosses over before tracking back to the predominant 'safe side' of the ridge which is on the L and along the southern face. A short, sharp climb follows up a steeply rising zigzag to reach an intermediate high point. In clear weather there are excellent views back from here towards Carrauntoohil and of the arête leading from there on to Beenkeragh. Severe fall-aways continue to accompany you on the R and always be mindful of these!

More interesting undulations follow along a rocky ledge before grassy areas are reached. These slopes then lead to the summit of Caher. Caher signifies 'stone fort' in the format of a protected, circular compound with dwellings sheltered inside. The summit stands at 1001 m (3285 ft) and commands more superb views, most of the details of which should by now be familiar to you. However, there are further absorbing revelations to the W, and from here more detailed perspectives of the Iveragh Peninsula stretching out in that direction with its diversity of mountain peaks and scattering of lakes may be assimilated.

The descent continues across a scree slope, now to the NW, and this leads to a wide, stony path marked by cairns which threads down through further sections of scree and loose stones.

The waters of Lough Acoose (Loch an Chuais) then appear below to the W. Broader slopes thereafter provide most of the easier continuation way down, but there are some further undulations and one final upward, craggy slope which has to be climbed. This contains more rocky outcrops and steeply plunging edges on the R. A wire fence is crossed along here and two cairns mark the top of this, the very last climb of the day!

Keep descending to the NW down a rough, rocky slope, zigzagging along the obvious path which will lead you down on to grassier slopes below changing your direction of travel slightly towards NNW. Lower down, the path performs a disappearing act in places but continue heading down across the grassy expanses now sprinkled with conglomerate rocks. The way becomes increasingly waterlogged lower down but keep walking along or towards the crest of the grassy spur following a clear and easy line of descent as this higher ground protrudes above the surrounding flatter slopes below.

Towards the termination of the ridge, where it begins to fall down more steeply, bear R across the heathery slopes and track N into the flatter ground below. Keep to this bearing to cross a difficult area of boggy ground, weaving a course across this which will avoid the worst places. This direction will take you to firmer, stony ground and across this you will connect with the bottom end of narrow Lough Eighter, once a natural lake but now a reservoir. A vehicle-width track leads further down the valley from here; turn L and follow it.

Clamber over a metal gate and a lengthy final descent along the wide track will bring you to the minor road below and a rendezvous with either your parked car or — hopefully — the transport that is awaiting your arrival there bang on time!

Alternative Ways

ESCAPES

This challenging, linear route is really not very suitable for shortening — that is apart from turning back early on, and an E or SE gale may cause you to do this! You could plan to return from the summit by way of Devil's Ladder as in Walk 13 and this of course will avoid the necessity of either using two vehicles or arranging a lift from the scheduled finish of the walk as previously indicated.

EXTENSIONS

There is a very feasible alternative descent from Carrauntoohil which will bring you to the same finishing point. This is the even more adventurous route over Beenkeragh to the N. You will need a head for heights to achieve this because the link between the two mountains is along an arête with some exposure in places. The route along the jagged ridge is awkward rather than difficult, and the more exacting pinnacles may be avoided by contouring around just below them. The ensuing descent from Beenkeragh is across wide, expansive, grassy slopes, and connection is made with the main route described just below Lough Eighter at MR 777856. Very strong and determined walkers could include both Beenkeragh and Caher in their itinerary but this will involve some backtracking.

Coomasaharn Lake Horseshoe

factfile

START/FINISH
Near N tip of Coomasaharn Lake — MR 636851

GRADING
Difficult/strenuous (colour-coded RED)

WALKING TIME ALLOWANCE
7 hours

DISTANCE
10.0 km (6.2 miles)

TOTAL HEIGHT GAINED
670 m (2200 ft)

PRINCIPAL HEIGHTS
- Knocknaman 561 m (1840 ft)
- Coomacarrea 772 m (2535 ft)

digest of walk

PARKING
Very limited parking on grass verges near the end of the approach road; space for about six cars. Additional space in front of nearby bungalow but you will need to seek permission to park there if necessary.

OVERVIEW/INTEREST
- Superb corrie lake, cradled by precipitously steep rock faces.
- Magnificent views down into the fantastic, wild, remote and awesome setting of the lake.
- Compelling, long-distance panoramas from the spaciousness of the surrounding mountains.
- The thrill of descending along a rocky arête.
- The opportunity to inspect nearby Rock Art (primitive paintings on rocks).

GRADIENTS
The walk commences with a steep climb up through difficult rock benches to reach the top of Knocknaman. Much of the hard work is then over, as the route circles around the lake at a high level and the remaining upward

COOMASAHARN LAKE HORSESHOE

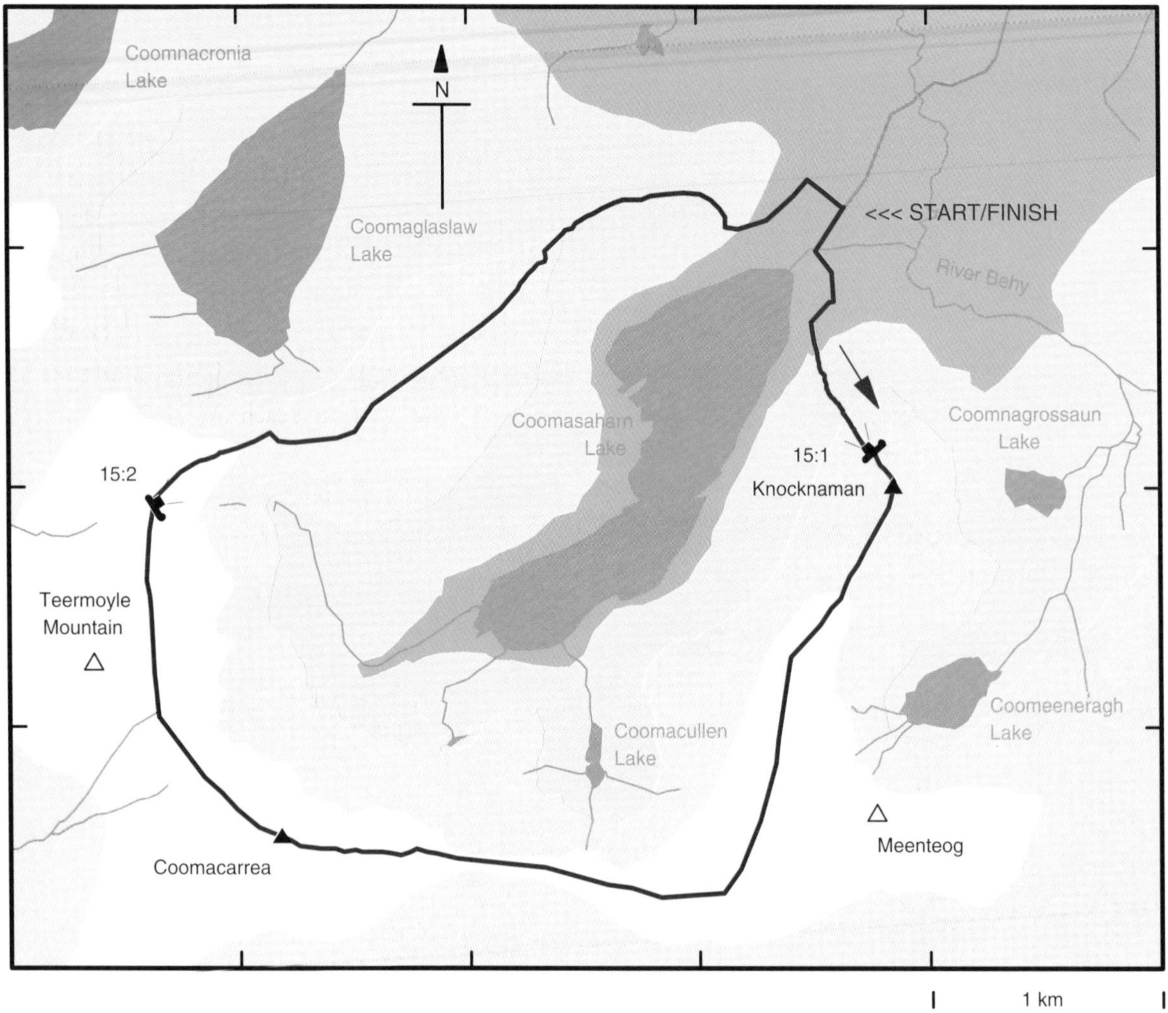

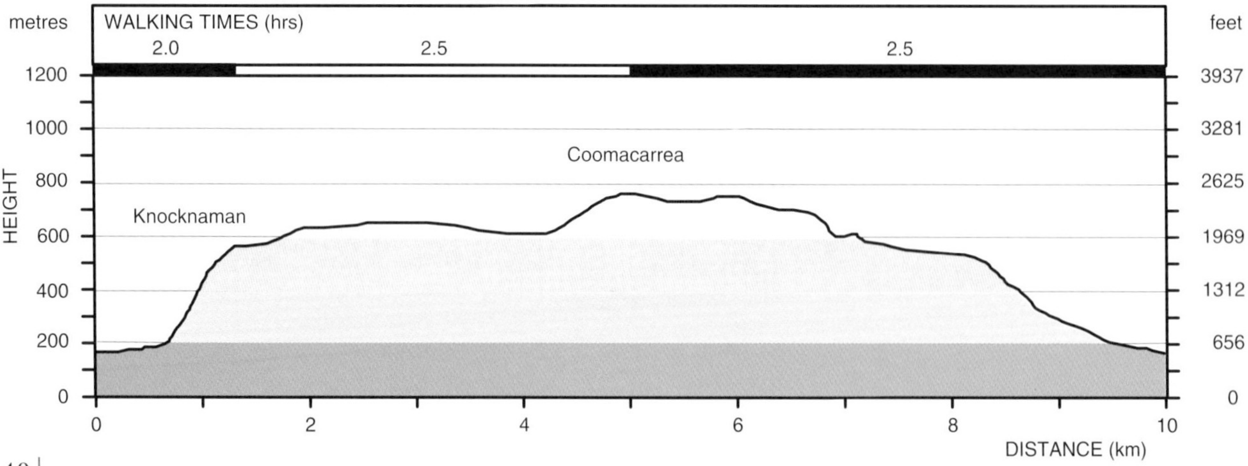

gradients are well spaced out, although the one leading to the summit of Coomacarrea does require some further moderate effort. The walk finishes with a prolonged descent which includes treading carefully along a narrow, rocky arête.

MAPS, FOOTPATHS AND WAYSIGNS

OS DISCOVERY SERIES 1:50 000 — NUMBER 78 (KERRY)

Much of this route is either climbing or descending over rough, rocky ground or walking across vast, high-level slopes covered mainly with a mixture of grasses and peat hags, devoid of any obvious paths or tracks. There are some sections of the way where use can be made of faint tracks or better-defined paths but these are few and far between. The starting and finishing sections do make use of minor access lanes.

There are no signs, and also cairns are rare on this route!

GETTING STARTED

The start of the walk is about 6 km (4 miles) SW of the busy village of Glenbeigh, which lies on the main N70 'Ring of Kerry' road. The suggested parking place may be reached either direct from the village or by turning off the N70 road at one of several places further W and then travelling southwards through the maze of minor lanes to reach the N tip of the lake.

Walk up the gravel-surfaced, walled lane, heading SW towards the vast combe directly ahead.

SUMMARY DESCRIPTION OF WALK

THE WAY TO KNOCKNAMAN — MR 638840 (Allow 2 hours)

The walk commences from a place which is low lying and fairly well hemmed in by nearby hedgerows and, therefore, to start with, distant views are fairly restricted. However, this will soon change for the better! The way winds marginally uphill and almost immediately you will observe the impressive rock faces and slabs of the steeply rising slopes of Knocknaman rearing up above on your L. This is just a taste of what is to come, for shortly you will be climbing up this formidable ground!

Emerging from the tree-fringed lane, you will obtain the first views of part of Coomasaharn Lake down to your R, its still waters stretching away to the SW towards the near vertical cliffs which cradle its upper reaches. The place is lovely, lonely, eerie and captivating. After passing through an ancient, metal gate, bear L up the rocky slopes on a diagonal line to the S veering SE, aiming to connect with the wire fence, now in view above, at its highest point. Continue to thread a way of your own choice between the rock benches and along intervening grassy strips where it is often wet and muddy. An upward series of zigzag manoeuvres will bring you to the fence, which you then cross.

Higher up, the whole length of the elongated and indented Coomasaharn Lake progressively comes into view. There are sublime perspectives from here of the rugged setting of the shimmering lake trapped within a deep, rocky basin which has been scooped out by powerful glacial forces. Vast, high mountains rise above and encircle the boulder-strewn shores of this remote corrie lake, save for the flattish entrance at the NNE end, through which you have just walked. Prominent amongst the lofty peaks which you can now see towering above the inky waters are those of Coomacarrea (An Tráigh) to the SW, Teermoyle Mountain further to the R towards WSW and, directly across the lough, Coomreagh to the W. You will walk across all of these summits later on in the day during the continuation of your horseshoe ramble high above Coomasaharn!

Plan your forward route upwards through the rock benches with care, avoiding all the more difficult rock pitches and overhangs and taking full advantage of the easier ways up the grassy sections when this is feasible. Further up, you will reach the vicinity of a distinctive stone jutting out, and here keep slightly to the R of this certain and helpful landmark, continuing to weave about seeking out the less exacting passages upwards. The way becomes easier towards the top of the challenging face as the rock pitches and stones diminish and the gradients of the slopes become progressively less steep.

More rounded, grassy slopes appear ahead, these now punctuated by only the occasional rocky outcrop, and as you continue to track SE, the welcome sighting of the top of the ridge appears quite suddenly above. From here, proceed to the rather unusual, squarish, stone cairn with its distinctive slab of rock pointing skywards. You have now reached the rounded, grassy summit of Knocknaman and are standing at a height of 561 m (1840 ft). Vast, panoramic views open up hereabouts, providing the weather is clear. The long ridge now visible to the NE culminates with Seefin and the higher mountains to the SE contain the separate peaks of Colly and Colly East, whilst in between these two groupings, through the gap in the middle, the distinctive, horn-shaped profiles of the MacGillycuddy's Reeks majestically pierce the sky, forming the far-away horizon to the E.

THE WAY TO COOMACARREA — MR 611825 (Allow $2\frac{1}{2}$ hours)

Head SW from the summit area of Knocknaman walking along the broad, rounded ridge where crossing a succession of peat hags will impede your otherwise rapid progress. Wide, expansive slopes lead further upwards towards the flattish summit of Meenteog to the S. (You actually circle away from this peak, passing by it to the W.) Just keep on tracking upwards between SSW and S, crossing eroded depressions when you have to and avoiding all those that you can without deviating too far off course.

Stretches of wet, boggy ground usually have to be crossed up here and the relatively featureless, grassy slopes which retain this water are then divided by a wire fence. Track around this fence at its westerly tip to the R, still heading predominantly S, and make for the higher ground ahead. More sodden ground is then crossed before you reach an isolated scattering of rocks and stones. Turn R at this point to continue SW veering W across comparatively drier, grassy ground which falls away gently. Unfortunately, bog and waterlogged areas quickly make an unwelcome return lower down the ridge where the continuation route crosses more substantial, shallow depressions.

The broad hause leading westwards to the approach slopes of Coomacarrea is then crossed. Track towards and then carefully walk along the edge over to your R to obtain the most fantastic views down into the deep void of the corrie below. Precipitously steep cliff faces plunge down many hundreds of feet towards a hanging valley which contains the trapped waters of tiny Coomacullen Lake, this still perched high above Coomasaharn. Pass through the unusual gate in the fence ahead, ducking under the strand of wire positioned above it. Route finding now becomes somewhat easier as you continue walking to the L of the remains of a stone wall and a wire fence which obligingly lead in the direction of Coomacarrea.

The way then passes by the end of an ugly-looking road, apparently constructed to bring up fencing material. (Helicopter trails would have disappeared much faster!) From here, climb steadily upwards beside the wire fence to reach and use a second metal gate. A short distance further on, around slightly to the R, is the summit of Coomacarrea. In getting there, be vigilant of the continuing precipitous fall-ways on your R as you pass by a line of redundant fence posts

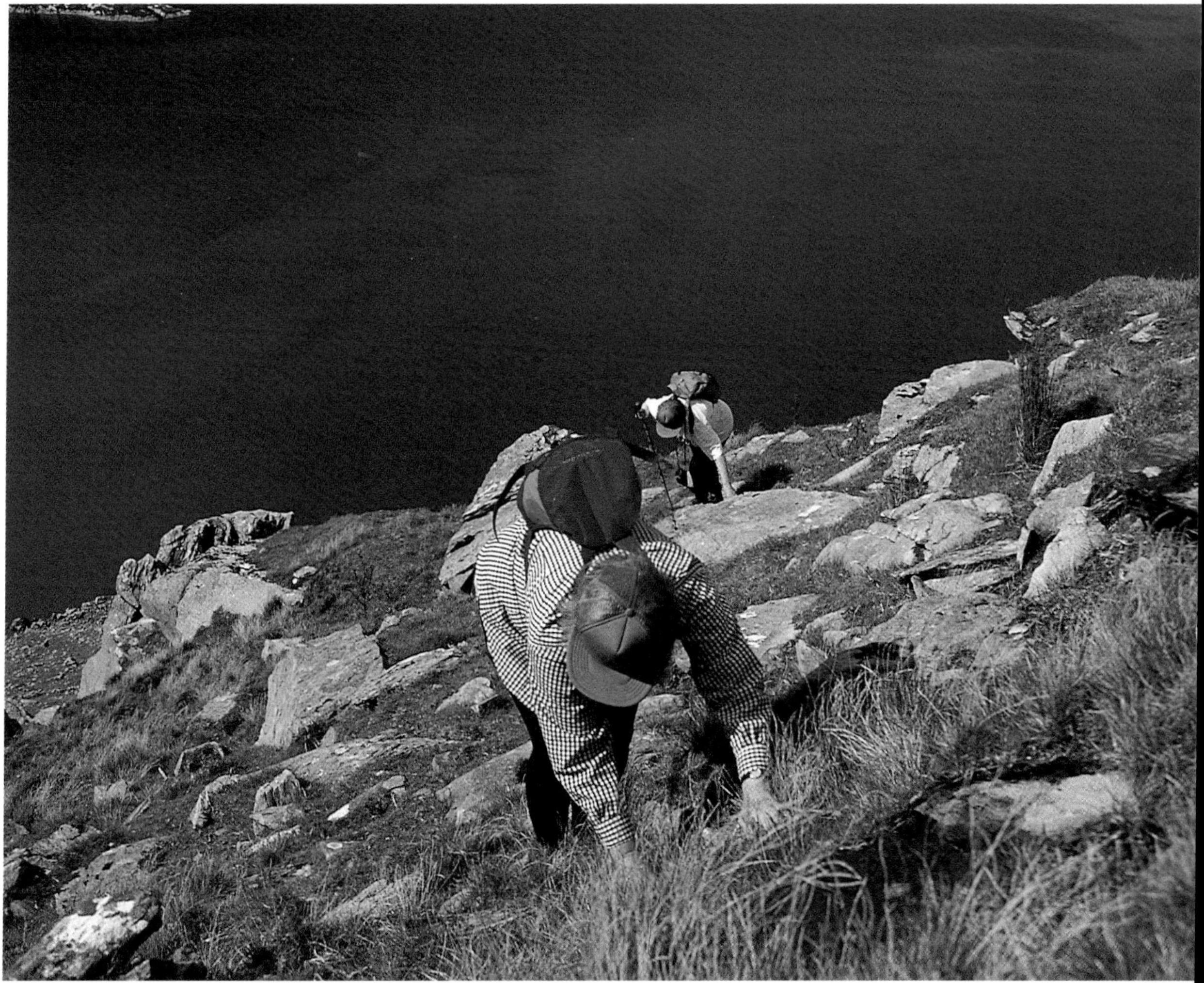

15:1 SCRAMBLING UP THE STEEP ROCK BENCHES WHICH LEAD TO THE SUMMIT OF KNOCKNAMAN

15:2 Mary-Frances Thompson, a Go Ireland guide, leading the way down along the Árete from Coomreagh

and stumps. The expansive, grassy top of Coomacarrea stands at 772 m (2535 ft) and its flattish top is rather featureless apart from the bog pools, being devoid of cairns, shelters, a trigonometrical point or even the more usual rocky outcrops. The views are rather restricted too by the contours of the slopes, and all in all it is not a particularly attractive place to linger.

THE WAY BACK TO THE PARKING AREA — MR 636851 (Allow 2½ hours)

After crossing another wide depression, descend to the NW across gently falling slopes, walking towards another wire fence which you cross. Then follow the line of more fencing as it bends around to the R, this obligingly tracking NW veering NNW which is exactly the way you need to continue along the elevated horseshoe. The views to the R along this stretch are quite superlative with Coomasaharn Lake spreadeagled far below, cupped by near vertical walls of rock and steep, craggy slopes which link your present precarious (be careful) position with the shimmering waters of the lake which impressively fill the massive, gouged-out, boulder-strewn corrie in the depths down below. In this vast landscape, spot the tiny lake of Loughacummeen trapped in the rocky ledge high up to the ESE.

A slight rise leads to the summit of Teermoyle Mountain, another flat, featureless, grassy expanse which you skirt around to the E. The eroded slopes of Mullaghnarakill rise ahead to the NNW but your route turns R towards NE before the next rise and thereby avoids climbing this mountain. Follow the line of the fence downhill but cross over it when it turns at right angles to your continued line of descent. (The top strand of this fence is barbed so exercise appropriate care.) Keep surrendering height to the NE near to the steep fall-away on your R to pass by a solitary, small cairn.

The grassy slopes then begin to fall more steeply as they funnel towards a rocky arête below. From above this narrow ridge there is a clear view, subject to favourable weather, of Coomaglaslaw Lake down to your L towards N. Unless it is blowing a gale or icy with a covering of snow, in which case only vastly experienced and suitably equipped walkers and climbers should be there, clambering along the arête is neither particularly difficult nor frightening and once under way it is nowhere near as exposed as it may appear from above. Exercise great care going along it, watching where you place each secure footstep. Further along the ridge, the more formidable, steep, grassy pinnacles may be circumvented by keeping to the easier, less exposed tracks which lead below these on the L.

The exacting but thrilling traverse surrenders to a broader, grassy band and this drops further towards lower ground to connect with wider, concave slopes below. When these grassy slopes flatten off, bear L towards NE to follow the spur as the ground ahead shelves marginally upwards to reach rocky outcrops. The remains of sections of stone walling are encountered ahead and when the ridge narrows and falls more steeply again, just keep towards the crest of it to reach another wire fence which again you need to exercise care getting over.

Continue your descent to the NE and then bear R lower down to trim your approach to connect with a cart or tractor track. This continues to lead you down the valley across rutted, fairly level ground. After a straightish traverse, the path zigzags down to reach a metal gate, its surface upgrading in this process. An attractive group of four bungalows are then passed, after which a surfaced lane leads you back to your starting-point.

Alternative Ways

ESCAPES

Do not attempt this challenging circuit unless the weather is reasonably good and you are confident and determined to complete the route as described. This is because, once you are committed to this horseshoe, there are no safe ways down other than the one described, and even to turn back from Knocknaman early on is fraught with considerable difficulties.

EXTENSIONS

Strong walkers in favourable weather may decide, whilst they maintain their altitude, to visit the additional summits of Meenteog and/or Mullaghnarakill, although to do the latter will involve some modest backtracking.

Overleaf: The Brandon Massif observed from near Cloghane

Dingle Peninsula Walks

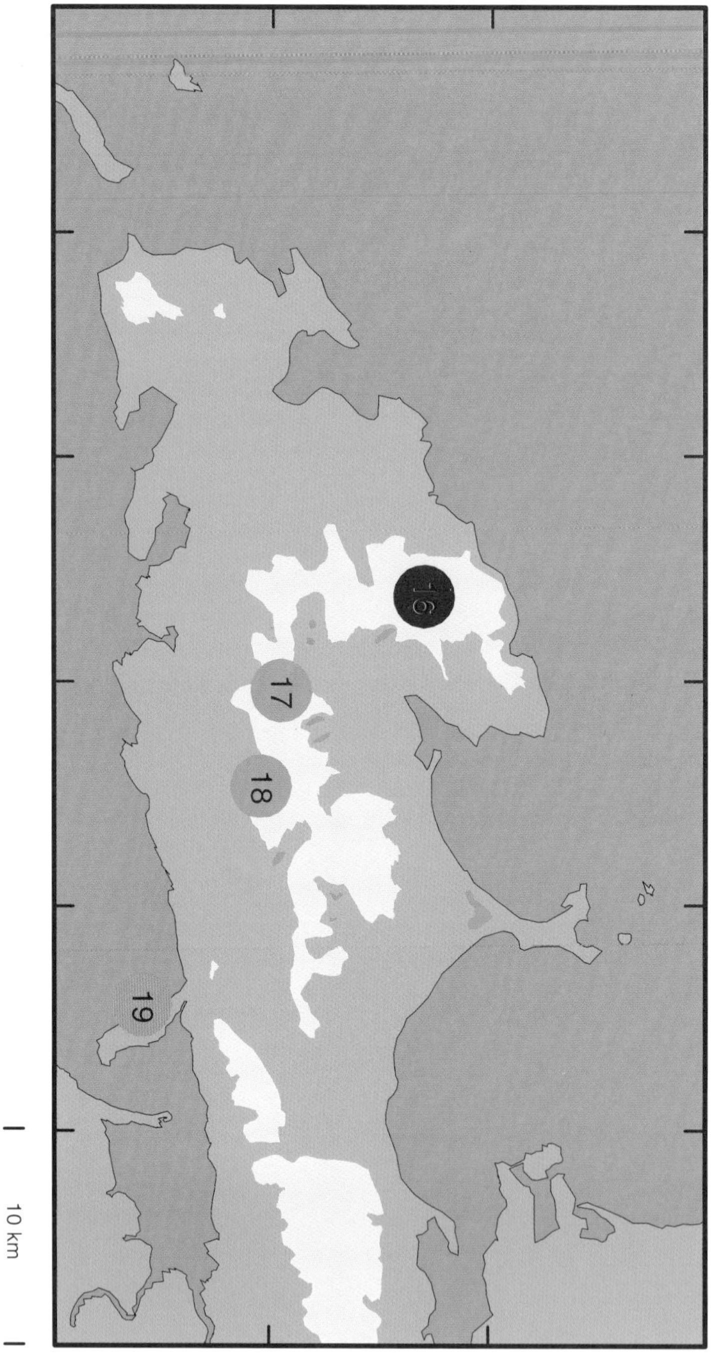
16
17
18
19
10 km

THE MOUNTAINS OF THE DINGLE PENINSULA

GETTING THERE

Tralee, apart from its world-famous roses and festival, is also the principal, northern gateway to the Dingle Peninsula. However, as you will be coming up from the S from the Iveragh Peninsula, you may avoid passing through Tralee for the time being, unless you wish to visit this attractive place *en route*. The way to bypass Tralee is to turn W when you reach Castlemaine to then head along the R561 coast road to connect with the main N86 road at Anascaul.

From here, it is a short journey to Dingle town, the heartthrob of the western end of the peninsula, where you may continue to all points further W or alternatively travel over the adventurous Connor Pass towards Cloghane and from there along the coastal strip to Castlegregory.

If you only have to journey from Killorglin you can be in Dingle within an hour or so, leaving most of the day free to exercise your leg muscles. From most other places in Iveragh you can make it to the western extremities of the Dingle Peninsula within half a day, which will still give you time to stand on the top of a modest mountain and get down again before dinner!

GEOLOGICAL PERSPECTIVE

The high spine of the Dingle Peninsula, with Brandon Mountain towards its western end and the Slieve Mish Mountains to the E, is composed of tough Old Red Sandstone and associated strata, all brought to the surface in the core of an anticline shaped like the hull of an upturned rowing boat. The youngest strata of the Old Red Sandstone are known as the Kiltorcan beds and are noted for their fossils, especially the remains of terrestrial plants which are amongst the earliest known. At about the time these beds were formed the ozone layer became sufficiently established to provide enough protection against ultraviolet radiation that colonisation of the land by both plants and animals took place.

The 'Old Red' has produced striking scenery along this peninsula. Erosion along its northern flank has formed spectacularly high sea cliffs, including those of Sauce Creek and Beennaman. The striking inlet of Smerwick Harbour has been shaped where the pounding seas have broken through the sandstone to reach and penetrate into older and softer Silurian rocks behind. The Blasket Islands, appearing off the westernmost tip of the peninsula, are noted for their outcrops of purple sandstones and their rugged coastlines including sea stacks.

The 'Old Red' dips beneath Carboniferous rocks to the E where a thin strip of Carboniferous limestone forms the vale of Tralee, providing rich pastures for the Kerry black cattle. Further E still, the limestone dips beneath Carboniferous sandstone and clayrocks known as the Namurian to form a heather-clad upland region.

There is much evidence of the Great Ice Age in this district. Numerous glacially striated rock surfaces, corries, moraines and U-shaped valleys testify to the action of glaciers, especially on northern and eastern slopes. Of special note are the corrie biting deep into Slievanea which contains Lough Doon and also the spectacular E face of Brandon Mountain where massive cliff faces cup an ice-deepened gully which contains a string of lakes linked together by a chain of waterfalls and which is referred to locally as the 'Glacial Staircase'.

Present-Day Landscapes and Opportunities for Walking

The Dingle Peninsula is reminiscent of the side view of some huge porcupine crouched, ready to launch itself out into the Atlantic Ocean. The spiky back of this, the most northerly of the three major peninsulas located in the SW of Ireland, bristles with mountains of all shapes and sizes.

To the E, the Slieve Mish Mountains are considered by some locals to be relatively dull. Conversely, the Brandon Massif, soaring to over 3000 ft and containing the separate summits of Brandon Mountain and Brandon Peak, is considered by many walkers to be one of the finest mountains in all Ireland! This grouping — with the spectacular cliff faces, combes, corrie lakes and glaciated topography of rock slabs, boulder fields and scree slopes which line its eastern flanks, the long, curving, approach ridge which sweeps up from the top of Connor Pass and the relatively benign, rounded, grassy gradients and rock outcrops which form its westerly slopes — offers an exceptionally wide variety of ascent routes which will appeal to all energetic walkers, be they looking for the most spectacular, adventurous challenges or be they content with having more docile slopes continuously around them. There are many other wild and wonderful high places on the Dingle Peninsula which will appeal to strong and experienced hillwalkers. The Beenoskee grouping and the high ground to the E of the top of Connor Pass, for example, are places where these walkers will be happy to explore.

Less energetic walkers will also find much of interest and to their liking in tramping across the lower hills towards the tip of the peninsula, and for them to stand on the top of Mount Eagle may be considered quite an impressive achievement. There are also many absorbing coastal walks, of which a leisurely saunter around Inch Point, captivated by the surrounding fine mountain panoramas, will not involve climbing more than just a few feet. Another trek of moderate severity is to walk across the peninsula using the mountain roads and tracks which link Lough Anscaul with the northern coast — you can walk back the following day!

Choice of Walking Routes

Standing on the summit of Brandon Mountain just had to be included. Walk 16 describes an exciting approach route from Faha, ascending by way of the eask with its spectacular scenery and fascinating string of paternoster lakes, a masterpiece of geological evolution. Two more high routes have also been selected: Walk 17, a criss-cross wander around the elevated ground and mountain peaks to the E of the top of Connor Pass, and Walk 18, a there-and-back route from the delightful setting of Lough Anscaul to the top of Beenoskee. By contrast, a day spent beachcombing along the vast sands of Inch Strand, described in Walk 19, completes this selection of varied walks in the Dingle area. Together, they will give you some feel of what it is like to grapple with this porcupine of a peninsula.

Local Walking Guides

Through contacts previously established whilst walking in the North Leitrim Glens, I had the good fortune to be put in touch with South West Walks, an organisation based in Tralee who specialise in arranging comprehensive walking holidays and guiding independent walkers both in the Dingle Peninsula and elsewhere in Ireland. A partner in this business, Linda Woods, who is a veritable human dynamo both physically and organisationally, became my walking mentor whilst in Dingle (and further afield!), and she kindly arranged for us to propel our feet in the directions suggested by Tony O'Callaghan, who is a native of these parts and employed as a local walking guide by South West Walks. Tony turned out to be a real charmer, a professional guide of the highest calibre, and we enjoyed some splendid times walking in his agreeable and knowledgeable company — the evenings spent with him weren't all that bad either!

Place your feet in the care of South West Walks and you will walk in safety, enjoy immensely pleasurable walking itineraries and acquire knowledge of the geology, flora, fauna, history and archaeology of the area which might otherwise pass you by unnoticed.

CONTACT DETAILS

South West Walks Ireland Ltd
40 Ashe Street
Tralee
Co Kerry
Tel: 066 28733
24-hour: 061 393419
Fax: 066 28762
Email: swwi@iol.ie

Accommodation, Eating Out and Local Transport

ACCOMMODATION

We have stayed at several bed and breakfast establishments in the Dingle Peninsula, some of these arranged through South West Walks. All of these guest houses are excellent and without the slightest hesitation I highly commend them to you. One of these, Ashe's Guest House, even has connections with Gregory Peck, who, on celluloid at least, scaled Mount Kilimanjaro! The various establishments are conveniently spread about the peninsula and, together with another guest house which was recommended by a fellow walking enthusiast when high up amongst the Wicklow Mountains, are listed in the table overleaf.

Hotel/Guest House	Rooms en suite	Rooms other	Charge B&B	Open	Visited by Author
Robert Ashe Ashe's Guest House Spa Road Dingle Co Kerry Tel: 066 51197	F 3 D 3 T 0 S 0	F 0 D 0 T 0 S 0	£16–20	All year	Yes
Bernie Bambury Bambury's Guest House Mail Road Dingle Co Kerry Tel: 066 51244/51786	F 8 D 4 T 0 S 0	F 0 D 0 T 0 S 0	£16–20	All year	Yes
Kathleen Dillon Dillon's Connor Pass Road Dingle Co Kerry Tel: 066 51724	F 1 D 3 T 0 S 0	F 0 D 0 T 0 S 0	£16	All year	Yes
Kathleen and P J O'Connor 'Four Winds' Anascaul Co Kerry Tel: 066 57168 (Also self-catering flats)	F 2 D 2 T 0 S 0	F 0 D 0 T 2 S 0	£16–20	All year	Yes
Kitty Brosnan Abhainn Mhór Cloghane Co Kerry Tel: 066 38211	F 1 D 1 T 1 S 0	F 0 D 0 T 0 S 1	£16–20	All year	Yes
John Curran Greenmont House Gortonora Dingle Co Kerry Tel: 066 51414	F 4 D 5 T 3 S 0	F 0 D 0 T 0 S 0	£16–30	All year	No

Rooms: F = Family; D = Double; T = Twin; S = Single

EATING OUT

Dingle town boasts a wide variety of hotels, restaurants, cafés and pubs which cater for tastes to suit all pockets. These range from expensive, gourmet meals consumed in elegant surroundings to pub grub washed down with a creamy, frothy-topped, black velvet liquid consumed whilst listening to traditional Irish music. Spread around the peninsula are many other isolated eating places waiting to be discovered during your wanderings. One such establishment which we found very much to our liking, situated along the northern coastline, was O'Connor's Bar and Restaurant at Cloghane (Tel: 066 38113).

LOCAL TRANSPORT

The walk over Brandon Mountain is a linear route and you will probably need to hire a taxi or minibus to support you on this exploration. We used John Browne, Dingle Cab Service (Tel: 066 51259; mobile 088 606500) who we found provides reliable, flexible and inexpensive services and who will charm you with an agreeable banter. Other taxi services in the area are operated by Kathleen Curran (Tel: 066 51229; mobile 087 549649), who has been recommended to us, and by ASAP Cabs (Tel: mobile 087 2322379).

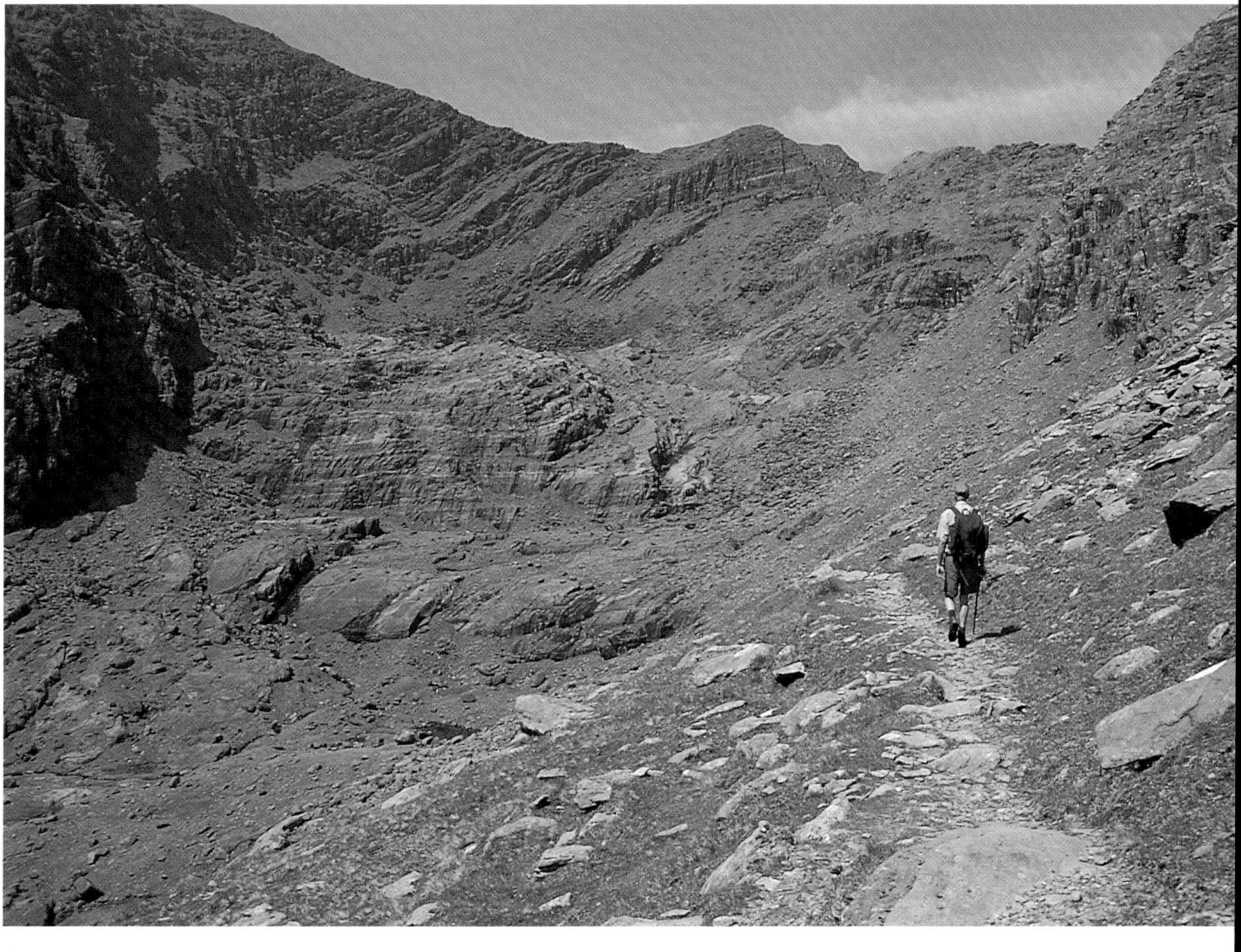

Tony O'Callaghan, local guide for South West Walks Ireland, leading the way along the eask, Brandon Mountain

BRANDON MOUNTAIN FROM FAHA

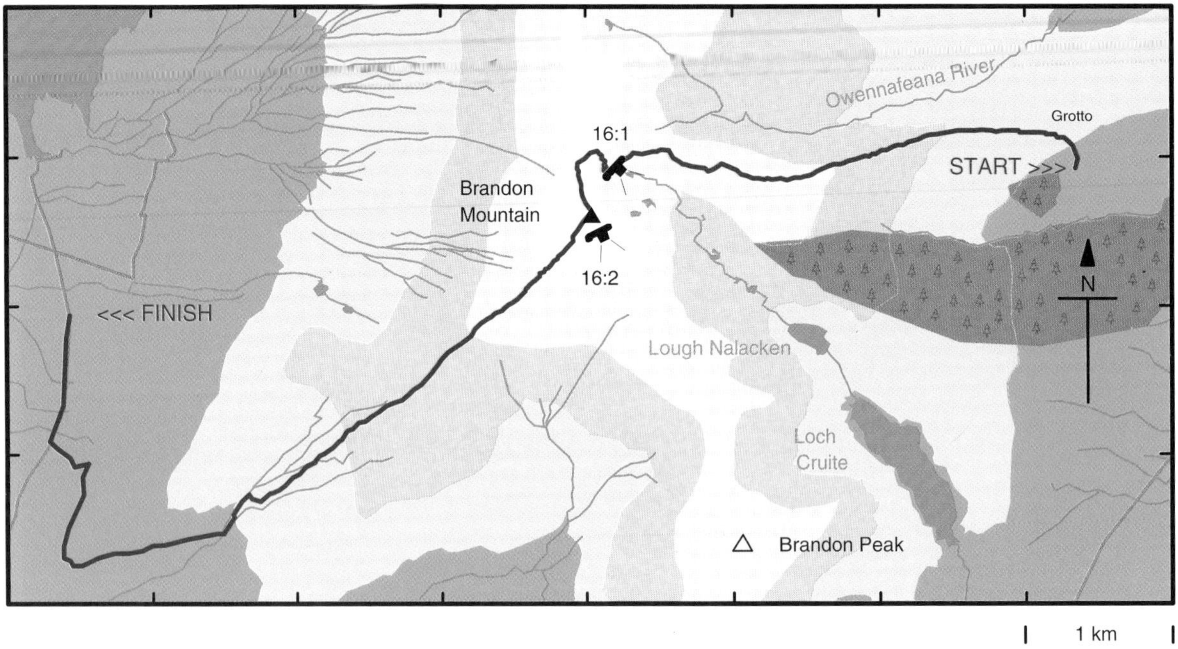

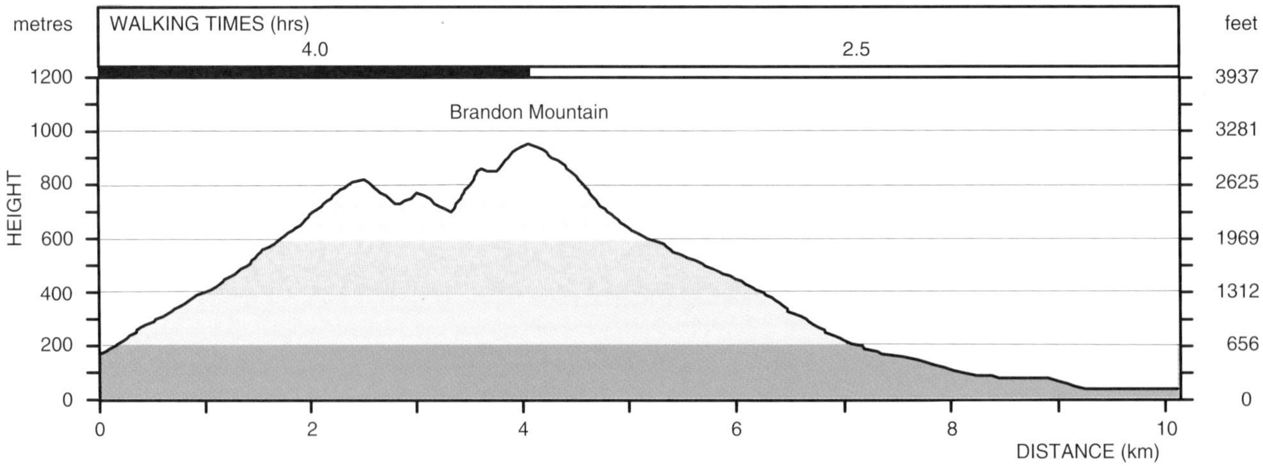

Brandon Mountain from Faha

fact file

START/FINISH

Start at Faha — MR 493119

Finish at the Walsh (Breathnach) Inn — MR 424108

GRADING

Difficult/strenuous (colour-coded RED)

WALKING TIME ALLOWANCE

6½ hours

DISTANCE

10.1 km (6.3 miles)

TOTAL HEIGHT GAINED

950 m (3110 ft)

PRINCIPAL HEIGHTS

- Brandon Mountain 952 m (3125 ft)

digest of walk

PARKING

Very restricted parking, with room for about six cars only, in front of the Lop-sided Tea Shop. (Note: This is a linear walk and, therefore, ideally two vehicles should be used, the second one positioned at the planned finish of the walk. Otherwise, arrange transport to collect you from the end of the walk at your estimated time of arrival there.)

OVERVIEW/INTEREST

- Great route full of geological discoveries along the way to the highest point in the Dingle Peninsula.
- Visit to a well-maintained grotto near the start.
- Fantastic assortment of corrie lakes, steep cliffs, rock benches, boulders and shattered rock.

- Superb, awesome, wild scenery as you cross the eask beneath the towering rock faces of Brandon Mountain.
- Good, long-distance views of surrounding mountains and coastline.

GRADIENTS

The walk commences with a gradual climb into and then along the eask to the E of Brandon Mountain. This leads to a steep climb, with some elementary scrambling involved, to ascend a narrow, eroded gully, which in turn leads on to the broad, rocky shoulder of the mountain. It is an easy walk from here to the summit up a gently rising slope. The descent is long and continuous with variable gradients, none of which are either particularly steep or troublesome. The final section to reach the finishing place is virtually on the flat, traversing across gently sloping ground.

MAPS, FOOTPATHS AND WAYSIGNS

OS Discovery Series 1:50 000 — Number 70 (Kerry)

There are narrow, rocky paths for most of the route which are usually quite well defined and relatively easy to follow. There is erosion in places, the most serious being along the rocky chute which leads above the eask up on to the shoulder of the mountain.

There are some signs at the start and finish and also marker posts to guide you on the first section of the way up and occasionally elsewhere. Cairns mark the summit and some other strategic positions.

GETTING STARTED

Faha, the starting-point of the walk, lies a couple of kilometres from the coast to the SW of Brandon Bay. Turn off the coastal road at either MR 512119 or MR 519127 and travel W down the minor lanes to arrive at the start which is part way up a hill.

Commence walking along the stony path on the R which immediately rises. Then bear R along the narrow way to pass through an iron gate, following the path signed 'Cnoc Bhréadain — Mount Brandon'.

Summary Description of Walk

THE WAY TO BRANDON MOUNTAIN — MR 461116 (Allow 4 hours)

Just above the start of the walk, there are the most wonderful views across the sweeping reaches of Brandon Bay with Beenoskee rising majestically above to the ESE. Brandon Peak (Barr an Ghéaráin) — resembling a near perfect, symmetrically shaped pyramid, with its exposed, E combes crumbling away into an assortment of steep, rocky ridges, buttresses, cliff faces, shattered rock fragments and scree — dominates the horizon to the SW. The steep, grassy path leads further uphill, through a second gate, heading NW to reach a grotto. This haven of peace and contentment is a spot to pause at for a few minutes to absorb the tranquil atmosphere and perhaps benefit from some quiet, private reflection on what you are about to receive.

An obviously well-used path continues to lead uphill to the NW veering W and additional height is quickly gained along a diagonal traverse which leads you to a fence and stile at which a red and white painted guiding post has been positioned. Keep climbing along this established diagonal, following the rocky path as it passes by several more such marker posts and over another cluster of stiles. Higher up still, a dilapidated stone wall is crossed. Then, if the visibility is good, undertake a small detour up the steeper, grassy slopes to your R to peer down into the wide Owennafeana Valley which falls between N and NE, from where you are standing, towards the coast. After absorbing this pleasant view, return to the security of the poled way below.

The upward gradient slackens off as you complete a long, straight, diagonal traverse, still going up. As you get nearer to the vast combes and cliff faces which form the exposed, easterly faces of the enormous land mass of Brandon Peak and Brandon Mountain (Cnoc Bréanainn), the sheer size and majesty of these mountains draw you towards them with a powerful gravitational pull and aura of excitement to which most walkers will gladly succumb. At this point the first, and largest, of several paternoster lakes (stringed like rosary beads) appears. This is the long and narrow Loch Cruite.

Progress continues to the WSW around the flank of the mountain slopes, and as you bear R into the eask (giant, glaciated, elongated combe and valley) proper, the awesome grandeur and size of this cavity are progressively revealed. The combination of cliffs, towering rock

16:1 The awesome, wild scenery of the eask ripping into Brandon Mountain

16:2 Time to relax on the sunny summit of Brandon Mountain

benches and the overdeepening of the valley floor by glaciers — these hollows now filled with a string of small lakes — exudes an atmosphere of enchantment, magic and mystery. Here you half expect some mythical creature to pop out from behind one of the boulders to demand a toll from you for daring to trespass into its mystical domain!

The narrow way threads deeper into this land of sheer delight. As you gain additional height more of the lakes are revealed down below and then the slopes of Brandon Mountain start to dominate the far side of the eask, these towering up as a great mass of sheer faces, formed by stacked, layered rock. Then the wild beauty of the head of the eask is exposed in the form of massive, contorted bands of Old Red Sandstone, which have been folded in several different directions by violent forces of nature pressing from S to N and subsequently sculptured by glaciers during protracted ice ages.

Higher up in the recesses of the eask, the path narrows as it crosses more rugged terrain in the form of boulder fields and shattered, fragmented rock in an area where the plant St Patrick's Cabbage flourishes. Take appropriate care along here, being mindful of the steep drop on your L! Following this, a less difficult final approach leads to the crossing of the eask, a relatively simple and unexposed walk over a series of flat bedding planes along a way that winds past large boulders and threads between tiny lakes and pools. There are poles and arrows to guide you here, and you may also be under the watchful eye of ravens who often soar overhead in this vicinity. A tiny watercourse is crossed and then the way leads below a rock overhang to reach an area where another tiny lake is concealed. More rock slabs and huge boulders are passed as your upward journey takes you beyond yet another lake, this one over to the R.

The gradient steepens as the route traverses to the R to avoid the towering rock faces which bar the way directly ahead. Butterwort are plentiful in this area. Then even steeper slopes have to be scaled, this by means of an eroded way that zigzags tightly up a rocky groove which leads you further N. Rock steps and loose stones have to be taken in your stride, and there are a few awkward places where some elementary scrambling or use of a steadying handhold is required. The saddle above in the form of a broad band of connecting rock is eventually reached, and it is relatively easy going from here. Your efforts are also rewarded in fine weather by seeing some magnificent views of the coastline to the W. These include the sheltered, almost land-locked bay of Smerwick Harbour with its splendid, sandy beaches and Mount Eagle rising to the SW.

Turn L and head S along the broad, rising shoulder, keeping well away from the crumbling edge of the sheer drop on your L. A good, wide path then escorts you to the top of Brandon Mountain, where there is an assortment of objects to interest you. These include a cairn, a trigonometrical point, a cross made from the spar of a plane, an oratory, a dried-up well and the remains of a clochán (small stone hut). These all rest at 952 m (3125 ft), which is the highest point on Dingle. The commanding views from here in fine weather are just fantastic: the graceful, concave edges linking the mountain to Brandon Peak and beyond fall away to the SE; many of the rises and falls of the mountainous spine of the Dingle Peninsula are exposed; and some of the titbits include sighting Carrauntoohil lording over the Iveragh Peninsula and looking down on the Blasket Islands, a short distance out to sea beyond Mount Eagle.

THE WAY TO THE FINISH AT THE WALSH INN — MR 424108 (Allow 2½ hours)

Depart from Brandon Mountain down a broad, grassy slope to quickly locate and pass two cairns to the SW. A stony path develops from here and this is known as the 'Saints' Road'. There is fine, springy grass beneath your boots as you pass by outcrops of conglomerate rocks. The forward descent is clearly visible, for you can follow with your eye the continuation of the path winding down for several hundred feet below you. Keep to the grassy surfaces wherever possible in places where the descent path either fragments or becomes obscure, threading a way of your own choice down between successive bands of rock.

Lower down, the path of sorts crosses a boulder field but these shattered rocks are not too tightly packed and there are good, grassy patches between the stones. Occasional guiding cairns are passed and these will serve to reassure you that your navigation is up to scratch. Keep towards the centre of the falling ridge to eventually pass by a large Standing Stone. Then, lower down still, wetter ground has to be crossed as you maintain your SW direction of descent. After this, the gradient eases as the grassy slopes that you are now crossing sweep down towards more sheltered, enclosed pastures of farmlands, these still some distance below.

Walk down towards these and you will then start to penetrate land divided into enclosed fields. Having reached the highest of these enclosures and just beyond the first dilapidated stone wall, cross over the gully and watercourse on your L at a place where a small cairn has been located on the opposite bank. Continue downhill from here, maintaining your SW bearing to then cross another watercourse which flows at right angles to your direction of approach. The way down then connects with a rough cart-track which you follow, surrendering more height as you do so.

A metal gate, which is rather difficult to open, then has to be negotiated and following this the surface of the path improves and there is the luxury of a bridge which spans the next stream barring your way. The tiny hamlet of An Baile Breac (MR 424092) is then reached. (There is room here for a few cars to be parked between the buildings and this would save a couple of kilometres of walking.) Turn R to continue along a grassy path that leads northwards. Further on, the surface of this path deteriorates as boulders and stones have to be avoided.

Turn L when you reach the first walled track leading down, squeezing around a metal gate. Walk down to the road below and turn R along it. The walk finishes less than a kilometre further on, at the Walsh (Breathnach) Inn, where a telephone, liquid refreshments and toilets await you.

Alternative Ways

ESCAPES

If you have made up your mind to stand on the top of Brandon Mountain and to get there from Faha via the eask, then the descent route suggested is both the easiest and the shortest way down.

EXTENSIONS

The obvious addition for strong, experienced walkers is to continue on to Brandon Peak. From here, there are a variety of further extensions and descent routes. Descending southwards along the massive main ridge will connect you with the 'Pilgrims' Route' and you can follow this either W or NE to reach a prearranged pick-up point or a vehicle positioned at one of the minor roads below. Probably the most challenging extension is to keep to the high ground and traverse around to the E to reach Connor Pass, having taken the summits of Ballysitteragh (Cnoc Bhaile Uí Shé) and Beennabrack (Macha na gCab) in your stride. Again, you will need to have planned this in advance and either have a vehicle in position at the viewing-point car park or have made suitable arrangements to be collected from there at the end of the walk.

An Cnapán Mór, Croaghskearda and Slievanea

factfile

START/FINISH
Viewing-point car park at top of Connor Pass — MR 491056

GRADING
Moderate (colour-coded BLUE)

WALKING TIME ALLOWANCE
5 hours

DISTANCE
9.9 km (6.2 miles)

TOTAL HEIGHT GAINED
370 m (1210 ft)

PRINCIPAL HEIGHTS

- An Cnapán Mór 649 m (2130 ft)
- Croaghskearda 608 m (1995 ft)
- Slievanea (top of the ridge to the NE) 670 m (2200 ft)

digest of walk

PARKING
Surfaced parking area holds up to 20 cars but is a very popular stopping place for transient tourists — the advice is get there early!

OVERVIEW/INTEREST

- Several peaks are visited in a route which criss-crosses a high-level mountainous area.
- Great variety of walking terrain across broad, rounded slopes and along a narrow, rocky ridge.
- An area of peat cutting is passed.
- Superb, long-distance views and sightings of nearby combes and corrie lakes.

An Cnapán Mór, Croaghskearda and Slievanea

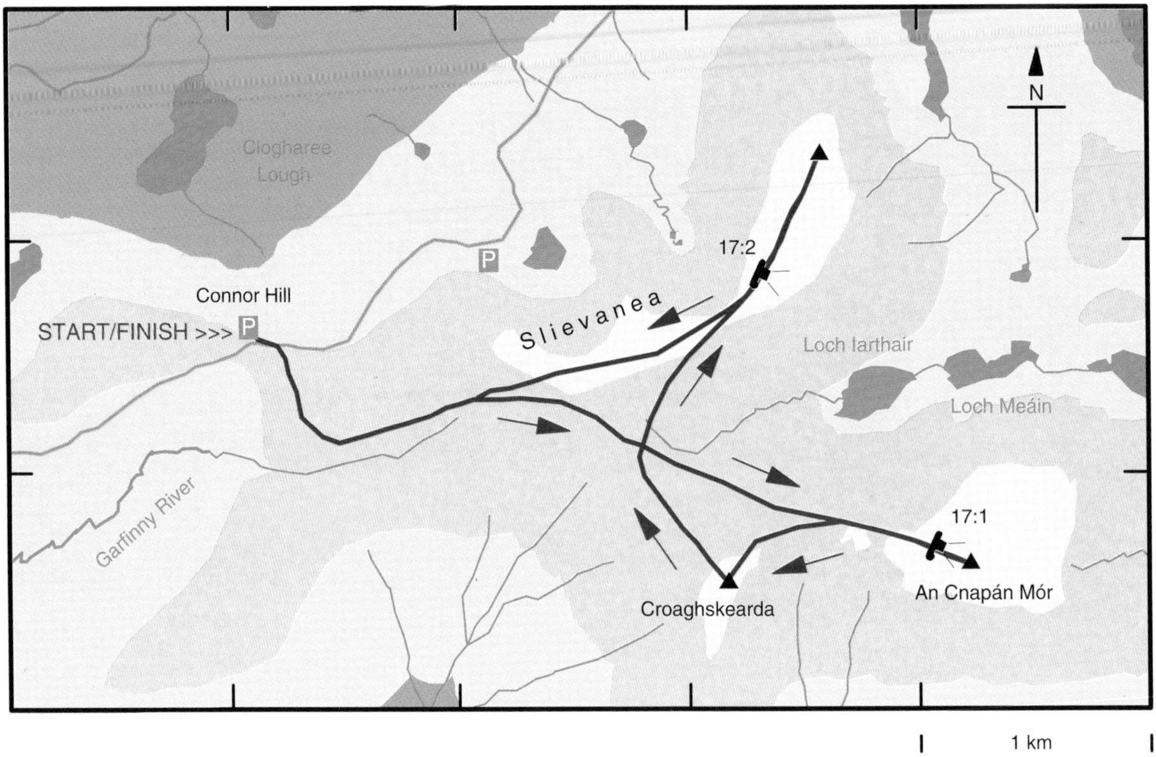

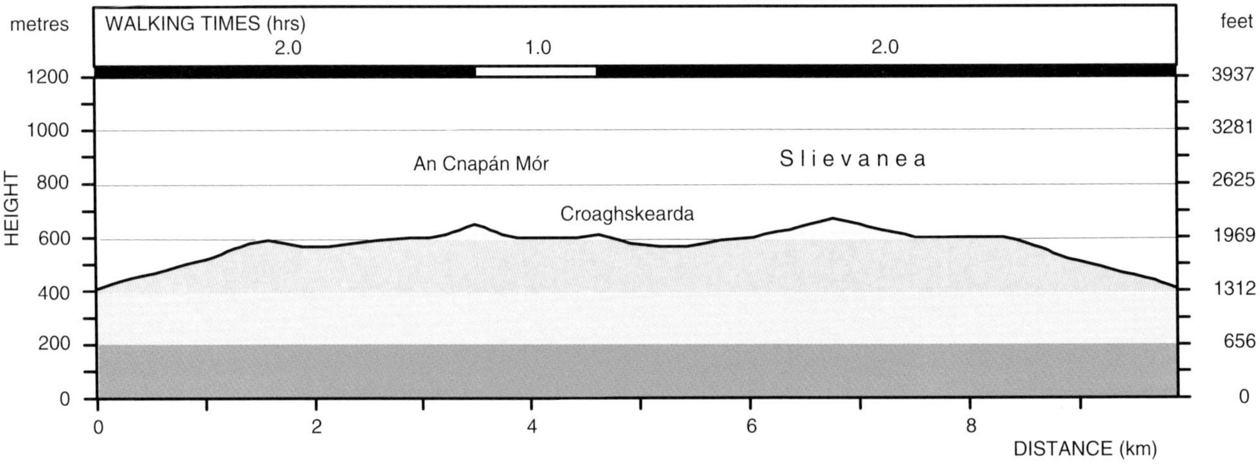

GRADIENTS

Moderate, sustained upward and downward slopes for most of the way. No severe climbs or awkward descents.

MAPS, FOOTPATHS AND WAYSIGNS

OS DISCOVERY SERIES 1:50 000 — NUMBER 70 (KERRY)

A wide track which winds uphill providing access to the turf-cutting area is used at the start and finish of the walk. After this, the route is mostly across uncharted high ground covered with a mixture of peat, grass, stones and rocky outcrops where there are few paths or tracks to guide you.

Apart from cairns and a stone shelter, you will need to rely on your map, compass and in-built navigational prowess.

GETTING STARTED

An adventurous, narrow road winds tortuously over Connor Pass to connect Dingle with Cloghane, cutting right across the spine of the peninsula in the process. The parking area is located at the high point of this difficult, twisting road and so some of the problems are already behind you when you reach this place!

From the car park, cross over the road and walk SE up the wide track which is surfaced with a mixture of grass, stones and compacted earth.

SUMMARY DESCRIPTION OF WALK

THE WAY TO AN CNAPÁN MÓR — MR 522046 (Allow 2 hours)

Given good weather, the views from the car park are really fantastic. The impressive spurs reaching up to the summits of Brandon Peak and Brandon Mountain curve majestically around to the NW, displaying some of the steep, eroded combes which line the crumbling eastern faces of this massive mountain configuration. Below and cradled in the lower folds of the rugged, rocky slopes are a number of corrie lakes, the overflow waters from which feed the Owenmore River winding through a wide, flat glaciated valley below. Between E and NE a series of rising peaks, culminating in Beenoskee, flank and protect the eastern side of the valley. Exploring the most southerly of these, Slievanea (Sliabh Mhaca Ré), is one of the principal objectives of the present walk.

The obvious way forward winds up around the massive hillside and then the wide track commences to curve progressively to the L, changing your direction of travel gradually towards ENE. Further up, it fans out into three separate ways. Select the middle course which leads more directly ahead, and from here continue climbing to the NE along an extension of the winding track. You will then pass by an area of turf cutting where you may actually witness this being done, usually by a man and wife team where it is dubious who has the most arduous task of the two!

Beyond this interesting place (it's never much trouble watching others at work!), abandon the clearly defined track when you reach the T-junction ahead. Walk straight on across the open moorland, heading ENE across the expansive slopes of the gradually rising ground. Be careful

17:1 The author and his wife decorating the summit of An Cnapán Mór

here not to crush underfoot any of the delicate, tiny, wild bog orchids which flower in May and June. The going along here is sound and firm, and fast progress is possible up these gently inclined, grassy slopes. Just keep moving ahead, staying towards the centre of the wide, rising spur.

The terrain hereabouts is fairly featureless and in low cloud it is possible to inadvertently stray over to the severe edge which falls away precipitously to the NE. If you happen to do this, immediately veer away from this towards SSE, to return towards the centre of the wide, grassy band and then concentrate on steering a middle course between ground which falls away rapidly to both L and R. Further on, the route descends gently to cross a series of eroded, boggy hollows but these cause no serious problems. This is followed by tracking across an area of flattish ground where eroded mounds of peat, several feet high in places, are scattered about.

In clear weather, veer to the L-hand edge of this flat ground to obtain a bird's-eye view of the three corrie lakes strung out below to the E. These are called the Coumanare Lakes (Locha Chom an Áir) and have the separate names of Loch Iarthair, Loch Meáin and An Loch Dubh. The stream flowing down to the R of your present viewing position feeds into the upper of these tiny lakes. Then head back to the safer crest of the wide ridge, following the bed of the stream uphill to regain the ground around MR 508052.

From this low spot along the spur, continue between SE and E (the way winds about as does the crest of the spur) up the gently rising slopes, this change in direction being made in the vicinity of a small Standing Stone. To your rear, on the L, another rounded, grassy ridge leads to the flat summit area to the NE of Slievanea which you will be visiting later in the day. In the other direction, on your R, part of the mountainous Iveragh Peninsula comes into view, together with the pointed, craggy peak of Croaghskearda (Cruach Sceirde) which is also on today's walking itinerary.

The route continues to the ESE up a slight incline covered with a pleasant, congruent mixture for walking over of grass, peat, sand, shale and stones. These broad, sweeping slopes lead you further eastwards to the rising, stony, final approach to the top of An Cnapán Mór, passing by clumps of St Patrick's Cabbage and sea pinks on the way there. The summit area of this mountain is quite expansive, a flattish area of shattered rocks which contains a trigonometrical point and a substantial cairn. These are positioned at 649 m (2130 ft). In clear weather, much of the Dingle Peninsula, stretching around this fairly central pivot, is in view. The geography of Dingle and Ventry Harbours is displayed to the SW, while to the SE and beyond the low, fertile, green pastures of the peninsula, the converging spits and sand bars of Inch and Cromane strive to close the narrow channel which flows between them in Dingle Bay. Further away still and also to the SE, the highest mountain in all Ireland, Carrauntoohil, just manages to poke its peak a little higher than several other nearby satellite summits which form the challenging arêtes of the MacGillycuddy's Reeks in the Iveragh Peninsula.

THE WAY TO CROAGHSKEARDA — MR 509039 (Allow 1 hour)

Commence your descent by retracing your final approach steps, on this occasion walking WNW veering W, away from the trigonometrical point. Again, keep towards the centre of the falling and narrowing spur. Continue walking due W to cross the slight rise, marked as 601 m on the OS map. Maintain this bearing for about another $\frac{1}{2}$ km ($\frac{1}{4}$ mile) and then bear L, following the edge of the steeper ground and progressively changing your direction of travel through SW towards S. This will take you on a direct course to your next main objective, standing at the far tip of the craggy, narrow promontory of Croaghskearda. In clear weather this high spot will be visible from here, with a grassy side spur off the main ridge leading there.

A large, well-constructed and preserved stone shelter is then passed and surprisingly quickly after this, you will be treading along the narrow projection towards its pointed peak, an adventurous scramble over rocks and large boulders leading you there. In very windy weather it is best to track on the western side of this spur, just below the exposed crest of the narrow, precarious ridge. The highest position at the end rises to 608 m (1995 ft) and in clear weather conditions there is another feast of excellent views to be digested from here. The highlights of these have previously been positioned but it is interesting to examine these again from a slightly different perspective.

THE WAY TO CONNOR PASS — MR 491056 (Allow 2 hours)

Return the way you came along the narrow ridge, now walking northwards. Towards the end of the promontory, bear around to the L, keeping to the contours of the higher ground and not surrendering any unnecessary height as you progress to the NNW across sloping, grassy ground. After an almost imperceptible dip, the expansive slopes rise again and your way continues towards and then through an area where there has been extensive erosion of the soft, peaty surface. You need to head N to reach and cross this.

The main ridge is then attained again and you have to alter your bearing slightly towards NNE to climb up on to this. During this approach, the pointed summit over to your R in the far distance is another view of Beenoskee, rising to the NE. You then cross over your outward route, almost at right angles, as you head NNE towards Slievanea and the tip of the ridge leading NE from it, to reach another fine viewing platform. The way there is up a gently sloping, grassy incline where more wild orchids add to the interest.

During this pleasant, final ascent, walk over to the crumbling edge on your L, being careful when you get there! The view from here in favourable weather conditions, across the deep combe below with its precipitous rock faces, then across the wide intervening valley towards the Brandon Massif, is breathtakingly supreme. Seen in the mellowing light of the late afternoon or early evening, when you are most likely to be there, the setting sun will illuminate to perfection the many ridges, rock faces, corrie lakes and areas of scree of this great and spectacular mountain.

Continue with care along the rising edge, using a faint path to reach the highest point towards the end of the grassy ridge which leads NE. This place commands an elevation of 670 m (2200 ft) and happens to be the highest point of the walk. In getting there, you will have the possibility of observing some of the best views along the famous paternoster lakes which occupy glaciated basins in the eask on the E flank of Brandon Mountain, these highlights observed as you diligently work your way around some peat hags, much closer to!

A tiny, quite pathetic cairn marks the climax of what, given clear weather, must rank as one of the very best viewing positions in the whole of Ireland. Go right to the end of the wedge-shaped summit area to marvel at the simply stunning 360 degree panorama, slowly swivelling around to absorb this at your leisure. Both Brandon and Carrauntoohil add their considerable presence to the sightings, these part of a mountainous landscape that includes much of the Dingle Peninsula and part of the Iveragh Peninsula also. Numerous corrie lakes are dotted about this fascinating, rugged countryside, adding their own inevitable attractiveness to elevate these views to sheer perfection.

Walk back south-westwards to regain the main spur, descending gradually to get there. Follow the steep edge, with this a few paces away, as it sweeps around to the R, initially surrendering more height and then devouring a gradual rise as the way swings around towards W. In misty conditions, keep well to the L to avoid the gouged-out corrie faces that have eaten into the mountainside. When visibility is seriously restricted, one certain identifying feature is a tiny but distinctive pond which has a grassy area extending into its otherwise symmetrical shape. Here, there is only a few feet between its western rim and a sheer drop on the R of this, so pass this stretch of water to the L on its eastern rim, well away from the edge. Some small but possibly treacherous bog pools are definitely other places which need avoiding as you continue this descent.

The return route bends further to the R and, always keeping a safe distance from the edge, follow the lip of the massive corrie WNW before leaving this on your R further down by then tracking W to walk slightly downhill across more gradually sloping terrain. Progressively change your direction of descent towards WSW to continue across steepening slopes. Some relatively boggy ground gets in your way as you track further downhill. Maintain your bearing but trim the final section of your descent directly towards the peat-cutting area which you passed near the start of the walk. From here, select the stony track which leads down, initially to the SSW. Then follow this around to the R, still descending, to finally head NW, retracing your outward steps back to the parking area.

Alternative Ways

ESCAPES

Once you have gained the high ground to the E of Connor Pass, the choice is really yours, and within certain confines you can do as little or as much as you like. The route as described may be shortened in a number of ways by missing out one, two or all three of the peaks suggested!

EXTENSIONS

In favourable weather conditions, strong walkers may venture further, perhaps considerably further, along the high ground to the E of An Cnapán Mór. However, beware that to do this will involve negotiating a steep down-and-up, with the reverse of this to be faced on the return journey!

17:2 Looking south-eastwards beyond the Coumanare Lakes from the heights near Slievanea

Lough Anscaul and Beenoskee

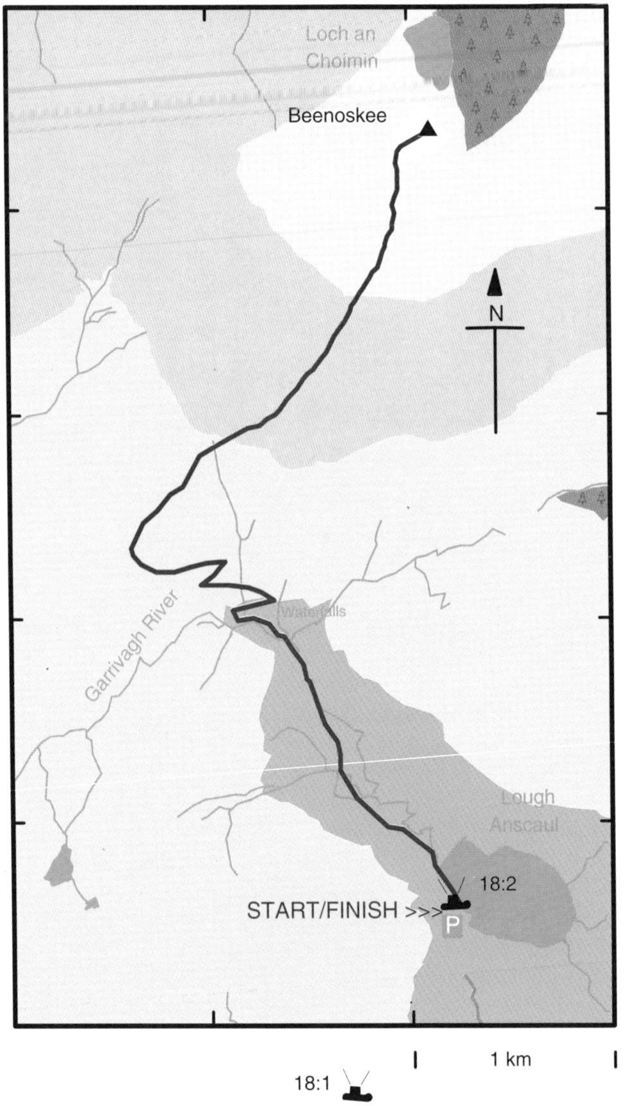

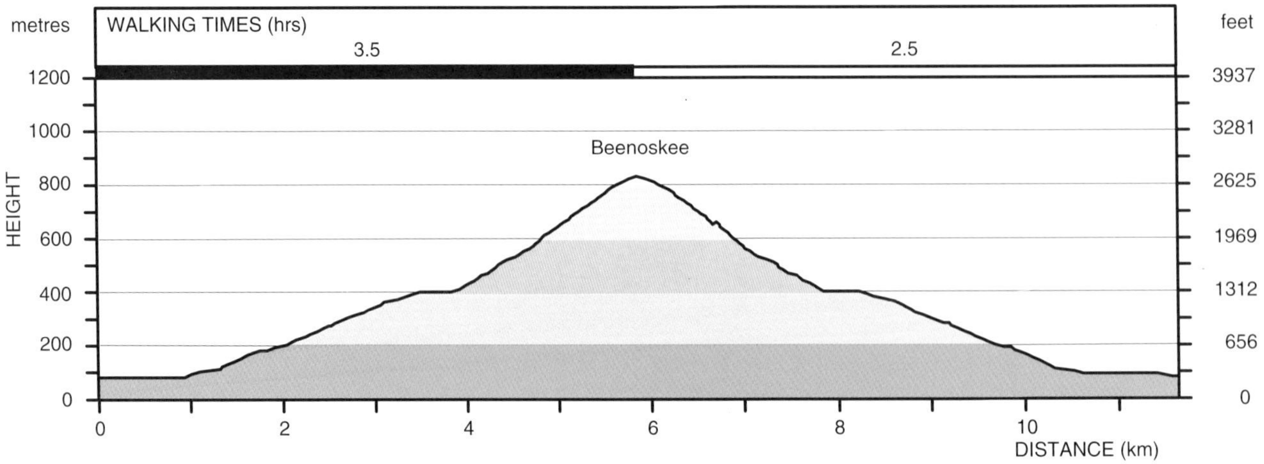

Lough Anscaul and Beenoskee

fact file

START/FINISH
Scenic car park at Lough Anscaul — MR 582052

GRADING
Moderate (colour-coded BLUE)

WALKING TIME ALLOWANCE
6 hours

DISTANCE
11.6 km (7.2 miles)

TOTAL HEIGHT GAINED
750 m (2460 ft)

PRINCIPAL HEIGHTS
- Beenoskee 826 m (2710 ft)

digest of walk

PARKING
Dedicated, remote and scenic car park holds about eight cars.

OVERVIEW/INTEREST
- Delights of Lough Anscaul and the magnificent, encompassing mountain scenery.
- Route passes by a series of waterfalls.
- Superb, panoramic views from the summit of Beenoskee.
- Great variety of walking, from treading along stony, mountain roads to trekking across challenging, open landscapes and avoiding peat hags.

GRADIENTS
There is a gradual climb all the way to the top of Beenoskee. This is mainly along moderate slopes but there are several steeper and more challenging sections. The descent is the reverse of this.

MAPS, FOOTPATHS AND WAYSIGNS

OS Discovery Series 1:50 000 — Number 70 (Kerry)

The walk commences with a lengthy upward section along a mountain road, the surface of which deteriorates into a rough, stony track towards the top of the pass. Then it is across open terrain; this is not too difficult to cross but there are few paths or tracks to guide you and some wet patches and peaty hags need to be avoided. The return is back, as near as possible, along the outward route.

There are no waysigns and the only cairns are those positioned on the summit of Beenoskee.

GETTING STARTED

Lough Anscaul is located just over 3 km (nearly 2 miles) to the NNW of the village of Anascaul. Turn N off the main N86 road at the village and follow the minor roads northwards through several tiny hamlets to reach the lough. A gate has to be opened but there is a surfaced — if potholed — road leading right to the car park.

The walk commences by continuing northwards under your own steam up the valley along the extension of the public road.

Summary Description of Walk

THE WAY TO BEENOSKEE — MR 581089 (Allow $3\frac{1}{2}$ hours)

Lough Anscaul (Loch an Scáil) occupies a majestic position surrounded by high, steeply rising, craggy peaks which direct your attention towards the remote head of the valley. This lies to the NW and it is up there that you will shortly be heading. The only lower, flatter ground is in the opposite direction to the SE and this is bisected by the exit stream from the lough, the Owenascaul River, as it flows southwards, down towards the village of Anascaul. Usually, the only sounds hereabouts are those made by the wind, the water in the lough lapping over the boulders which form its shore and transient bird-life; peace and solitude reign supreme at this place of quite outstanding natural beauty.

Right from the start of the walk you are treading beneath steeply rising, rocky crags and boulder fields. These are on your L and they form the lower slopes of Cnoc Mhaoilionáin, the summit of which rises, out of view, to the W. The end of the lough is soon reached and left far behind, as is a metal gate which you have to pass through. Continue up the wide, glaciated valley, threading your way along the track between imposing crags which now start to enclose the glen on either side. Initially you proceed along a flat section beside the meandering stream on an excellent track for walking; pass through a rusty metal gate and then between redundant stone pillars.

Then the continuation way starts to rise. The upward incline is moderate at first but this steepens further on as the surface of the track changes from compacted earth and stones to grass. Another metal gate is then reached, and from this higher position there are good views back down along the valley. Following this, a pleasant grassy ledge, high above a steepish drop down to the Garrivagh River below, provides the continuation route. Several tributary watercourses feed into the main stream, each of these eroding irregular, deep V-nicks into the hillsides opposite, down which tiny waterfalls cascade.

The way bends around to the L, tracking NW above a series of more impressive waterfalls fed by the greater torrents of the main river, these plunging down through a narrow gully over exposed, layered rocks. Nearer to, the ground beneath your boots becomes rougher as you tread across boulders and loose stones along a narrowing path which continues to lead upwards. The track curves further to the L up the rising valley, before it commences to zigzag up the steeper slopes on the R, then bridging the stream several times as it continues to gain height. More captivating waterfalls are passed along here, these located above on your L.

Further up, when you reach a suitable vantage point, turn around to gain an overall impression of the vastness of the mountains which surround Lough Anscaul and of the sheer cliff faces which plunge down and cup the still waters of the distant lake, now far below. A series of long traverses, interspersed with acute bends at their ends, will lead you towards the top of the broad ridge above. There are some badly drained wet patches along here! Fork to the R higher up, keeping to the stony track and heading NW, and then turn R along a continuation of this track, changing your direction towards NE. This is towards the vast, rounded slopes that rise to the summit of Beenoskee (Binn os Gaoith).

More mountains, including rounded peaks and craggy ridges, come into view as you near the crest of the spur, and towering above them all is the massive bulk of Brandon Mountain

18:1 Distant Beenoskee rising above the lush meadows surrounding the Owenascaul River

which rises majestically to the WNW. Just before you reach the apex, turn off the track, full R, to continue NE, then heading across open ground which is covered with a layer of soft peat that is often waterlogged. The way traverses across expansive, grassy slopes which rise slightly. Outwit the wet peat hags lying in wait along here by locating and using a series of connecting sandy hollows which lead NE, the way you need to progress, to eventually gain further height and in so doing get above the more difficult ground below. However, before this drier, stony terrain is reached, you have to cross a wide, shallow hause, maintaining your now established NE bearing. When making this crossing be careful to surrender only the minimum height necessary, and in misty conditions be vigilant not to get drawn downhill to your R!

An infant watercourse then has to be crossed and following this head uphill, making directly for the pointed, rocky hillock, now visible straight ahead further NE. The open ground to get there is relatively easy to cross and, once they spot it, most walkers will reach this certain landmark surprisingly quickly. The approach slopes to the rocky outcrop rise slightly more steeply and an intermittent, faint, narrow path will sporadically guide you through the surrounding jumble of boulders and stones to get there. The fascinating craggy tor is composed of weathered red sandstone, in places more pink than red, and this makeshift look-out point will enable you to spy part of the mountainous Iveragh Peninsula, far away to the S.

Change your direction of travel slightly towards NNE and continue climbing, seeking out the less severe gradients ahead, before veering marginally L to follow a definite spur leading to higher ground above. One devious way of pausing for breath as you climb further up is to turn around to admire, at your leisure, the simply splendid views of the cradle of mountains which includes Cnoc Mhaoilionáin to the SSW, and An Cnapán Mór and Slievanea to the SW, linked together by high, rocky bands. Beyond these and far away to the WNW, your eyes could feast on the delights of Brandon Mountain and Brandon Peak for some time longer than that necessary to regain your puff!

18:2 Early morning sunshine at Lough Anscaul, the start of the walk

Afterwards, zigzag up the steeper, heather-covered slopes and then veer more to the L to head N in order to gain the more rounded contours which support a mixture of bilberry, heathers and mosses in a vastly more exposed environment. It seems a long way up, so pace yourself accordingly. Then, when you reach another broad spur above, bear slightly to the R along this to continue climbing to the NE up a more gently rising incline. The final approach to the summit is across barren ground covered with rocks and stones, and this will lead you to the conical top of Beenoskee, which is composed of weathered sandstone.

Beenoskee, with its two cairns and toppled-over trigonometrical point, commands a height of

826 m (2710 ft) and, as it rises above all of the nearby summits, it offers superb, unrestricted, long-distance views when the weather is clear. Many of the highlights in the fascinating panoramas to be observed from here have previously been positioned, but there are new and compulsive sightings to the N where most of the attractive coastline between Brandon Point to the NW and the great sweep of Tralee Bay to the NE may be studied in some detail. Much closer to, Stradbally Mountain (Cnoc an tSráidbhaile) rises majestically to the NE. When absorbing these fine views also pay heed to the nearby crumbling edges which line the N and E flanks of the summit area and be careful never to get too close to these! Before you depart, venture a little further on just below the main summit area in order to observe a fine, bird's-eye view of pear-shaped Loch an Choimín, hundreds of feet down below to the N. Once again treat the approach edge and steep fall-away with respect!

THE WAY BACK TO LOUGH ANSCAUL — MR 582052 (Allow $2\frac{1}{2}$ hours)

Simply retrace your outward steps! To recapitulate briefly on these, commence your descent from the summit area to the SW and lower down, when it reappears, trim your line of fall to reach the rocky knoll of red/pink sandstone. (From above, this feature resembles a mini-escarpment.) Pass below this weathered outcrop and continue downhill into the wetter ground below, still heading SW. Recross the shallow hause, take the subsequent slight rise in your stride, and then reconnect with the wide track which threads through the mountain pass further W. Turn L and follow this obvious way down to the parking area.

Alternative Ways

ESCAPES

Some groups of family walkers may come under pressure from their children to venture no further than the waterfalls, and these cascades are in fact often the main objective of many such walkers during hot, sunny, summer weather. Less serious walkers may also be content just to walk to the crest of the ridge along the mountain road-cum-track. Should you decide to do only this, just pop across to the far side and, without descending any real distance, walk down a little to admire the splendid views to the NNW along the steep-sided valley through which the Glennahoo River gently meanders.

EXTENSIONS

The obvious, short addition from the summit of Beenoskee is to visit nearby Stradbally Mountain. For very strong and experienced walkers only, there is the possibility of a much longer and vastly more adventurous itinerary. This includes descending from Beenoskee along the connecting ridges to the NW (walking in strict sequence WSW, NW, SW, W, N and finally NW) to cross over An Com Bán and Binn an Tuair before descending to reach a track adjacent to the coast road at MR 549106. Here, you have the choice of either being collected by prearranged transport or walking the long way back SE across the mountain pass to recover your vehicle from the car park at Lough Anscaul.

INCH STRAND AND POINT

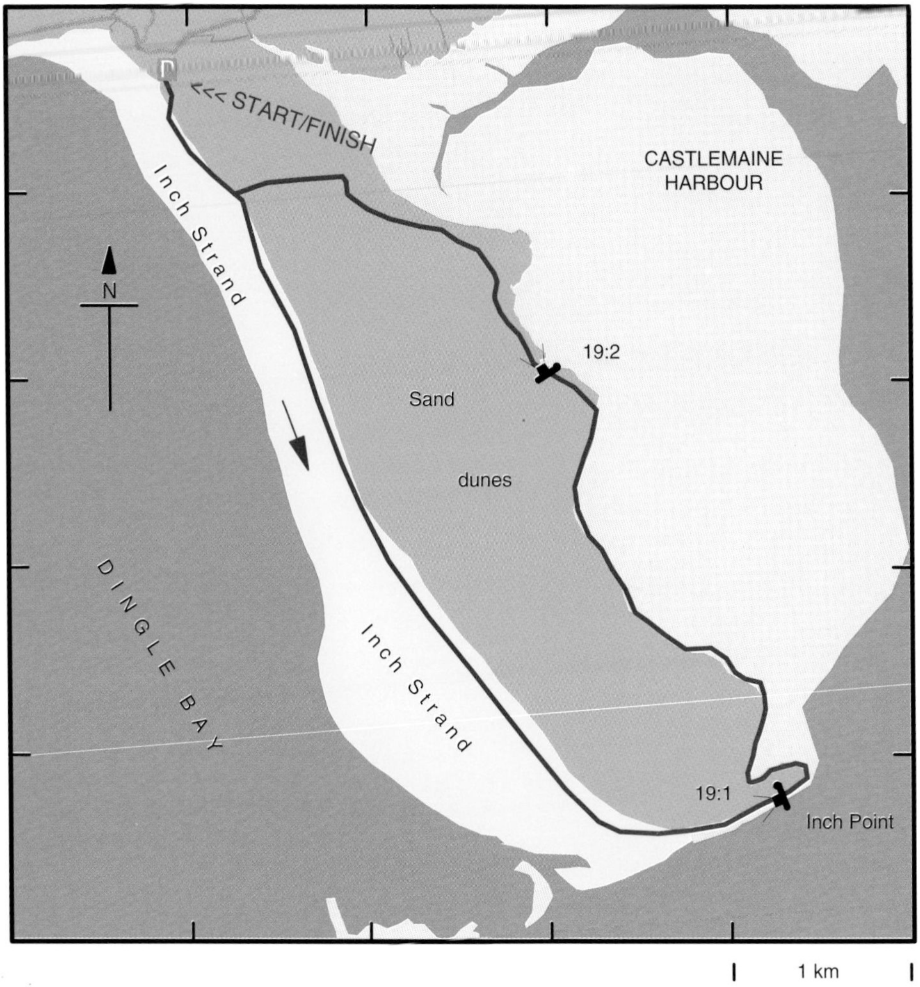

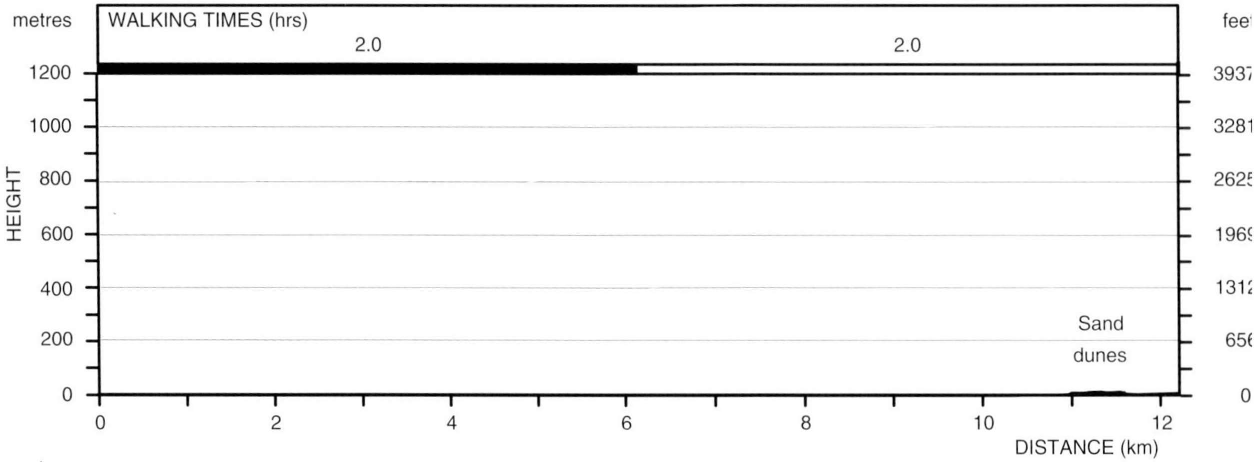

INCH STRAND AND POINT

fact file

START/FINISH	DISTANCE
Beach car park at Inch Strand — MR 644006	12.2 km (7.6 miles)

GRADING	TOTAL HEIGHT GAINED
Easy/straightforward (colour-coded GREEN)	20 m (70 ft)

WALKING TIME ALLOWANCE	PRINCIPAL HEIGHTS
4 hours	• Just above sea level!

digest of walk

PARKING

Extensive parking areas near to beach but these are very popular with holiday-makers during the summer months, especially at weekends, and quickly get filled up.

There are toilets and an enterprising café-cum-souvenir shop nearby at Sammy's Store.

OVERVIEW/INTEREST

- Lovely, leisurely walk along the beach and around the sand dunes.
- Opportunity for having a paddle or even getting wet all over.
- Plenty of wildlife associated with sand bars, salt marshes and mud flats.
- Extensive flora along the sheltered east flank of the promontory.
- A nature reserve dedicated to the protection of the fauna and to safeguarding the environment, delicate ecology and natural beauty of the area.
- Marvellous seascapes all the way, and the MacGillycuddy's Reeks in full view as you walk around Inch Point.

GRADIENTS

Virtually none!

MAPS, FOOTPATHS AND WAYSIGNS

OS DISCOVERY SERIES 1:50 000 — NUMBERS 71 AND 78 (KERRY)

Most of the walking is either along the beach or on grassy cart-tracks. The sand dunes are crossed on the way back but this strip of land is quite narrow and these ups and downs are quite quickly left behind.

There are virtually no directional indicators but none are needed. There are the occasional warning signs which provide information about tides etc. and these must be heeded!

GETTING STARTED

The R561 coastal road passes by Inch Strand which is located about half-way between Dingle and Castlemaine. The main car park for the beach is just below this road.

Walk down to the beach and head southwards towards Inch Point with the Iveragh Peninsula in view across the bay and you are on your way, treading sand.

SUMMARY DESCRIPTION OF WALK

THE WAY TO INCH POINT — MR 675967 (Allow 2 hours)

As you walk onto the beach you will pass a notice warning you about the tides, mud flats and salt marshes. You should take great care to comply with these sensible precautions at all times in order to avoid any difficulties subsequently arising.

In good weather, the mountainous backbone of the Iveragh Peninsula forms an intriguing skyline, the pointed peaks towering up as a faint, bluish silhouette on the far side of Dingle Bay. The highest of these are the MacGillycuddy's Reeks rising to the SE; you will obtain the best views of these later on when you walk around Inch Point. Behind you a range of attractive, rounded, green hills baulk — for the time being — any more distant views of the higher mountains of the Dingle Peninsula. Ahead, vast areas of virgin sand are ready to record as imprints the pattern on the soles of your boots, and at low tide a wide strip of this connects the hardy, fluttering grasses of the sand dunes on your L with the waves breaking on the shoreline. You will soon leave behind most of the other visitors who tend to congregate in the area nearest to the car park and café. Then you will have the beach virtually to yourselves, and gradually solitude and a closeness with nature will most likely pervade your thinking and generate such thoughts as when, how and why did this wonderful place come into being.

There are miles and miles of firm, clean, crusty sand to walk over and this is as flat as a pancake. When the tide is out, and this is the best time to undertake this exploration, make your way down to and then along the water's edge during the first part of the walk. Then as you saunter along you may experience the joys of beachcombing by inspecting the numerous shells, seaweed, remains of crabs and starfish, tell-tale signs of creatures buried in the sand and other flotsam which has been left behind by the receding tide. Further on, the extensive flats further out to sea do become softer, muddier and covered with small pools of water, and when you approach this area it is best to head back towards the firmer sands to your L which line the sand dunes.

Just keep walking SSE with not a care in the world, revelling in the spaciousness and experiencing a seldom-felt freedom for hillwalkers of it not mattering in the slightest exactly where you plonk each of your footsteps! This immensely enjoyable safari extends for about 5 km (3 miles) before you begin to bear L to walk around the tip of Inch Point at the far end of the sand bar. Towards the very end of the terra firma you are not all that far away from the Iveragh Peninsula, this jutting out towards you in the form of Rosbehy Point, a not dissimilar strip of land just over a couple of kilometres away at its nearest point across the tidal straits separating the two converging promontories.

When heading towards and around the point, always keep close to the higher ground of the sand dunes on your L and be constantly vigilant of incoming tides, especially so the high spring ones. This precaution will ensure that you constantly tread on firm sands which will hold the weight of a car and that you consequently avoid any softer spots further away from the dunes.

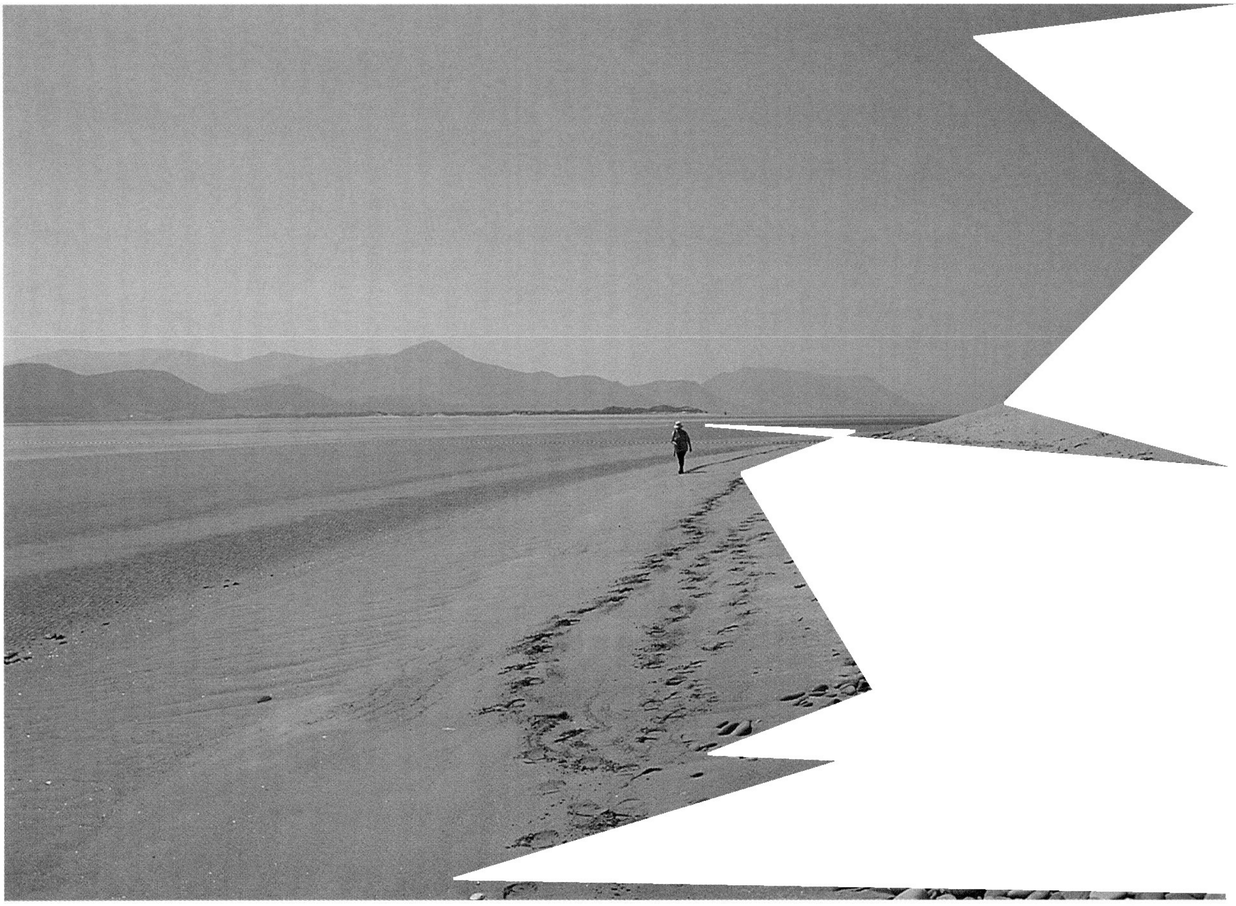

19:1 Walking around a sandy Inch Point

Now is the time to look back towards the mainland of Dingle Peninsula, as from this better vantage point, in favourable weather, you will be able to identify some of the high peaks which form its mountainous spine. Two prominent summits to look out for are the wide shoulder of the Brandon Massif to the NW and the twin peaks of Beenoskee to the NNW. Much closure to, hordes of flies can be somewhat tiresome along here during the hot, summer months and millions of worm holes punctuate the sands.

Inch Point is invariably a good place to stop for refreshments and there are several suitable resting spots on or near to areas of stones and pebbles where the sand is less likely to get mixed up with your sandwiches! The panoramic views, as you contentedly eat and drink your fill, across the strait to the S are terrific. In clear weather, many of the individual peaks which form the MacGillycuddy's Reeks to the SE may be sorted out. The highest of them all is Carrauntoohil, the rooftop of Ireland.

THE WAY BACK TO THE PARKING AREA — MR 644006 (Allow 2 hours)

As previously warned, for reasons of safety keep close to the edge of the dunes at all times when walking around Inch Point. In particular, when the tide is out, avoid approaching either the exposed sand bars or the mud flats which lie beyond. There is an indent just beyond the point and at low tide it is feasible to cross this over the firm, rippled sands; otherwise stick close to the line of sand dunes as they curve around ahead to your R.

19:2 THE SECRETS OF A TINY ROCK POOL ARE REVEALED

Then, depending upon the state of the tide, track just below or along the fringe of the dunes as you continue to make your way back towards the parking area, heading NW. The absorbing return route winds around a series of bays, indents and points and past mud flats away on your R which you continue to steer well away from. Further on, a strip of salt marsh bars your way: it is not possible to cross this and you should, therefore, refrain from attempting to do so! When you come to this, bear L into the safety of the dunes to outflank it. This manoeuvre is made near to MR 668988 and just before you reach the point marked 'Dromdarrig' on the OS map.

Walk towards the gently undulating spur of higher ground to locate and follow a grassy-surfaced cart-track which winds through the dunes seeking out the easiest passage. This conveniently leads northwards in your intended direction of travel. The track then curves to the L to avoid more difficult ground and for a short distance your heading changes temporarily towards W. Keep walking along this wide track, avoiding all narrower and less well-defined side paths as you penetrate deeper into the enclosing dunes.

Further on, the well-established track curves back to the R, again changing your direction, on this occasion to your predominant heading of NW. It then curves to the W of more low-lying salt marshes, leaving these over to your R to then pass through an area where feeding-hoppers for animals have been located. Around here during the summer months, the ground is attractively patterned with vivid yellow and white movements resulting from the sea breeze causing a crowded assortment of buttercups, daisies and wild lilies to flutter about as it disturbs them. You will probably see many timid rabbits along here when your unwelcome presence invariably causes them to disappear fast down their burrows.

Just keep following the track which winds around the flatter edges of the hillocky dunes, further on passing a wooden guiding stake on your R. Then fork L ahead to arrive at a gate and wire fence. Turn full L at this point and walk due W to cut across the narrow strip of land which supports the sand dunes. Keep near to the wire fence on your R but deviate from this along a wide channel further to the L when you are nearly across, this in order to seek out the easiest way forward and to avoid crossing some relatively steep, loose, sandy hillocks which can be tiresome. Climb up across the final sandy rises and the beach which you walked along during your outward journey will then appear just below. Turn R and retrace your steps the short remaining distance which now separates you from the parking areas.

ALTERNATIVE WAYS

ESCAPES AND EXTENSIONS

Such variants are not really appropriate on this walk, although you can always either stop and set up camp to allow the children to enjoy themselves anywhere along the beach during the outward stretch or turn back if time is short, you do not like sand getting into your boots or any other reason suggests itself to you.

OVERLEAF: LOOKING OUT TO SEA TOWARDS THE ARAN ISLANDS

The Burren Walks

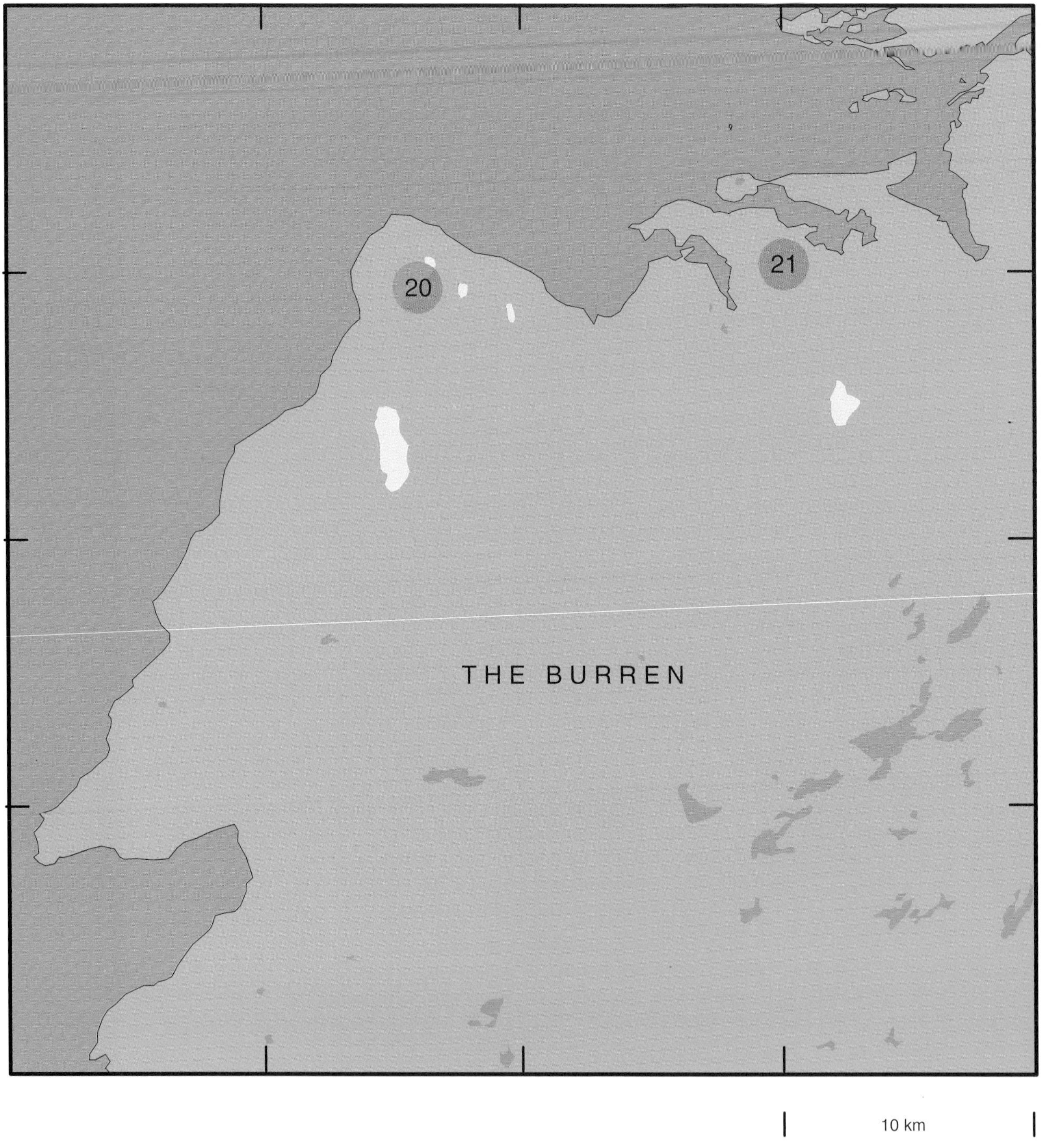
20
21
THE BURREN
10 km

The Mountains of the Burren

Getting There

Now is the opportunity to visit Tralee if you have not already done so, for passing through this town is on the obvious northern exit route from the Dingle Peninsula when travelling towards the Burren.

Use the 20 minutes' ferry crossing from Tarbert to Killimer over the Shannon; it's not cheap but it does save the longer and more tedious road journey around the mighty estuary via Limerick, and on these grounds it is economically justified. The direct way to this ferry crossing from Tralee is along the N69 road, but you may prefer, and be prepared to allow more time, to detour up the R551 road, using this far more scenic, coastal route to visit Kerry Head and perhaps also stop in Ballybunnion.

On the north side of the River Shannon, head for Kilrush along the N67 road. From this busy town, travel northwards again, on this occasion along the R483 road. Connection is then made with the N67 road and this will take you further northwards through Milltown Malbay to the attractive, bustling, seaside resort of Lahinch (Lehinch on OS map), where you may also wish to spend some time. More choices await you here. You can remain on the N67 road to motor through Ennistymon (Emistimon on OS map) and on to either Lisdoonvarna or, further on, Ballyvaughan (Ballyvaghan on OS map). Alternatively, you can opt to use the interconnecting, and much more scenic, R478, R479 and R477 coastal roads where, before you round the impressive promontory of Black Head to reach Ballyvaghan from the W, you may be tempted to set up base camp at accommodation around either Liscannor or Doolin. There is also the seduction, irresistible to most passers-by, of spending some time marvelling at the impressive Cliffs of Moher and perhaps also having a coffee at the interesting visitor centre located there. Allow a full day for this travel, assuming you are going to include some of the attractive diversions along the way.

Geological Perspective

The coastal region of Co Clare between the Burren to the N and the Cliffs of Moher in the S is underlain with Carboniferous rocks. The strata dip gently to the SW so that the older beds of Carboniferous limestone occur in the N and the younger Clare shales of the Namurian occupy the S. The region around the Burren is largely one of bare limestone, with only thin pockets of glacial drift and soil. Natural, vertical breaks, or joints, in the limestone have been opened up by solution to produce a surface of limestone blocks ('clints') separated by deep fissures ('grykes'). This topography is known as 'karstic'.

Except where there are deposits of glacial drift, such as along the bed of the Caher River, there are no surface streams as all drainage disappears through the fissured limestone into extensive cave systems, for example those open to the public at Aillwee near to Ballyvaughan. Where unstable cave roofs have collapsed, depressions have formed at the surface. These depressions may become extended by further solution underground, as exemplified by the Carran Depression, some 60 m (200 ft) deep.

To the S, the Carboniferous limestone passes beneath thin sandstones and clayrocks of the Namurian. These beds of sandstone or flagstone, generally fine grained, have been quarried for use in building. In the Liscannor area the flagstones contain conspicuous fossil trails of animal origin, observed as ridges or furrows about a centimetre across. The Namurian rocks are generally impermeable and, therefore, in contrast to limestone landscapes, the drainage is retained on the surface. Weathering of these rocks, together with the glacial drift derived from them, has produced acid soils where bogs are common. The Namurian, with its flagstones and clayrocks, is dramatically exposed in the vertical or overhanging Cliffs of Moher, which rise dramatically from the sea to a height of over 180 m (about 600 ft).

Present-Day Landscapes and Opportunities for Walking

The vast and unique upthrust limestone plateau of the Burren offers superb walking opportunities, especially so to all those nimble-footed people who are also interested in wild flowers and who will take in their stride the occasional whiff of that peculiar scent which emanates far afield from nomadic, wild goats which roam these heights!

The pearly whites and greys of the limestone outcrops effortlessly intermingle with vast stretches of green vegetation to produce pleasing landscapes of modestly sized, rounded hills and mountains, a particularly alluring feature of which is their terraced slopes which rise in steps to flattish and extensive summit areas. However, it is the expansive limestone pavements criss-crossed with clints and grykes, the abundance of wild flowers and the assorted megalithic burial tombs and stone forts which elevate this region to world-class interest, appealing to geologists, botanists and archaeologists alike and attracting experts on these subjects from far and wide.

It is quite popular with walkers too, who are able to roam freely across much of its interesting terrain, choosing routes which suit their experience and physical capabilities to explore, at their leisure, large parts of these rolling landscapes. The topography of the region combines with its mild, wet climate and poor alkaline soils to create an environment that supports one of the widest ranges of wild plants to be discovered anywhere in the world. On the Burren, Arctic and Alpine flowers intermingle with species more common in hot Mediterranean lands. Walkers, please tread with care so as not to crush any of these delicate blooms, especially so the rare, wild orchids some of which take many years to flower.

Choice of Walking Routes

Due to its limited size and variability, only two walking routes have been selected in the Burren, but what superb walks both of these are. The more challenging one covered in Walk 20, but still only classified as moderate, encompasses a visit to Black Head and Gleninagh

Mountain. On this walk you can revel in climbing up a succession of limestone ledges that resemble an elongated staircase before trekking across virtually flat and expansive limestone pavements. Walk 21, the second route, explores the limestone table of Abbey Hill with its splendid views across Galway Bay.

LOCAL WALKING GUIDES

Deserved recommendations from several sources advised me to seek the wise counsel of local guides Christopher Browne and Shane Connolly before deciding on what walks to cover in the Burren. Christopher accompanied us on the Black Head route, where his in-depth knowledge of the natural history, geology and flora of the area proved to be quite fascinating. Shane was already committed to undertaking two walks each day whilst we were in the vicinity and so we reluctantly resisted trying to persuade him to get his torch out as a prelude to accompanying us on midnight rambles!

CONTACT DETAILS

Christopher Browne
Fertile Rock Study Tours
Station Road
Lahinch
Co Clare
Tel: 065 81168
Fax: 065 81228

Shane Connolly
Burren Hill Walks Ltd
Corkscrew Hill
Ballyvaughan
Co Clare
Tel: 065 77168; mobile 088 654810

ACCOMMODATION, EATING OUT AND LOCAL TRANSPORT

ACCOMMODATION

We have sampled four places to stay at in and around the Burren, three of these recommended to us by local walking guides. Ita and John Coughlan, who invite visitors into their comfortable home at Lahinch during the summer months, will lavish warm hospitality on you and will fill you up with wholesome breakfasts and generous offers of tea and cake at every conceivable opportunity. Cullinan's Restaurant and Guest House is another very comfortable place to stay at, with the added advantage of serving delicious evening meals which could joyfully confine you to barracks each evening. Benrue Farmhouse and Rockhaven Farmhouse are located away from it all in the heart of the Burren and this makes them very convenient bases for your explorations; Bríd Casey at Benrue caters specially for walkers, to whom an exceptionally warm welcome is extended.

These guest houses, together with three other accommodation establishments which have been recommended to the author and which have a special empathy towards the needs of walkers, are listed in the table overleaf.

ACCOMMODATION REGISTER

Hotel/Guest House	Rooms en suite	Rooms other	Charge B&B	Open	Visited by Author
Ita and John Coughlan Ocean Breeze Station Road Lahinch Co Clare Tel: 065 81616	F 2 D 1 T 0 S 0	F 0 D 1 T 0 S 0	£16	July and August	Yes
James and Carol Cullinan Cullinan's Restaurant and Guest House Doolin Co Clare Tel: 065 74183	F 5 D 1 T 0 S 0	F 0 D 0 T 0 S 0	£16–20	All year	Yes
Bríd Casey Benrue Farmhouse Lisdoonvarna Co Clare Tel: 065 74059	F 2 D 3 T 1 S 0	F 0 D 0 T 0 S 0	£15–17	Feb to Nov	Yes
Theresa McDonagh Rockhaven Farmhouse Cahermacnaughton Ballyvaughan Co Clare Tel: 065 74454	F 2 D 0 T 0 S 0	F 0 D 1 T 0 S 0	£16	April to Sept	Yes
Teresa Donnellan Slieve Elva Farmhouse Kelmoon Lisdoonvarna Co Clare Tel: 065 74318	F 0 D 6 T 0 S 0	F 0 D 0 T 0 S 0	£16	Mar to Nov	No
Patsy O'Connor Castleview Farmhouse Cliffs of Moher Road Clahane Liscannor Co Clare Tel: 065 81590	F 0 D 5 T 0 S 0	F 0 D 0 T 0 S 0	£14–16	Easter to Oct	No
Mary Doorty Burren Farmhouse Ballybreen Kilfenora Co Clare Tel: 065 71363	F 0 D 0 T 0 S 0	F 0 D 3 T 0 S 0	£15	All year	No

Rooms: F = Family; D = Double; T = Twin; S = Single

EATING OUT

With dining and wining at Cullinan's Restaurant we have limited experience of eating out in the Burren, and whilst those places we sampled were all right, I feel you may do better discovering the delights of eating at venues of your own choosing. However, do place Cullinan's on your 'hit list' as this is very good indeed.

LOCAL TRANSPORT

Taxi and minibus services, should you need these, are operated throughout the Burren by Gerard Hartigan (Tel: 065 81737) and John Creedon (Tel: 065 81247; mobile 087 478049), both firms operating from Lahinch.

BLACK HEAD AND GLENINAGH MOUNTAIN

fact file

START/FINISH

Church at Fanore — MR 147089

GRADING

Easy/straightforward to moderate, depending on the weather (colour-coded GREEN/BLUE)

WALKING TIME ALLOWANCE

6 hours

DISTANCE

14.0 km (8.7 miles)

TOTAL HEIGHT GAINED

350 m (1150 ft)

PRINCIPAL HEIGHTS

- Peak (not named) 314 m (1030 ft)
- Gleninagh Mountain 317 m (1040 ft)

digest of walk

PARKING

Large car park at church; avoid parking there during Mass times.

OVERVIEW/INTEREST

- Magnificent, limestone scenery with extensive areas of pavements and intriguing rock features.
- Riveting landscapes, a mixture of green and white, with rounded hills falling gently to the sea.
- Extensive and extremely varied flora ranging from Arctic and Alpine species to Mediterranean plants.
- Area rich in ringforts and other features of archaeological interest.
- Distant views across Galway Bay towards the high mountains of Connemara.
- Sightings of the Aran Islands.

BLACK HEAD AND GLENINAGH MOUNTAIN

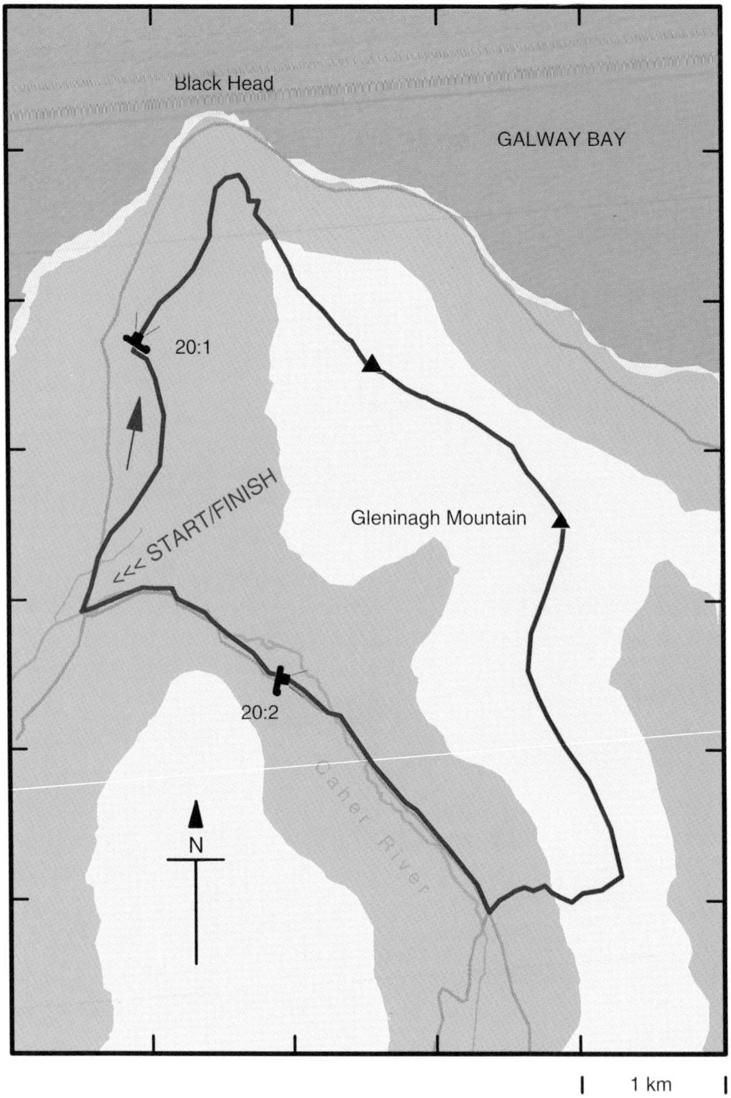

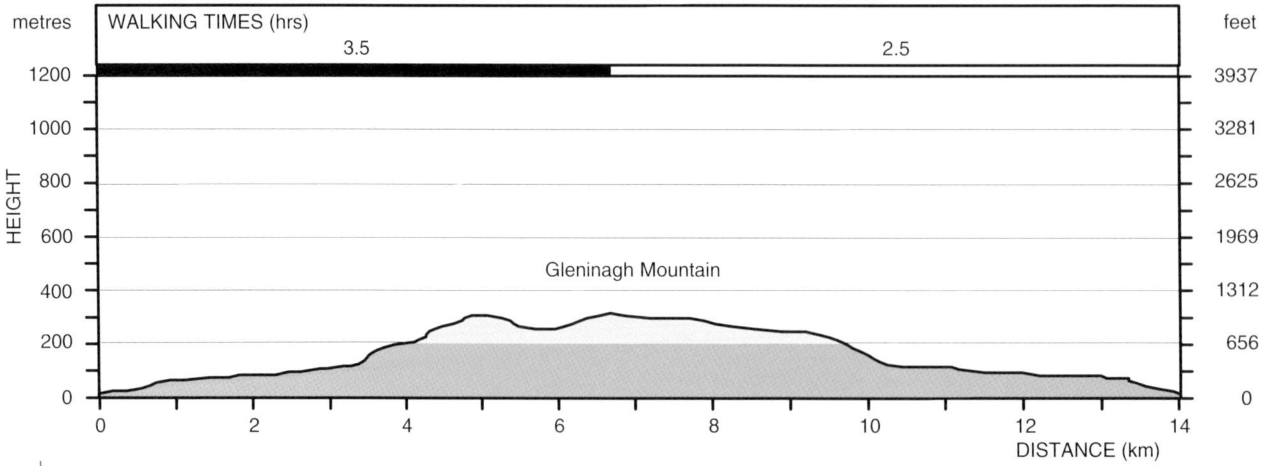

GRADIENTS

Following a gentle approach, there is a steady climb up moderate, stepped gradients to reach the two high points of the walk which are separated by a lower band of rock. From the second of these, Gleninagh Mountain, there is a gradual descent southwards across expansive slopes to reach the Burren Way. A sharper, twisting section downhill then leads to a minor road, which in turn descends more gradually to lead you back to your starting-point.

MAPS, FOOTPATHS AND WAYSIGNS

OS Discovery Series 1:50 000 — Number 51 (Clare and Galway)

The start and finish of the walk are along a series of connecting roads, tracks and paths along which it is easy to navigate. The central section, including the summits of the two mountains, is across open countryside where there are only intermittent, faint tracks to guide you across challenging, rocky terrain.

Apart from road signs, cairns and the marking of the Burren Way, there are no signs to guide you.

GETTING STARTED

The area of Fanore lies along the coast a few kilometres to the S of Black Head. It can be reached by travelling along the R477 coast road either westwards from Ballyvaughan or northwards from Lisdoonvarna. At MR 145089 turn E off the R477 road and the parking area is a short distance further on to your R.

Turn L out of the car park and walk back to the coast road. Turn R along the R477 to continue N in the direction signed 'Ballyvaughan 12'.

Summary Description of Walk

THE WAY TO GLENINAGH MOUNTAIN — MR 179095 (Allow $3\frac{1}{2}$ hours)

The gushing waters of the Caher River are crossed almost immediately by means of Fanore Bridge and on your R, way beyond this meandering stream, the limestone terraces of the Murrooghkilly hillsides rise in impressive, uniform layers. In the opposite direction, to the W, fleeting glimpses of the coastline appear across the intervening sand dunes as you continue along a straight section of the road. Traffic is frequent on this coastal route in summer and you will need to be alert as you walk along the side of the road.

Just past a bungalow, turn R off the R477 and follow a track which then bends sharply to the L to lead slightly uphill parallel to the road below. The way continues up a gentle gradient, passing between the dwellings and farm buildings situated at Murroogh. In favourable weather and as further height is gained, there are revealing views of the low-lying Aran Islands out to sea in the W and also the first sightings of the high mountains of Connemara, including the Twelve Pins, which form the distant horizon beyond the sheltered waters of Galway Bay to the NW.

The track curves to the R to lead you to a large, isolated bungalow and this approach then swings more abruptly to the R around the building. When you reach this point, continue straight ahead along the green road (an enclosed, grassy way along which cattle were led, eating as they went) which is accessed by clambering over a stone wall. Turn immediately R through a gap in the hedge, walk for about 30 paces beside this hedge and then turn back L to continue along the enclosed green road which leads further uphill towards the limestone terracing and pavements rising ahead to the N and NE.

The elevated green road, which you may have to share with grazing cattle, winds impressively around the hillside at a more or less constant height, affording clear views of the interesting limestone pavements extending below towards the coast. Three low, stone walls have to be crossed in this section before the way widens and the grassy surface becomes flatter and easier to negotiate as it swings around to the L in an elegant loop below a layered, limestone ridge. A fourth, and higher, wall is then crossed as the green road starts a prolonged curve back to the R to round Black Head, edging below low cliffs.

The continuation way passes through gaps in two sections of stone walling before it mounts a limestone terrace on the R. Along here, select a convenient gap in the walling on your R to abandon the grassy band as a prelude to heading SE up the steeper, rockier slopes. This turning is made at about MR 156118. Quickly establish a line of approach which will lead you directly towards a distinctive cairn on the horizon above. The way there is up layered limestone, reminiscent of treading up a stretched-out staircase. Proceed to a second cairn, a short distance higher up on a continued SE alignment, clambering up more terraced limestone to get there.

Beyond these helpful markers, a less severe slope which you consume on your established SE bearing will bring you to an impressive ringfort which is remarkably well preserved. Take

20:1 Descending along one of the green roads which forms part of the Burren Way

time to walk around this interesting structure, being careful to preserve the ecology of this historic site by not dislodging any of the stones or building material. From the far side of the fort, continue to progress to the SE towards the more challenging, flaky, shattered rock above, being careful to climb up the terraced limestone directly ahead, keeping well to the L of the steeper cliffs to the S as these are considerably more difficult to scale in safety.

The immediately surrounding landscapes assume a progressively more lunar-looking appearance, and as you climb higher this relatively barren ground is divided by a stone wall which runs at right angles to your direction of approach. Cross through the walling at one of several gaps to continue heading uphill to the SE across steepening slopes. Your continuation way then arrives at a second stone wall to the L. Ascend further beside this feature for a short distance and then clamber over it at a convenient low spot, to then repeat this manoeuvre when you reach the next walling.

Maintain your SE direction of travel to scale the low, limestone bluff ahead, selecting one of several less steep, grassy channels running across its face to achieve this. Expansive, gentler slopes lie above and these lead to another terrace which you need to scale in a similar fashion. The crossing of successive, fairly level areas followed by climbing up short sections of terraced cliffs of varying height is repeated five more times, making seven replications of these features in total as you continue to gain further height to the SE. The relative monotony of repeating this may be punctuated by observing herds of goats who roam this rocky environment which is much to their liking. Try to keep up-wind of these animals if this is possible!

The first summit now lies just above and this is identified by a pointed cairn placed upon a significant mound. Before you dash to the top, at the edge of the last cliff face, turn around to observe the most fantastic, panoramic view in clear weather of the whole of Galway Bay spreadeagled below you, with the high mountains of Connemara drawing your gaze across the vast inlet towards their distant, riveting shapes forming the horizon in the NW. The summit lies at 314 m (1030 ft), and from here there are fascinating views into the heart of the Burren where spacious, upthrust, limestone hills, plateaus and ridges occupy the segment between SE and SW.

Continue SE from the summit area, again heading across limestone slabs and paving but on this occasion descending slightly. Work a way of your own choice to the L around the linking band of rock, being careful in misty weather not to get drawn towards the lower ground to the S which progressively tumbles down into a chasm below. The surrender of some height is unavoidable along this traverse but keep it to a minimum, for you will soon need to recover all of this and a bit more!

Also be careful as you nimbly stride over the numerous clints and grykes in the limestone pavements and slopes which divide a succession of low terraces that have to be negotiated during the limited and controlled descent. Beyond this layering, the ground flattens off to form a broad hause which connects the two peaks. Across this band, further stratified bands of limestone lead uphill towards the summit area of Gleninagh Mountain. A wide gap in another stone wall has to be negotiated to reach these upward slopes.

Through this gap, continue to head SE, threading your way with care up some challenging cliff faces which lie directly above. Again choose grassy gullies running across these steeper banks, as these afford by far the easiest and safest ways up. The summit area resides on a confined, grassy plateau which is surrounded by limestone outcrops. There is an unusual trigonometrical point in the form of a low column set into a semi-sphere of concrete positioned on this peak. This is located at 317 m (1040 ft), which is ever so slightly higher than the first summit. The all round views to be observed from this summit given good weather are very similar to those visible from the previous top, which may be seen on the skyline to the NW.

THE WAY BACK TO THE CAR PARK — MR 147089 (Allow $2\frac{1}{2}$ hours)

At the summit of Gleninagh Mountain turn through about 100 degrees to your R to commence your descent to the SSW, keeping to the broad crest of the falling ridge. Exercise great care during the initial sections of the way down as you cross over a shallow covering of soil and flora which hides holes and crevices in the limestone rock just below. Keep to the secure, exposed limestone where you can and avoid treading on any overhanging foliage which you perceive could just possibly conceal a crevice or hollow beneath it. Prod anything suspicious with your walking stick if you happen to be carrying one with you!

The progressive descent reveals more extensive sightings of the interesting topography of Blackhead Bay and of the inlets to the E. After about a further $1\frac{1}{2}$ km (1 mile) of walking, the descending ridge bends progressively around to the L, changing your direction of progress towards SSE. If you look back at this point, both of the summits previously visited are visible in clear weather to the NNW and NNE respectively. Further on, a slight rise has to be accommodated before a pointed cairn is passed, and a short distance beyond this marker you will need to cross, at some conveniently selected low point, a stone wall which runs directly across your line of approach.

Continue descending to the SSE and very soon, over the brow ahead, identifying features including farmhouses will appear in the valley below. The gradual way down crosses three more stone walls, and following these your line of descent leads to another stone wall to your R. Follow this feature further downhill, walking southwards to scale one more wall before your route connects with a wide track at MR 183071. Turn R along this track which forms part of the Burren Way and follow it as it winds quite rapidly downhill in a series of twists and turns. The dilapidated buildings which you pass by on your L are the remains of a shebeen, an illegal drinking place which at one time was daringly popular.

The rough, loose surface of the descending track is compensated for by the hedgerows which line it further down, these profuse with shrubbery and wild flowers. The track descends to a minor road which is accessed through a redundant gateway. Turn R along this narrow, side road and refrain from immediately turning off L along the signed continuation of the Burren Way. Your new heading is to the NNW veering NW. About $3\frac{1}{2}$ km ($2\frac{1}{4}$ miles) of gently descending road walking now remain before you arrive back at the starting-point.

This section of the route tracks close by the Caher River, one of the very few surface waterways to avoid disappearing without trace down notorious sinkholes into the porous limestone of the Burren. Some distance further down the valley the river is crossed at Carha Bridge, after which the descending waters and your accompanying way pass through the narrowing jaws of a rocky gorge. This is known locally as the 'Khyber Pass'. Near to the end of a section of retaining walling on your R here, look out for an unusual stone boot cemented on to the top of the stonework. The poignant inscription on this memorial, in which flowers are regularly placed, reads 'In memory — Tony — Friend — Fellow Walker'.

From here, the rest of the way leads uneventfully downhill back to the church and parking area.

20:2 SWEEPING LIMESTONE PAVEMENTS OBSERVED FROM THE CAHER VALLEY

ALTERNATIVE WAYS

ESCAPES

There are a number of alternative ways up and down the first summit, all of which avoid the more difficult ground and cliff faces to the S and SW. Therefore, it is possible to return to the green road which winds around Black Head by a different route before retracing your outward steps back to the starting-point, thus simultaneously avoiding any further climbing and considerably shortening the route described.

EXTENSIONS

It is feasible to continue further SW along the Burren Way before using the connecting minor roads and a short stretch of the R477 coast road from Fanore More to track northwards back to the church. However, some considerable more climbing is involved in doing this!

ABBEY HILL

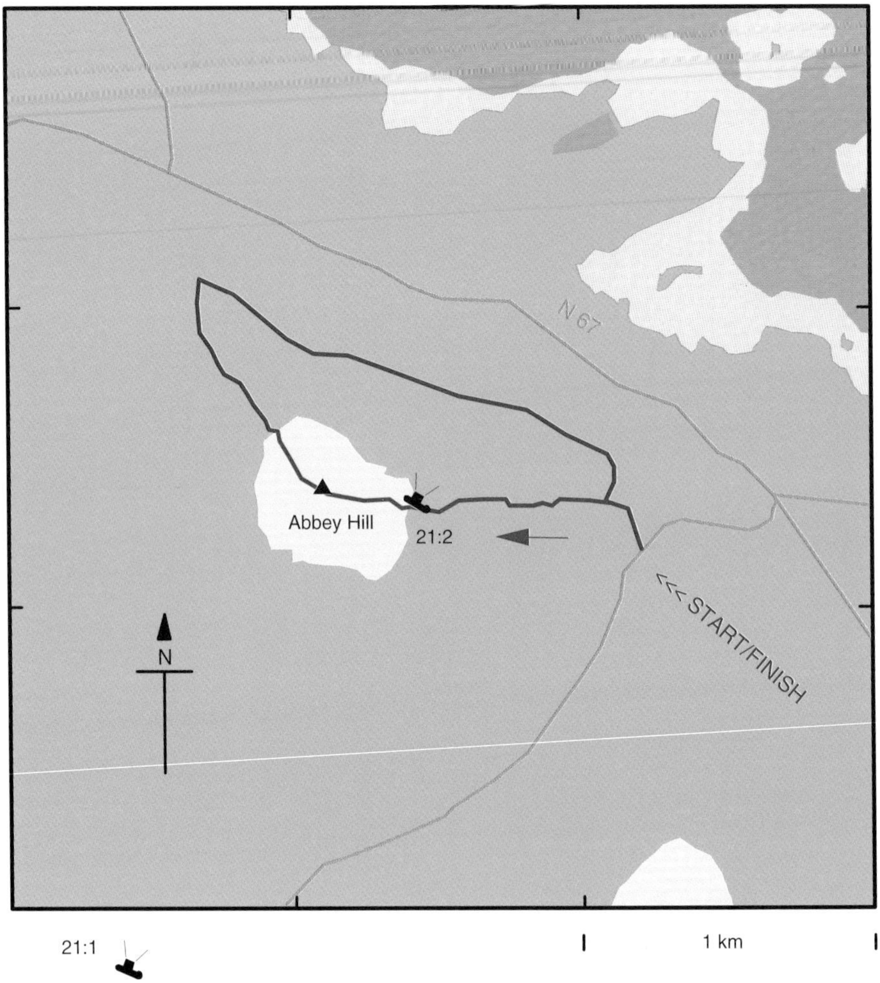
N 67
Abbey Hill
21:2
<<< START/FINISH
N
21:1
1 km

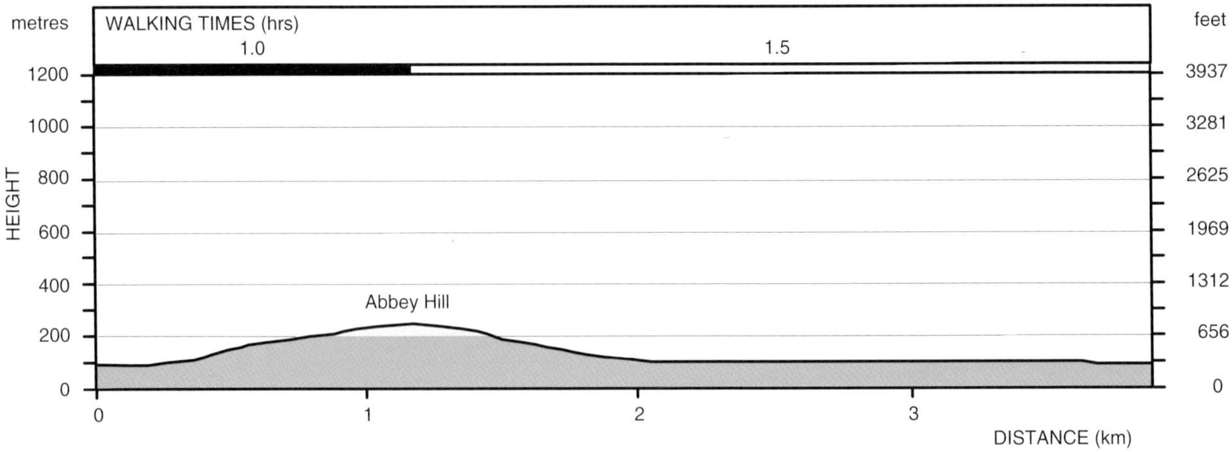
metres
WALKING TIMES (hrs)
1.0
1.5
feet
HEIGHT
1200
1000
800
600
400
200
0
3937
3281
2625
1969
1312
656
0
Abbey Hill
0
1
2
3
DISTANCE (km)

ABBEY HILL

fact file

START/FINISH

Junction of minor road and track — MR 312102

GRADING

Easy/straightforward (colour-coded GREEN)

WALKING TIME ALLOWANCE

2½ hours

DISTANCE

3.9 km (2.4 miles)

TOTAL HEIGHT GAINED

160 m (520 ft)

PRINCIPAL HEIGHTS

- Abbey Hill 240 m (785 ft)

digest of walk

PARKING

Limited space for about six cars.

OVERVIEW/INTEREST

- Delightful short walk to the top of a dome-shaped hill.
- The route is across limestone pavements and passes by fascinating rock formations.
- Extensive flora ranging from Arctic and Alpine plants to those which thrive in a Mediterranean climate.
- Superb, panoramic views, especially so the magnificent seascapes.

GRADIENTS

A moderate climb to the top followed by a similar gradient on the way down, both of these short and sweet!

MAPS, FOOTPATHS AND WAYSIGNS

OS DISCOVERY SERIES 1:50 000 — NUMBER 51 (CLARE AND GALWAY)

There are short stretches of walking along a walled lane at the start and finish of the route. However, the core of the walk is up and then down limestone pavements and threading a way between rocky outcrops. There are sections of path which assist you in doing this, parts of which are clearly defined and parts of which are barely distinguishable. Despite this, route finding never presents any significant difficulties and the challenge is to pick a way that presents minimum effort in either striding over or outflanking the numerous rocky protrusions.

There are no waysigns but this does not present any serious navigational problems as the continuation way is mostly obvious, even where there are no defined paths to follow.

GETTING STARTED

The starting-point is located just above the main N67 road on the stretch linking Kinvara to the E with Ballyvaughan to the W. Turn off the N67 at MR 317104 and the parking place is up the hill about $\frac{1}{2}$ km ($\frac{1}{4}$ mile) to the SW.

Head northwards along the walled lane and you are on your way under your own power.

Summary Description of Walk

THE WAY TO ABBEY HILL — MR 301104 (Allow 1 hour)

Exciting views surround the starting-point. To the WNW your principal objective, the undulating summit area of Abbey Hill (Cnoc na Mainistreach), rises beyond green fields and a cluster of limestone terracing and jumbled rocks; between N and E the indented coastline presents a fascinating, kaleidoscopic pattern of colourful, irregular inlets and intervening promontories jutting out to sea; and to the SSW Turlough Hill, another vast, limestone upthrust, forms the distant horizon.

Head northwards along the walled lane and follow this as it winds almost imperceptibly uphill. A short distance further on, be vigilant to spot and use the narrow gap stile in the walling on your L to then continue uphill along the grassy path, following a changed direction to the W. A well-trodden and obvious path winds through limestone outcrops heading up towards the summit rim of the hill directly ahead. During the late spring and summer months the ground which you now cross is a blaze of colour and the yellows, purples and whites of a variety of wild flowers which thrive in this unique environment sway about and intermingle in any light breeze which fans these delicate blooms.

The path leads directly to the edge of a gigantic and elongated limestone staircase and boulder field. Climb across this, still heading W and deftly darting over the numerous clints and grykes which criss-cross the extensively weathered surface of the exposed rock hereabouts. Select a route up of your own choice, being particularly careful where you place your footsteps when the surface is wet as limestone can be notoriously slippery in such conditions. A spur on the L provides one of the easier ascents, but avoid getting trapped in a gully further over in that direction as this terminates in a relatively difficult rock face which will require you to retrace your final approach steps in order to find a more acceptable way up.

Further on, make for a distinctively shaped, pointed Standing Stone which will appear above to the L. In clear weather, the summit cairn should now be visible further W as you pass by more pointed stones. The rate of climb then slackens off as you track across a vast, rounded slope which is composed of layers of weathered limestone which have been sculptured by the elements into fantastic, flattened patterns. A cairn is positioned to the R and in this direction, to the N, more and more of the enormous size of Galway Bay is revealed as you gain further height.

A narrow, flattish strip of grass is crossed near to the top, and beyond this a steeper, grassy bank covered with boulders and rocky ledges leads to gentler slopes which stretch to the summit area. This approach is speckled with characteristic limestone outcrops angled in a way which assists your ascent. The summit is reached immediately after you have outflanked, to the L, one final, small ridge.

Abbey Hill rises to 240 m (785 ft) and its flattish summit area is graced by a large, symmetrical cairn shaped like a gigantic beehive. This dwarfs several smaller cairns which have also been built here. The dominant cairn is at the axis of three dry-stone walls which converge there. In fine weather the panoramic views from this modestly sized but isolated peak are quite magnificent. In addition to the features and landscapes previously mentioned, there are extensive new vistas to the W towards the huge promontory of Black Head with most of the intervening, rounded, limestone hills and ridges also revealing their topography and relative positioning. Nearer to, in the WNW, the snaking inlet which terminates at Bell Harbour rips into the shoreline. This is a mud flat at low tide but a picturesque, curving expanse of clear, blue water when the tide is in.

21:1 THE REMAINS OF CORCOMROE ABBEY AND ABBEY HILL BEYOND

21:2 The northern slopes of Abbey Hill provide fine vistas across Galway Bay

THE WAY BACK TO THE PARKING AREA — MR 312102 (Allow $1\frac{1}{2}$ hours)

Depart from the summit area to the NW, following the line of a wall downhill. More limestone pavements and terracing form part of your descent, and when you reach a small cliff face make use of a narrow gully which starts adjacent to the walling to provide an easy passage down. Cross over the flatter pavements below to pass by a reassuring marker cairn, this positioned over to your R. Following this, another modest ridge is descended, again keeping close by the walling.

Continue to track downhill to reach and cross some relatively lush meadows containing an abundance of wild flowers. More steep, rocky sections interspersed with grassy areas are then encountered as the walling curves around to the R, towards N. Keep on surrendering height near to the wall, circling around patches of brambles when you have to. You will probably detect the distinctive smell of goats in this vicinity even if you do not actually spot any of these hardy animals whilst walking by!

Further down, pass through a gap in the wall near to its terminus in order to avoid having to cross a relatively difficult strip of scrubland containing dense brambles. After this, head straight down to reach the track below, accessing this at a low point in the containing walling. Be careful to drop down on to the lane without disturbing further any of the loose stonework in this wall.

Turn R and follow this elevated, walled way the 2 km ($1\frac{1}{4}$ miles) back to where your vehicle is parked. This final section is gently downhill, with continued fine views down on your L extending across the vastness of sheltered Galway Bay.

Alternative Ways

ESCAPES

This is a very short walk to start with and the only sensible way of curtailing it any further, assuming you have made it to the top, is to retrace your outward steps directly back to the parking area.

EXTENSIONS

From the summit of Abbey Hill there is an alternative and longer descent to the SW which could include a visit to the remains of the nearby Corcomroe Abbey *en route*. From this site you will need to use the minor roads and work your way NE back to the parking place.

Overleaf: Bundorragha River and Ben Gorm

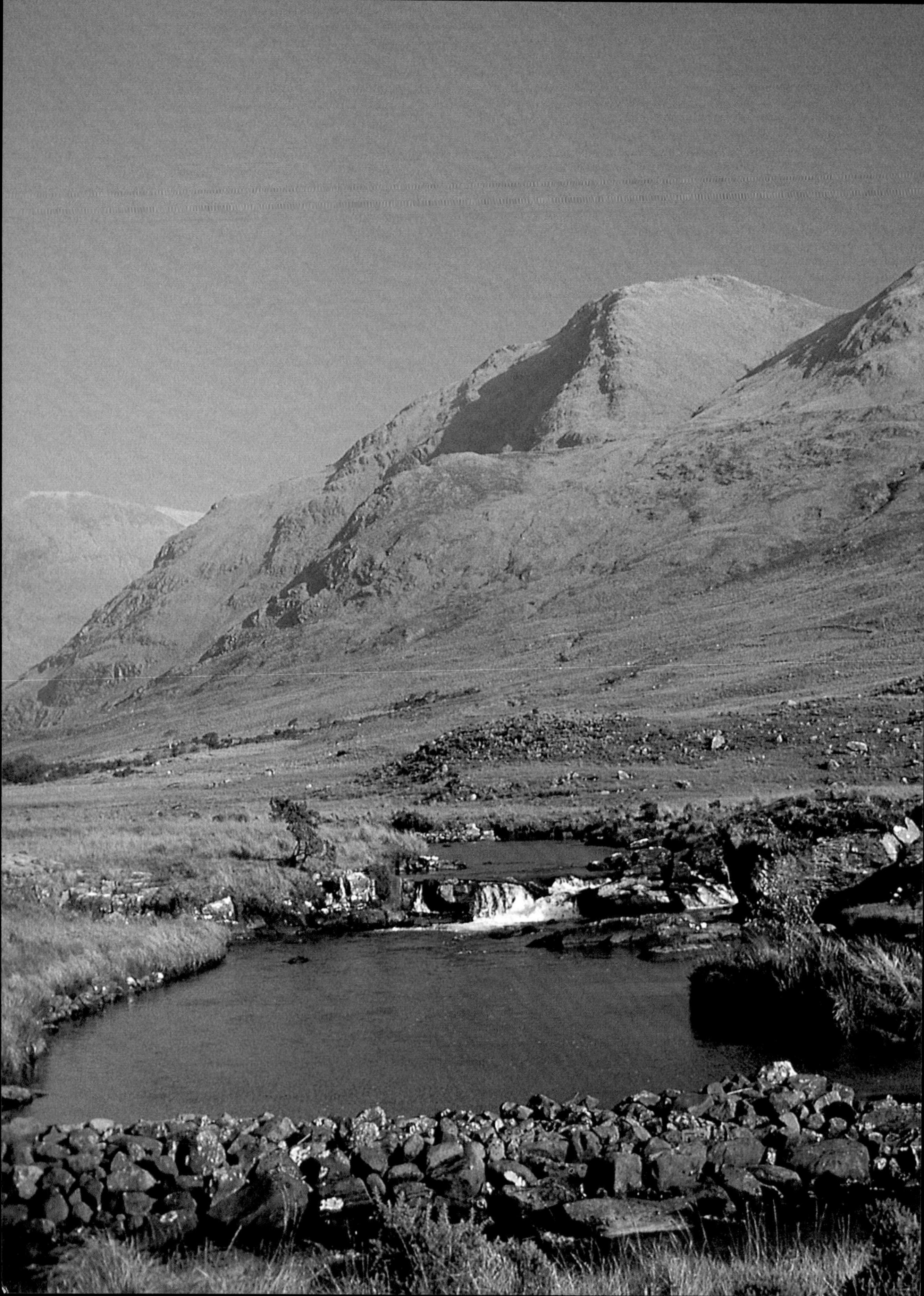

Connemara and Mayo Walks

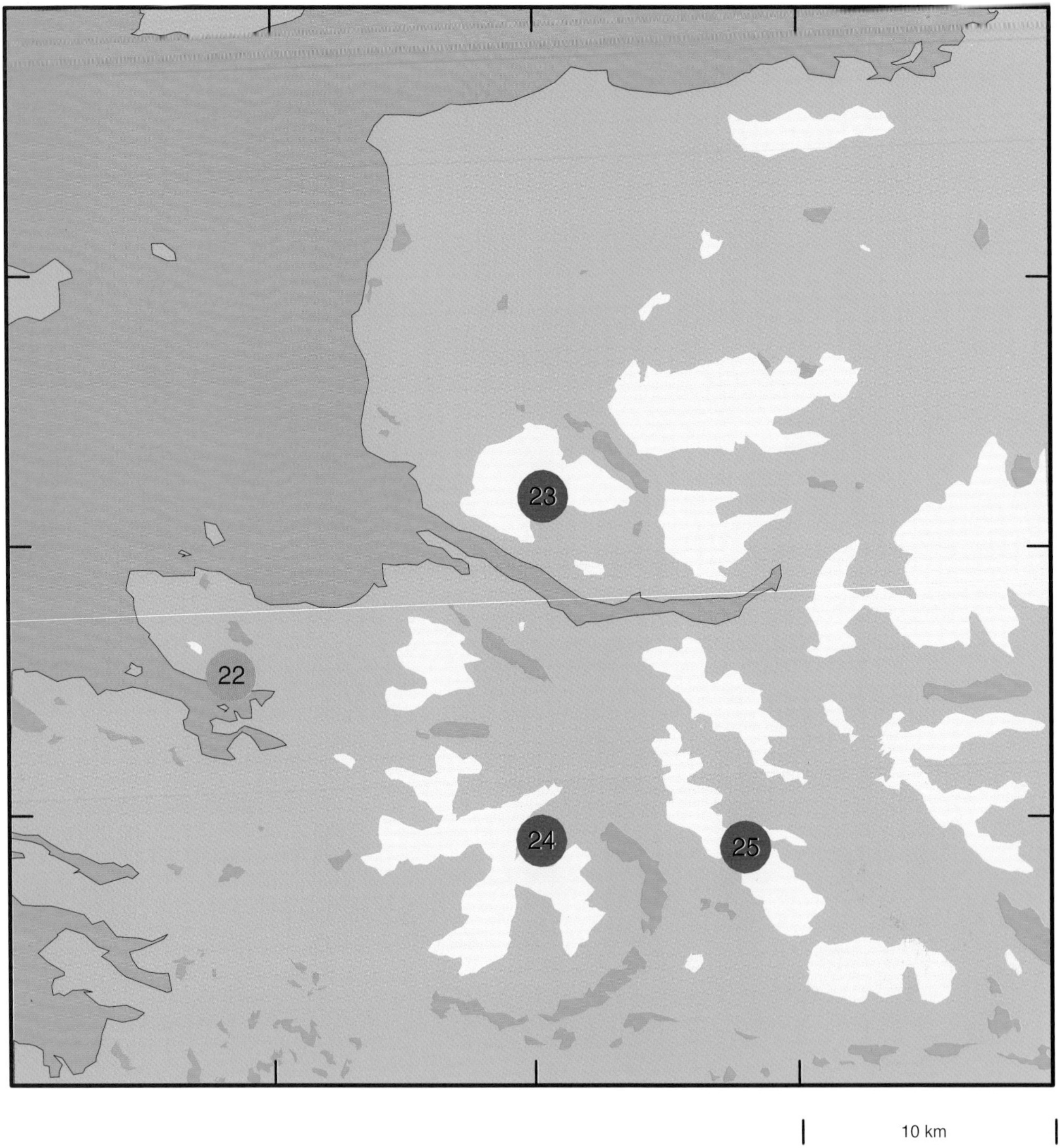
23
22
24
25
10 km

The Mountains of Connemara and Mayo

Getting There

From the Burren, you can observe the spectacular, high, pointed mountains of Connemara rising across the vastness of Galway Bay and only the fine city of Galway will temporarily delay a fast journey there to enable you to walk amongst this wild, rugged, untamed beauty.

Leave the Burren along the N67 road, following this as it snakes along the indented coastline NE to connect with the N18 road. Then travel northwards towards Galway. There is a clearly signed ring road to the N of the city and, unless you wish to do some walking on the flat around this fair place, you are recommended to faithfully follow this by-pass to connect with the N59 road to the W of Galway. Then use the N59 road to travel NW right into the heartland of Connemara's magnificent lakes and mountains. These features loom up ahead quite quickly as, full of keen anticipation, you commence to enter them and, a short distance further on, they are wrapped around you. What a mouth-watering feast of walks to look forward to in the days, or perhaps years, to come!

Continue along the N59 road either as far as the attractive town of Clifden near to the coast or until you reach either of the spur roads, R336 and R344, which lead northwards through the mountains, this choice depending upon the location of your initial destination.

Geological Perspective

The region is composed of an east–west outcrop of Precambrian rocks (formed more than 590 million years ago), flanked to the N by younger Ordovician and Silurian rocks (500 to 400 years in age). The high mountains of Connemara are formed of Precambrian quartzite. This is a sandstone where the quartz sand grains are bound by quartz cement to form a remarkably tough rock. This quartzite formation is known as the Twelve Pins quartzite, after the mountain mass of that name. The same formation may be observed in the Clifden area and also in the Maumturk Mountains.

Other rock types associated with the quartzites, but less resistant to erosion, include the Connemara marble; this was originally a kind of limestone (dolomite) but subsequently was altered by heat to form the white–green decorative stone formerly used extensively in buildings but now mainly reserved for tourist gifts. Whereas the hard quartzites form the distinctive, steep-sided peaks, the less resistant rocks form a lower, undulating surface largely covered by bog. It is probable that during the Great Ice Age of the Pleistocene these high quartzite peaks stood proud of the ice surface as nunataks.

The northern boundary of Connemara is formed by Killary Harbour which is a gigantic fjord; further N the Ordovician and Silurian rocks of Murrisk, which also include quartzite beds, are responsible for the high, white mountain mass of Croagh Patrick. A short distance further

N still is an important fault line trending east–west which is probably a continuation of the Highland Boundary Fault in Scotland. This fault continues westwards to run through Clare Island.

Finally, the coastline of the region contains a number of white beaches. These are composed, not of sand grains, but of fragments of organic skeletal or shell material which are of great interest when examined under a hand lens or magnifying glass.

Present-Day Landscapes and Opportunities for Walking

Even superlatives will do only scant justice to the superb walking terrain of wild and wonderful Connemara. Spectacular, quartzite mountain peaks pop up all over the place and these offer a wide variety of challenging walking routes which will test the stamina, resolve and, in severe weather, route-finding abilities of even the most experienced, fittest and best-equipped hillwalkers. In particular, the steep, rugged, rocky slopes of the Twelve Pins (or Bens), the craggy, undulating, in places precariously steep traverse of the ridge of the Maumturk Mountains, the vast, sweeping horseshoe of the Mweelrea Mountains and the discrete, steep hillsides of the Sheeffry Hills and of Ben Creggan and Ben Gorm collectively provide a challenging, high-level paradise for serious walkers which it will prove extremely difficult to better either in the rest of Ireland or elsewhere.

The Pins or Bens deserve some further amplification. Here, magnificent, steep slopes — their concave symmetry disturbed by bristly ridges, cliff faces, rocky protrusions, massive boulders and areas of shattered rocks and scree — sweep up towards serrated peaks which tower high above. Long, straight, glaciated valleys penetrate into this mountainous wonderland with placid streams meandering across their wide, flat floors, these having been honed down to this shape by valley glaciers slowly moving across their surfaces during successive ice ages of the last two million years or so.

The Partry Mountains rise in the E of the area but these heights are relatively flat-topped and featureless and are regarded by some local experts to be significantly less interesting than the compulsively impressive mountain groupings previously mentioned. However, not so are the attractive, lower landscapes of the coastal fringe together with some of the intervening valleys, as these cater well for the needs of less energetic walkers who may trek across these more modest hills and the flatter ground marvelling at the mighty peaks rising all around them.

Choice of Walking Routes

Three challenging walks have been selected, one each in the Mweelrea Mountains (Walk 23), the Twelve Pins (Walk 24) and the Maumturk Mountains (Walk 25). Each of these high-level routes is fascinatingly different, and together they will provide dedicated hillwalkers with a varied introduction to the delights of treading amongst the high places of Connemara. By contrast, Walk 22 is a gentle and undemanding ascent of Tully Mountain which is located near to the coast; this interesting route, with a plethora of superb views in fine weather, is suitable for more casual walkers and it should also appeal to family groups because a visit to a fine aquarium and maritime museum may also be included in the exploration.

Local Walking Guides

Christopher Stacey of Wicklow fame (see page 17 for contact details) joined me and steered me safely and enjoyably along the more adventurous walking routes undertaken in Connemara, including those presented as Walks 23, 24 and 25. Bill Byrne, the leader of the Wicklow Mountain Rescue Team, and his charming wife Margaret joined us for some of the walks, so for once I was surrounded by a bevy of experts.

Gerry Greensmyth is a local walking guide operating from Belclare near Westport. Gerry is yet another vastly experienced guide and he does market a rather unique walking package. Groups of walkers are accommodated at his attractive and comfortable home-cum-guest house and the inclusive price of these energetic holidays covers full board and transport, in addition to a varied and comprehensive programme of interesting, guided walks. The guest house side of the business is sensibly left in the capable hands of Bernie, his wife, and apart from delicious, wholesome home cooking you will be pampered there until you purr!

Michael Gibbons, a leading archaeologist, is an acknowledged authority on the landscapes and features of interest of this area and he leads and organises comprehensive heritage and walking holidays from his base at Clifden.

CONTACT DETAILS

Gerry Greensmyth
Croagh Patrick Walking Holidays
Belclare View
Belclare
Westport
Co Mayo
Tel/Fax: 098 26090

Michael Gibbons
Connemara Walking Centre
Island House
Market Street
Clifden
Co Galway
Tel: 095 21379; mobile: 087 2349545
Fax: 095 21845
Email: walkwest@indigo.ie

ACCOMMODATION, EATING OUT AND LOCAL TRANSPORT

ACCOMMODATION

Through South West Walks Ireland Ltd, who use the place for some of their walking holidays, we were directed to The Pass Inn and Restaurant near Kylemore. Here we had the great pleasure of meeting and tapping into the considerable 'local knowledge' of Rose Rima, the mercurial and friendly owner of this quite superbly located and extremely well-appointed, family-run hotel. If ever a place was positioned and built to suit perfectly the needs of walkers The Pass Inn must be it, for this splendidly remote and isolated establishment is surrounded by vast, rugged landscapes of high mountains, whilst the benign waters of Kylemore Lough lap peacefully just below your open bedroom window as you breath in the pure, clean mountain air, pondering in just which direction upwards you should propel your feet during each successive day of sheer delight.

One of our other overnight resting spots was with our good acquaintances, the Greensmyths, and yes we did purr! Another place we visited was the luxury holiday apartment development at The Harbour Mill, Westport. Activity holidays, especially hillwalking, feature at this splendid centre and there are guided walks led by experienced and enthusiastic local guides.

These hotels and guest houses etc., together with a selection of other accommodation establishments which have been recommended to the author and which have a special empathy towards the needs of walkers, are listed in the table below.

ACCOMMODATION REGISTER

Rooms: F = Family; D = Double; T = Twin; S = Single

Hotel/Guest House	Rooms en suite	Rooms other	Charge B&B	Open	Visited by Author
Rose Rima The Pass Inn and Restaurant Kylemore Connemara Co Galway Tel: 095 41141	F 3 D 3 T 5 S 0	F 0 D 0 T 0 S 0	£22–27	All year	Yes
Gerry and Bernie Greensmyth Belclare View Belclare Westport Co Mayo Tel: 098 26090	F 3 D 0 T 1 S 0	F 2 D 0 T 0 S 0	£16 Also, 'all-inclusive' walking holiday (c. £400 per week)	April to Oct	Yes
Eldon's Hotel Roundstone Connemara Co Galway Tel: 095 35933	F 3 D 7 T 9 S 0	F 0 D 0 T 0 S 0	£22–40	March to Nov	No
Theresa Walsh Kylemore Connemara Co Galway Tel: 095 41019	F 0 D 0 T 0 S 0	F 0 D 2 T 2 S 0	£14–16	April to Nov	No

Hotel/Guest House	Rooms en suite	Rooms other	Charge B&B	Open	Visited by Author
Noreen Staunton Kylemore Connemara Co Galway Tel: 095 41395	F 0 D 0 T 0 S 0	F 1 D 1 T 2 S 0	£14–16	May to Oct	No
Harry and Nora Conroy Kylemore Lodge Kylemore Connemara Co Galway Tel: 095 41148	F 0 D 0 T 0 S 0	F 0 D 2 T 1 S 1	£15–18	April to Nov	No
The Harbour Mill Westport Harbour Westport Co Mayo Tel: 098 28555	• Luxury holiday apartments • Sleep 3 to 6 • Inclusive weekly rentals range from £125 to £550				Yes

EATING OUT

When you return to The Pass Inn each evening you need not go out again because this establishment boasts both a fine, elegant restaurant and a cosy, congenial bar where meals and snacks are served. Down below in the snug bar area, having enjoyably eaten your fill, you can converse with the local characters, one with exceptional musical talent, and they will contribute greatly to rounding the evenings off in fine style — although these could just conceivably be quite long ones!

Clifden and Westport both contain a wide range of eating places to choose from, but whilst in the Westport area, do sample the delicious home cooking and seafood served at 'The Sheebeen' which is situated near to Gerry and Bernie's place. Here, if you have a hearty appetite, the huge, fresh cod, caught each day, and the plate full of chips will absorb great quantities of whatever you decide to wash them down with!

LOCAL TRANSPORT

Taxi and minibus services are operated in Connemara by John Wallace (Tel: 095 41699) and Michael Nee (Tel: 095 51082), and from Westport by Brendan McGing (Tel: 098 25529; mobile 087 417466/404993).

Getting Back to Dublin

The quickest and most direct way of getting back to Dublin from the Westport area is to travel along the N5, N4 and M4 main roads and motorway to reach the outer M50 ring road arcing around the capital city to the W. This will involve passing through or near to Castlebar, Charlestown, Tulsk, Longford, Mullingar and Kinnegad.

Should you have time to spare, this journey back could be agreeably extended by either stopping off at Mullingar which has several fine attractions, spending some time exploring the city of Dublin or even staying overnight at some convenient place in the nearby Wicklow Mountains, where you might even be tempted into putting your precious walking boots on once again! *Bon voyage!*

Tully Mountain

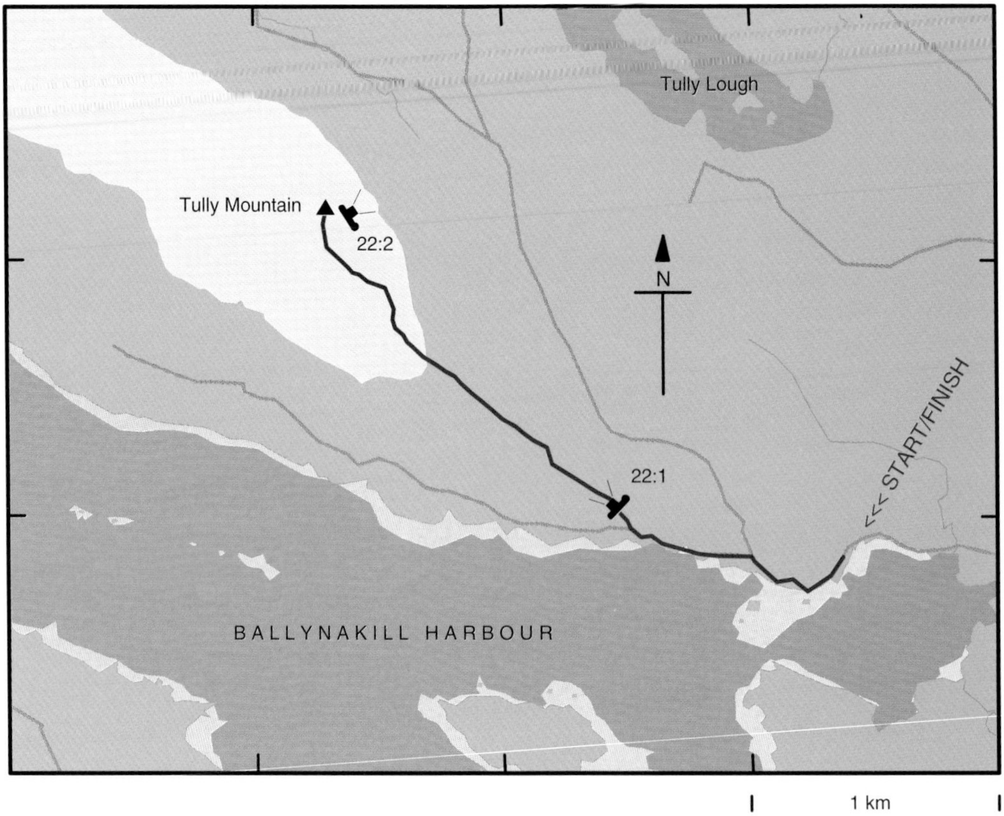

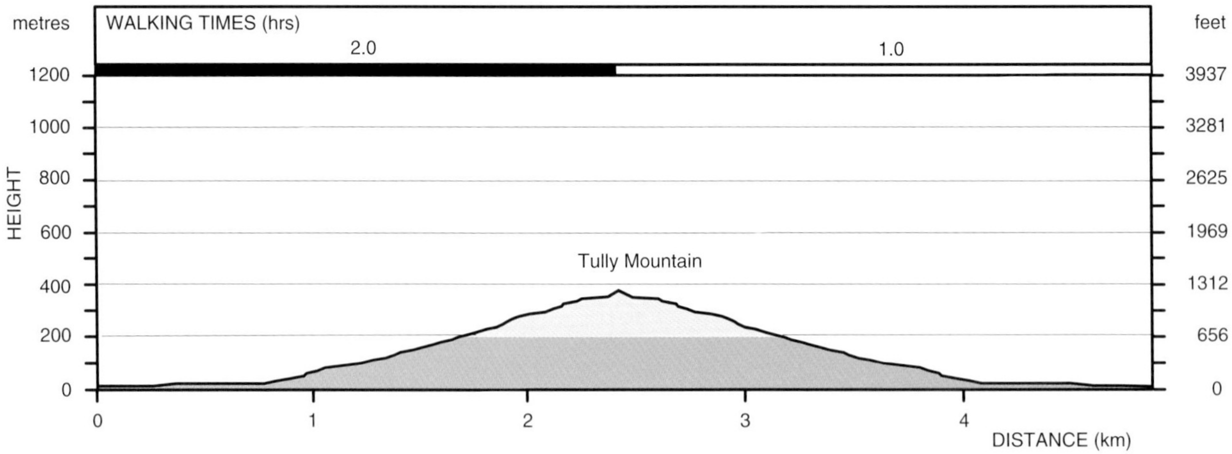

Tully Mountain

fact file

START/FINISH
Just E of the 'Quay' at Ballynakill Harbour — MR 694598

GRADING
Easy/straightforward (colour-coded GREEN)

WALKING TIME ALLOWANCE
3 hours

DISTANCE
4.9 km (3.0 miles)

TOTAL HEIGHT GAINED
360 m (1180 ft)

PRINCIPAL HEIGHTS
- Tully Mountain 356 m (1170 ft)

digest of walk

PARKING
Obtain permission to park at the 'Ocean's Alive Visitor Centre'. Additional parking near 'Quay'.

OVERVIEW/INTEREST
- Short, 'there-and-back' walk to the top of a modest but commanding mountain.
- Fantastic views both along the coastline and also into the mountainous heartland of captivating Connemara.
- Magnificent sunsets may be observed if you time your walk during the late afternoon or early evening.
- Opportunity to combine the walk with a visit to an aquarium and maritime museum, and perhaps also indulge in a boat trip.
- This exploration definitely has special appeal to family groups.

GRADIENTS
Following a gentle initial stretch, a moderate climb with some steeper sections needs to be accomplished to reach the summit of Tully

Mountain. The return descent simply retraces the outward steps.

MAPS, FOOTPATHS AND WAYSIGNS

OS Discovery Series 1:50 000 — Number 37 (Mayo and Galway)

Minor roads and fairly continuous, reasonably well-defined footpaths accompany a substantial part of the route. In a few sections where the paths are less clear, the continuation way is pretty obvious.

The route is not signed but this is no hardship.

GETTING STARTED

Turn off the main N59 road connecting Westport with Clifden at Letterfrack to head northwards. Just over 2 km ($1\frac{1}{4}$ miles) further on, after passing over Dawros Bridge, turn L and the starting-point of the walk is about another 1 km ($\frac{1}{2}$ mile) along the shores of Ballynakill Harbour.

Commence the walk by striding out westwards along the minor road which skirts the northern shore of the harbour.

Summary Description of Walk

THE WAY TO TULLY MOUNTAIN — MR 673612 (Allow 2 hours)

At the start of the walk allow some time to absorb the main features of the picturesque inlet of Ballynakill Harbour and to register the fine views to the SE of some of the high mountains of Connemara, dominated by the pointed peaks of the Twelve Pins. As you walk along the gently rising road, in clear weather you will soon be able to identify your main objective, the arresting, conical summit of Tully Mountain which rises to the NW, over on your R. Attractively located, white-painted cottages dot the lower slopes of the mountain, adding perspective and additional interest to the superb landscapes now rearing up ahead.

An unusual, ancient water hydrant, still apparently in sound working order, is then passed, its yellow paint and the vivid reds of the fuchsia hedging together adding a blaze of contrasting colour to the many shades of green which dominate the surrounding scenery. Keep walking along the coastal fringe by forking L when you reach a road junction ahead and this, for the time being at least, allows you to remain on lower ground.

A tiny breakwater and slipway, named 'Quay' on the OS map, is then passed; a rusting coaster and a number of more attractive small boats still in active use are usually found anchored in these protected waters. The narrow road then gradually rises, winding up the hillside and passing residences on the R. At the far end of these dwellings, turn R up the next track, passing by a disused area of rock extraction on your L. A short distance further on, bear L along a rougher, grassy track to continue uphill beside a wire fence. Go through the metal gate ahead and continue climbing along a wide, recently excavated roadway. (Note: This was undergoing further development when last visited during the summer of 1997.)

The man-made surface soon peters out (but this could change!), and, when it does, continue climbing NW to reach the crest of the ridge ahead which leads towards the summit area of Tully Mountain. The pleasant way up to this ridge is across closely cropped pastures, the dedicated barbers of these being flocks of sheep. The correct continuation way will bring you to a derelict stone building which may be passed on either side. After this, when you reach the brow of the next rise, turn around to feast your eyes on the splendid views of coast and mountains to your rear.

22:1 A woolly sentinel guards the approach to Tully Mountain

Skirt around to the R of a more formidable, rough hillock ahead, crossing over ground which is often soft and boggy in this vicinity. Following this, continue tracking uphill to the NW, making directly for the pointed peak, still some considerable height above you. Keep either along or near to the crest of the rising ridge in order to avoid wetter ground below. The way up is over relatively easy ground and the moderately rising slopes provide gradients which are not too difficult to scale at a reasonable pace. The ground covering here is a mixture of low-growing heathers, grass, sedges and moss.

Further up, a number of connecting narrow paths and tracks become better established, and those leading in your continuing direction of upward travel to the NW may be used with advantage. More impressive views continue to appear as further height is progressively gained, and in particular the magnificent coastal scenery to both the NE and SW provides, in clear weather, an irresistible seduction to activate, almost continuously, the shutter of your camera. Included in the views to the NE is the attractive, elongated shape of Tully Lough, its placid waters gently lapping the myriad of tiny, tree-covered islands which pop up above its surface.

A good and clearly defined path now leads along the apex of the ridge, and further on, when the heather-covered slopes steepen, resort to a series of sweeping zigzags in order to reduce the rate of climb to one which you continue to find comfortable. The upper slopes of the mountain are covered with stones, fragments of rock and the occasional bluff or steep bank, and progress through these will bring you ever closer to the conical peak above. Near to the top, be careful to skirt to the R around a steeper, craggy rock face and then continue scaling the safer, heather-covered slopes to the L just beyond this feature.

The first cairned peak that you reach will turn out to be something of a false horizon, for the highest point of the mountain is located a short distance further on to the NW. In clear weather this will now be in full view and it is a relatively short and easy climb to get there by walking across the intervening shallow depression.

Tully Mountain rises to 356 m (1170 ft) and this high spot is marked by a trigonometrical point positioned on top of a substantial mound of stones. When the visibility is good, the coastal panoramas revealed from this modestly sized but detached summit are simply fantastic. To the S the tremendous, irregular shape of Ballynakill Harbour and the lowlands cupping this provide riveting and prolonged viewing whilst their secrets are gradually absorbed. Looking between W and N out to sea, the craggier extension of the ridges tumbling down from the mountain

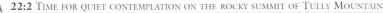

22:2 Time for quiet contemplation on the rocky summit of Tully Mountain

disappear in a series of regressive humps, leading the eyes across the intervening waters towards the island of Inishbofin. To the NE, the sea funnels into the massive indent of the fjord of Killary Harbour with the serrated peaks of the Mweelrea Mountains sweeping up majestically beyond this deep intrusion. Looking inland towards the SE, the pointed peaks of the Twelve Pins pierce the skies forming a fascinating horizon in that direction, whilst to the L of these the high ground spanning the heights of Benchoona and Doughruagh competes for your prolonged attention.

THE WAY BACK TO THE PARKING AREA — MR 694598 (Allow 1 hour)

There is no more agreeable or easier descent than to retrace your outward steps. Therefore, head SE back along the ridge you came up, walking directly towards the 'Quay' below. As previously, paths and tracks come and go during your descent. Similar to the climb up, use those that are aligned with your direction of progress and abandon these when they diverge from this, continuing to head down on a SE diagonal across open ground until you connect with the next section of path going your way!

During the descent you will be continuously looking eastwards towards several of the major mountain groupings in south-western Connemara, and this will give you another opportunity to admire these at leisure, particularly so if the weather was inclement on the way up and the clouds happen to be clearing as you descend. In this event your journey down could take some considerable time!

At the bottom of the slope, walk past the disused quarrying area again, turn L along the minor road and return to the area of human activity at the 'Quay' and the Ocean's Alive Visitor Centre. The Ocean's Alive aquarium and maritime museum is exceptionally interesting and well worth a visit. Toilets, refreshment facilities and a gift shop are located there, and the children in particular may need to be eventually dragged away from these seductive attractions. (The telephone number of this delightful and unusual visitor centre is 095 43473.)

ALTERNATIVE WAYS

ESCAPES

Assuming you are determined to stand on the top of Tully Mountain you can forget about these!

EXTENSIONS

The walk is primarily intended as a short, half-day, undemanding climb to the top of an isolated mountain to admire the splendid panoramic views which may be observed from here, given fine weather. There are alternative, longer descent routes which extend further to the NW along the continuation of the ridge. However, these penetrate significantly more craggy and demanding ground and involve walking down rougher and steeper slopes. Therefore, these extensions are not recommended for casual walkers and family groups, but they may well appeal to more dedicated hillwalkers who have additional time at their disposal.

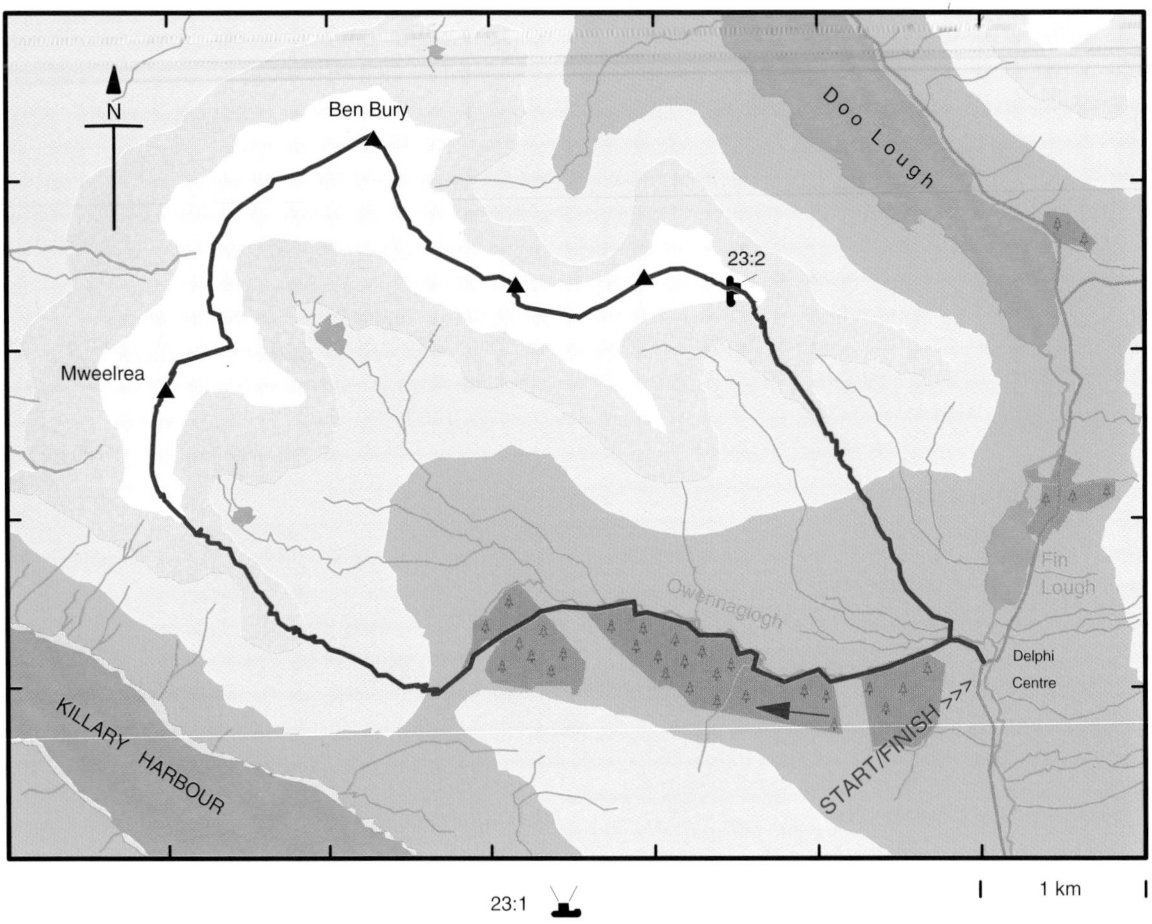
N
Ben Bury
Doo Lough
23:2
Mweelrea
Owennaglogh
Fin Lough
Delphi Centre
KILLARY HARBOUR
START/FINISH >>>
23:1
1 km

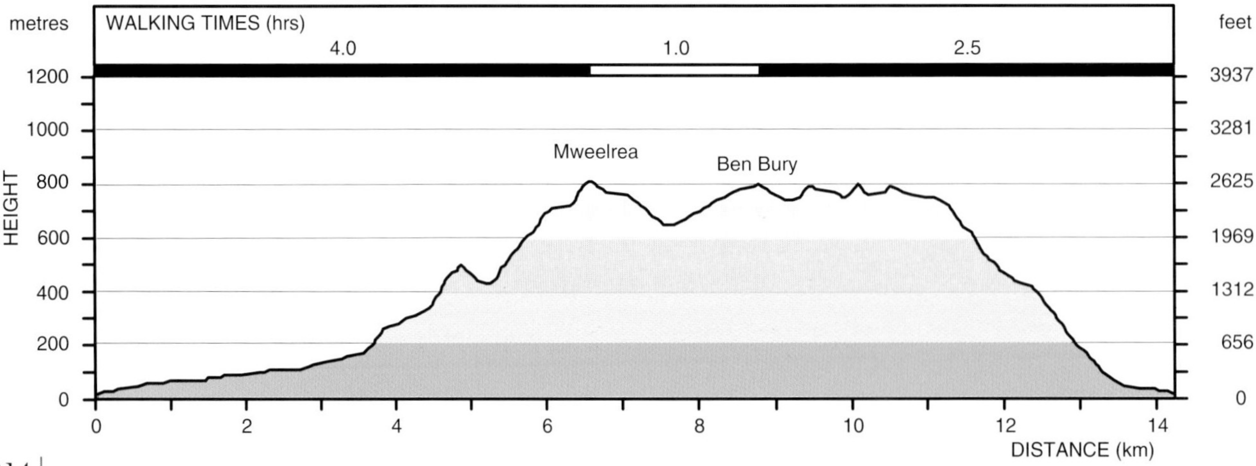
metres
WALKING TIMES (hrs)
4.0
1.0
2.5
feet
1200
1000
800
600
400
200
0
3937
3281
2625
1969
1312
656
0
HEIGHT
Mweelrea
Ben Bury
0
2
4
6
8
10
12
14
DISTANCE (km)

THE MWEELREA HORSESHOE

fact file

START/FINISH

Delphi Outdoor Activities Centre — MR 840652

GRADING

Difficult/strenuous (colour-coded RED)

WALKING TIME ALLOWANCE

7½ hours

DISTANCE

14.2 km (8.8 miles)

TOTAL HEIGHT GAINED

1140 m (3740 ft)

PRINCIPAL HEIGHTS

• Mweelrea	814 m (2670 ft)
• Ben Bury	795 m (2610 ft)
• Peak (not named)	803 m (2635 ft)
• Peak (not named)	760 m (2495 ft)

digest of walk

PARKING

There are extensive parking and other facilities at the splendid Delphi Centre and the owner, Frank Noone, allows independent walkers to park there and to walk across his land providing they keep to recognised paths and use the stiles and bridges provided to cross fences and streams respectively. Please observe these sensible rules.

OVERVIEW/INTEREST

- A magnificent walk amongst wild, wonderful and untamed countryside where the spirits soar.
- Several separate peaks are scaled along a linked, high-level route.
- Great variety of terrain including a sheltered stretch of valley beside a gushing stream, steep, rugged slopes both up and down, and

some adventurous walking along narrow, craggy, connecting ridges.

- Fabulous views all day long, first up to the mountains above and then down into the valleys and towards the coast below.

GRADIENTS

Following a fairly flat approach along a wide valley, there is a sustained climb, with several very steep sections, to gain the main height of the horseshoe. From here, there is a real roller-coaster of a continuation route which climbs up and down several more peaks where more steep slopes have to be negotiated. The prolonged descent is down a ridge which narrows in places and has some steepish sections before levelling off into wider, more gentle slopes.

MAPS, FOOTPATHS AND WAYSIGNS

OS Discovery Series 1:50 000 — Number 37 (Mayo and Galway)

There is a footpath of sorts along the valley which tracks quite close to the stream. Sections of this are often waterlogged and muddy, and several tributary watercourses can be exacting to cross. Much of the higher ground is devoid of clear paths, but there are some sections of faint, intermittent tracks which may be used to advantage as you work your way around and then down the massive horseshoe.

There are no signs to point the way but you will come across a number of strategically positioned cairns which are reassuring navigational aids.

GETTING STARTED

The Delphi Centre lies between Doo Lough to the N and Killary Harbour to the S. It is conveniently located adjacent to the R335 road which connects Louisburgh with the main N59 road at the easterly tip of Killary Harbour.

Leave the Delphi Centre along the path which leads northwards past the abseiling ramp and then beyond a storage area of large Calor gas tanks. Turn immediately L to walk up the brow of the slope ahead along a wide, stony path which changes your direction towards W. Follow this track around to the R, ignoring a branch path off to the L and then another of these a short distance further on.

Summary Description of Walk

THE WAY TO MWEELREA — MR 790668 (Allow 4 hours)

The walk starts amongst superb scenery as the Delphi Centre is surrounded by high, craggy mountains. The Sheeffry Hills rise to the NE, the twin peaks of Ben Creggan and Ben Gorm block any more distant views to the E, the Maumturk Mountains regress to the SSE, the Twelve Pins dominate the landscapes to the SW and the gigantic horseshoe of the Mweelrea Mountains (Sléibhte Chnoc Maol Réidh), your objective for today, lures you towards them in the W.

Continue heading W up the wide valley floor to reach a wooden gate and stile positioned to your L which you use to access and then walk through a plantation of Scots pines. The waters of the Owennaglogh stream tumble down merrily on your R. Avoid crossing this river either over the thoughtfully positioned footbridge which you now pass or indeed at any other place further upstream. Keep to the broad, winding track until you reach a second abseiling ramp and at this point, when the track bends around to the L, abandon it by climbing up the bank ahead near to the stream to locate and use a stile above. This is positioned in a wire fence in surrounds that do become quite boggy.

Continue W across the marshy ground, veering R to keep close to the stream to then progress further up the valley, walking between the watercourse and the boundary fence of an extensive forestry plantation on your L. A narrow path leads on and, when this divides, opt for the higher way nearest to the forest fence. Continue close by the river to walk around several promontories, avoiding wherever you can walking through clinging, high grasses which can become somewhat tedious. Several wet and boggy patches have to be crossed with care, these quite often associated with tributary watercourses which flow across your approach to spill their contents into the main stream still on your R. Fortunately, there is a narrow path along here for most of the way which obviously has been used by other walkers.

About $2\frac{1}{2}$ km ($1\frac{1}{2}$ miles) from the Delphi Centre, the forest fence turns back acutely to the L to form a pointed, V-shaped corner. At this point, continue straight on along a faint path which leads WSW, veering SW, towards the hause ahead which separates the ridge to the S from the higher, craggy spur which rises in a series of steep slopes towards the summit of Mweelrea in the NW. Make directly for the lowest point of this connecting grassy hause, which is located at MR 806649.

23:1 The Mweelrea Horseshoe reveals its secrets in soft autumn twilight

A challenging climb on a NW heading up rough ground along the main ridge now commences. At first, this is over grassy slopes which progressively steepen as you gain further height. Reduce the rate of climb by zigzagging where you need to, working your way up pathless ground which is pierced by rocky outcrops, slabs and boulders. The compensation for your toils are both the superb views beyond Killary Harbour to the S and also the revelations of the greater part of the massive horseshoe circling above on your R.

Quite surprisingly, over an obstructing brow ahead you reach a virtually flat bit of ground, and walking across this will allow your suffering lungs to achieve a temporary recovery! This respite is quickly followed by further formidably steep ground. Again, tight zigzags are called for to lessen the rate of ascent, and further up there is another place where you can have another breather in the form of a shallow hollow. Rocks and boulders abound in this vicinity, making this area wild and wonderful.

A gradual descent follows to reach a rounded, connecting spur of rock which then leads higher along the narrowing ridge. The views along here in fine, clear weather are quite supreme, particularly so those down to the L towards the coast which reveal a pleasing assortment of inlets, sandy beaches and a huge, encircling bay speckled with offshore islands. Then glimpses of tiny Lough Lugaloughan may be registered down on your R, these trapped waters appearing many hundreds of feet below, cupped by mighty cliffs. This is part of a gigantic, gouged-out corrie which is enclosed by near vertical rock faces that plunge down into the dark recesses far below.

23:2 Clearing skies reveal the splendour of Doo Lough during the exhilarating descent above Teevaree Rocks

Another steep upward section follows and commence this climb by heading up the scar of a previous landslip over ground which is now stable. This is followed by another more gradual slope, and then one final steep push will get you on to a narrow but secure ridge. Along here, the edge to your R progressively steepens, and higher up this develops into a precipitous, sheer drop which you need to constantly be mindful of, steering clear of its crumbling, upper lip. The narrowing, rocky spur edges around to the R passing through N, where a section of well-trodden path of compacted earth sensibly maintains a distance of some several feet between its users and the sheer edge to the R.

The rounded, flattish summit area of Mweelrea is eventually reached. This commands a height of 814 m (2670 ft), is the highest point along the horseshoe and accounts for most of the sustained climbing which has to be accomplished in circling around the tops of these fine mountains. The peaty surface of Mweelrea supports two modestly sized cairns. The all-round panoramas from the top of this mountain, given favourable weather, are fantastic but most of these have been progressively revealed on the way up and previously disclosed in this description of the route there.

THE WAY TO BEN BURY — MR 802683 (Allow 1 hour)

Leave the summit area by descending to the N. Be careful in misty conditions to keep along the crest of the falling ridge, walking down a fairly gentle gradient prior to this spur then levelling off. From here, the ridge progressively curves around to the R to head NE and then E, where the ground covering changes from moss and grasses to stonier terrain. Massive, rounded slopes rise ahead as you again change your direction towards N to cross a connecting strip of ground before tackling the next rise along the undulating ridge.

Along here, there are revealing views on the R down towards Lough Bellawaum, with precipitous rock pitches plunging down towards its inky blackness. The continuation route then passes through spasmodic boulder fields and rock debris where an intermittent path leads across these features. Following a gentle drop, the broad shoulder of the spur bends around to the R, rising once more as it does this. Near here, several small pools of stagnant water are passed, these providing a congenial environment for frogs and the like.

Your heading changes to NE, climbing once again, and along a lengthy but gently rising slope the fickle continuation direction subtly changes once more, on this occasion to ENE. An isolated cairn is passed and, following this, head up the still gradually rising slope, changing your bearing more towards E. A second cairn is passed, this positioned in a desolate landscape covered with shattered rock. Then a third cairn is located and this one marks the summit of Ben Bury, alternatively named Oughty Craggy on the OS map; this stands at a height of 795 m (2610 ft).

Proceed with care to the edge on the L of the summit area of Ben Bury to observe the spectacular views in favourable weather down below towards NE. The highlights in these are Glencullin Lough and the larger Doo Lough cradled within precipitous cliffs which rise almost sheer towards your present viewing position.

THE WAY BACK TO THE PARKING AREA — MR 840652 (Allow 2½ hours)

Your continuation way is now to the SE veering E down a gentle, grassy slope which is speckled with stones and rock fragments. Be vigilant to always maintain a safe distance between your descent footsteps and the precipitously steep edge which falls away on your L, to then pass by a distinctively shaped cairn which contains a pointed centre-stone. From this certain point, follow the line of the edge down to the SE. More cairns are passed, marking the potentially dangerous edge, as the ground rises again across a surface covered with more stones, splintered rock fragments and gravel.

Undulations follow as the route tracks close, but not too close, by the steep, crumbling edge on your L where the ground to the R varies between a broad shoulder with rounded, benign slopes and a narrow, rocky ridge which borders on an arête in places. Another insignificant cairn is passed during this section of the way. Eventually, another high spot at 803 m (2635 ft), which is not named on the OS map, is reached. Descend to the SSE from this point, veering E to walk across another slight rise marked by a cairn.

Then head NE to cross an area of fairly flat ground where further marker cairns are positioned. There are more good views down towards Killary Harbour along this stretch. The continuation route bends progressively to the R, passing back through E as it contours along the crest of the ridge. In the vicinity of MR 826674 turn progressively through another 45 degrees to then head SE down a narrow, grassy spur following a well-used section of path. There are magnificent landscapes around and below you as you continue to descend, including the Sheeffry Hills to the NE, Tawnyard Lough to the E, the twin peaks of Ben Creggan and Ben Gorm to the SE and the upper, easterly reaches of Killary Harbour to the SSE.

Some steep, rocky sections will be encountered on the way down, but these are spaced out between easier, grassy areas which may be crossed at speed. Much lower down, bear R along the wider, grassy slopes to head towards the valley below. High grasslands, acres of them, then have to be crossed, where no sooner have you discovered a track leading your way through this tedious obstacle than it heads off in a different direction, leaving you to search for another one!

Strike a diagonal line towards the Delphi Centre to the SE and keep steadfastly to this with as few deviations as possible. Lower down, trim your direction of approach to walk directly towards the footbridge which spans the powerfully flowing Owennaglogh stream below. Cross this thoughtfully positioned bridge and then turn L along the forest road. This leads gently downhill back to your starting-point.

Alternative Ways

ESCAPES

Once committed to the main ridge, safe ways off are few and far between and, therefore, it is advisable to choose a day for this walk when the weather is fine and settled. Early on, if the weather suddenly deteriorates or for any other reason you do not wish to continue, retrace your outward steps back to the hause at MR 806649 and from here you may complete your return over the relatively unchallenging hillside to the ESE, keeping always either along or near to the crest of this lower ridge.

EXTENSIONS

The route described is a fairly demanding one with some steep climbs and lots of ups and downs along a discrete, high-level, horseshoe circuit. Sensible, realistic and safe extensions are not easy to find and none are recommended, as dangerous slopes, difficult ground and fast-flowing streams will often be encountered away from the main route suggested.

Gleninagh and Bencollaghduff (Part of the Twelve Pins)

fact file

START/FINISH
Along the side lane just off the R344 road — MR 819561

GRADING
Difficult/strenuous (colour-coded RED)

WALKING TIME ALLOWANCE
$6\frac{1}{2}$ hours

DISTANCE
10.7 km (6.7 miles)

TOTAL HEIGHT GAINED
880 m (2890 ft)

PRINCIPAL HEIGHTS
- Bencollaghduff 696 m (2285 ft)

digest of walk

PARKING
Park near to the first cottage along the side lane; space for about 10 cars.

OVERVIEW/INTEREST
- Challenging route across magnificent, mountainous terrain.
- Valley, river, steep slopes, boulder fields, loose scree, rocky ledges, craggy pointed summits — the lot!
- Some relatively easy scrambling may be added.
- Fantastic views of wild Connemara spreadeagled around and below you.
- The walk is most suitable for strong, experienced hillwalkers and is best undertaken on a fine, sunny day when there is minimum wind and maximum visibility.

GLENINAGH AND BENCOLLAGHDUFF

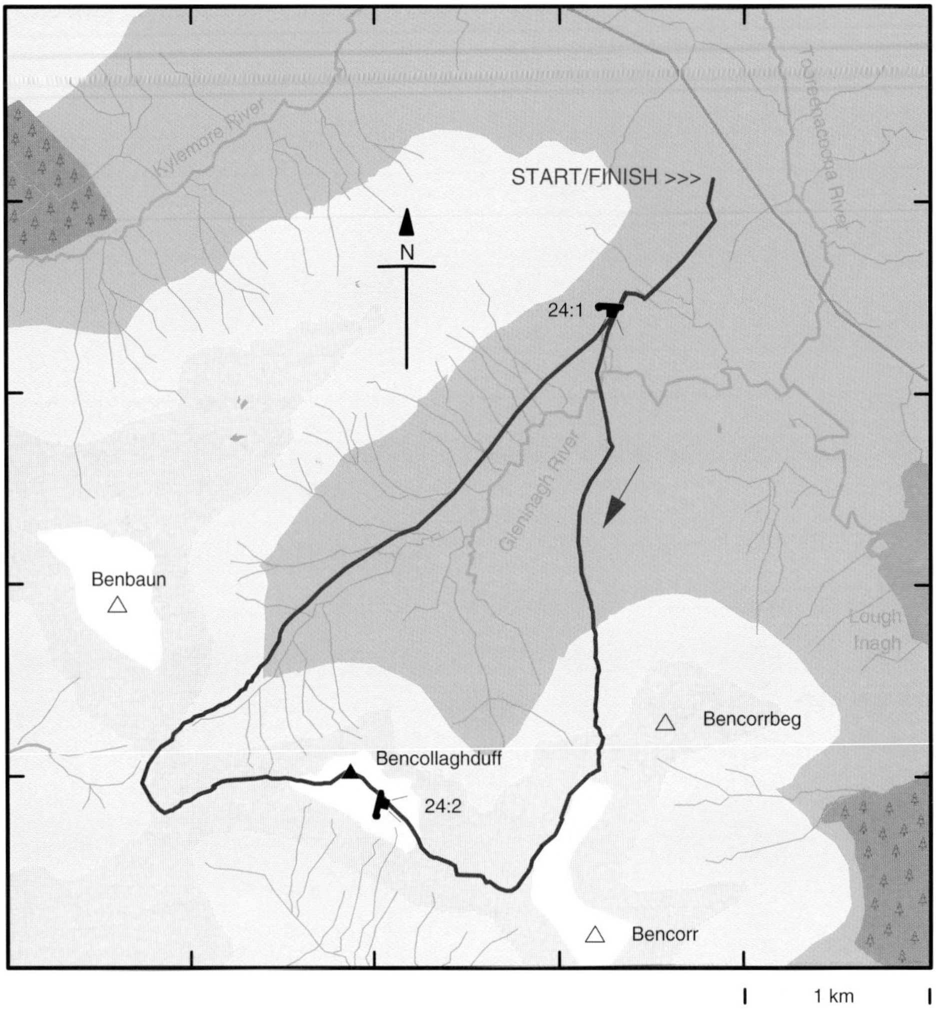

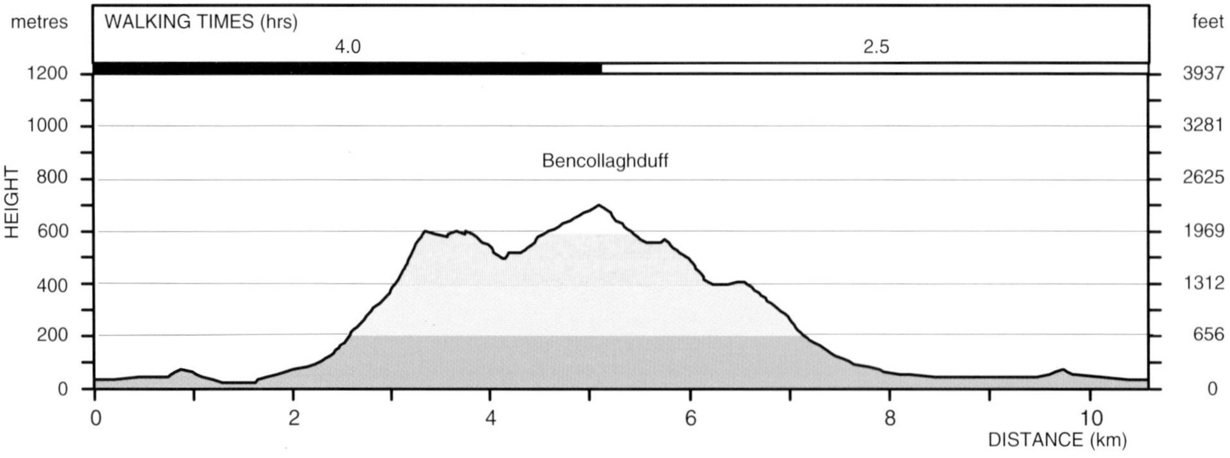

GRADIENTS

The approach along the valley is fairly flat but, following this, a very demanding climb up increasingly steep slopes is necessary to gain the heights of the connecting, high-level ridges above. Further steep ups and downs follow, and the tricky, exceptionally steep descent from the summit of Bencollaghduff demands care and expertise. After this, there is a prolonged descent from the hause below, this NE down the valley along a moderate gradient which levels off lower down.

MAPS, FOOTPATHS AND WAYSIGNS

OS DISCOVERY SERIES 1:50 000 — NUMBER 37 (MAYO AND GALWAY)
THE MOUNTAINS OF CONNEMARA 1:50 000
CONNEMARA BY TIM ROBINSON 1: 63 360
There are few well-defined and continuous footpaths, although the upper parts of the route have obviously been used by many other walkers as part of several routes around different parts of the Twelve Pins. On these sections the way is fairly obvious, but in many other places you will need to rely on your map and compass, together with your navigational skills. There is a narrow but clear descent path leading down NE back into the valley from the hause at MR 788531, but this becomes more obscure lower down.

The route is not signed and cairns are few and far between.

GETTING STARTED

The minor R344 road short circuits the westerly loop of the N59 road which passes through Clifden. It connects the northern section of the major road near to Kylemore Lough with the southern (Clifden to Galway) section near to Recess. The parking spot is about 2 km ($1\frac{1}{4}$ miles) further N of the northern tip of Lough Inagh, a short way down a side lane to the W.

To commence the walk just continue striding along the surfaced, valley road, walking SW up Gleninagh.

SUMMARY DESCRIPTION OF WALK

THE WAY TO BENCOLLAGHDUFF — MR 798530 (Allow 4 hours)

A magnificent, mountain setting surrounds you as you commence the walk. Across the flatness of the wide, glaciated valley to the E, the craggy spurs and peaks of the Maumturk Mountains rear up into the skies above, forming a riveting horizon. To the N, further away, the giant horseshoe, combes and pinnacles of the Mweelrea Mountains do likewise, whilst in your direction of travel the breathtaking, pointed, quartzite peaks of the Twelve Pins confirm that you have nevertheless chosen well for today's exploration. Prominent amongst these towering heights are the summits of Bencorrbeg (Binn an Choire Bhig) to the SSW, and Bencollaghduff (Binn Dhubh) and Benbaun (Binn Bhán) to the SW. These impressive peaks form a mighty cauldron of rock faces, spiky ridges, boulder fields and areas of scree, with massive, rough, grassy slopes sweeping up from the Gleninagh Valley towards these awesome features towering above. The total effect is both electrifying and magnetic, drawing you eagerly into its challenging embraces.

Beyond a metal gate you can see part of Lough Inagh nestling placidly below to the SE. Around the next bend the full splendour of the remote glen and its mountainous setting becomes progressively revealed, and you should allow yourself some time to take it all in and to position exactly those features and peaks which could be helpful later on, should the weather deteriorate. The lane rises slightly to pass by sheep pens and a stable followed by a secluded bungalow. Bear L ahead to avoid passing through an iron gate and then, almost immediately, cross a trickle of a stream. From here, a rougher, stony path threads further up the narrowing valley.

Then veer further L to walk southwards down the grassy slopes leading towards the meandering Gleninagh River below; several tributary watercourses and some often boggy ground have to be negotiated hereabouts. Cross the main river at some convenient point, the gravel bar providing a good place to achieve this. Then head SW towards the high combe rising ahead on your R where more soft, waterlogged, peaty ground will get in your way. This diagonal approach will lead you to a stony path; turn along this to continue heading gently uphill towards the boulder fields and formidable cliff faces rising above.

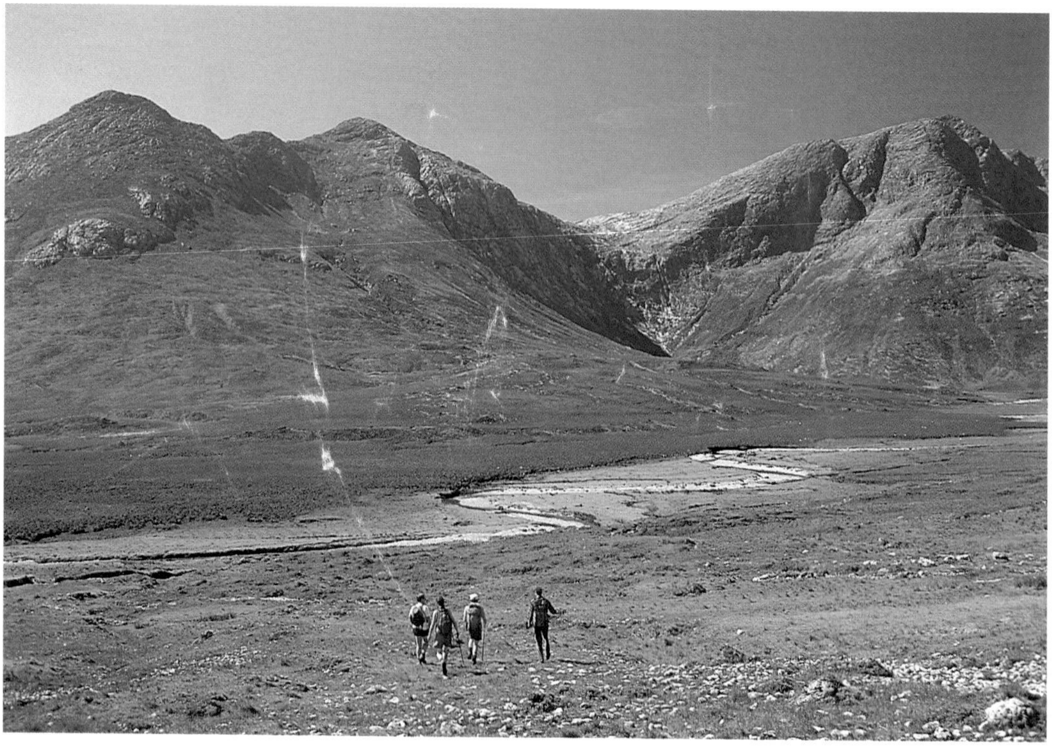

24:1 The approach to the Twelve Pins across the spaciousness of tranquil Gleninagh

The way up tracks along the course of a diminutive stream, and as you gain further height you will be able to identify the rock features of a famous and severe rock climb above on your R; this is Carrot Ridge and the sheer climb is named 'Seventh Heaven'. An isolated, venerable holly tree is then passed, and this will provide a certain landmark as you continue to track up along the western flank of the stream before crossing over a R-hand branch of this, just above a miniature waterfall. After this, the gradient progressively steepens as acres of bracken are crossed and then, higher up, you will encounter the first fragments of surface rock, where you need to watch out for loose stones and unstable debris underfoot.

There is now a section of sustained climbing to the S where you gain further height of several hundred feet. Zigzag up the steeper sections, avoiding areas of loose scree and the worst of the boulder fields wherever you can. Higher up, head towards the R-hand side of the massive, scooped-out basin which in places has the characteristics of a hanging valley. Then keep well to the W of an infant watercourse which seeps down the rock faces, rendering these slimy and slippery. An intermittent, stony path-of-sorts leads up across a rough, loose surface avoiding this hazard but caution is still demanded. Also make full use of the occasional grassy strips in order to avoid as much unstable ground as is possible.

Higher up still, traverse towards the rock wall on the R to connect with a faintly defined, narrow path; then follow this as it zigzags steeply upwards through more stones and loose scree where maintaining and controlling your balance is precarious. Thread your way with considerable care through the fixed rock pitches and over more scree, keeping towards the edge of the cliff faces on your R, and then traverse L again to reach and use another section of narrow path which leads across more scree to the exit gap above.

Fantastic, new and exciting vistas and perspectives open up to greet you in the vicinity of the gap. Craggy, jagged, quartzite peaks rear up in all directions. These include Benbreen and Glengower to the SW, Benbaun to the WNW and, just poking up above the near ridge, the tips of Altnagaighera (Binn Fhraoigh) and Benchoona (Binn Chuanna) far away to the NW. A downhill section follows and this leads to a traverse around the broad, craggy shoulder of Bencorr as you head SW, allowing a faint, stony path to determine your continuation way.

Take care to keep to this path, as in places it becomes less well defined as it leads over areas of rock, and on no account allow yourself to be drawn down to the R as you maintain a diagonal approach to the rocky hause ahead to the SW which separates Bencorr from Bencollaghduff. Keeping a fairly constant height for some distance, traverse below the formidable, rocky pitches rising steeply above on your L. Beyond these, climb up a gully to then traverse around further L still, climbing steadily up the rocky slope. Along here, the mountain plants, St Patrick's Cabbage and bedstraw, have invaded many of the deep crevices, well out of the reach of ravenous sheep.

Eventually, your faint and at times undefined way will connect with a clearer path which leads down from the summit of Bencorr. This important connection is achieved at MR 807524. Turn R along the path and use it to descend over difficult ground, which includes huge rock slabs, to reach the remote hause below. Progress here is to the W along a way that starts off wide and grassy but which lower down deteriorates into rougher terrain that includes the crossing of a rocky mound which you bear R to safely negotiate.

Cross over the peaty gap below, where there are further superb views in clear weather to both N and S. Those to the N should by now be well known, but new revelations appear in the opposite direction, leading your eyes beyond the heights of Benlettery across the southern wild and desolate landscapes of Connemara which are dotted with loughs of all shapes and sizes towards the irregular, distant coastline.

Move down a gear to commence climbing once again, now tackling the steep, rocky slopes leading upwards to the W and using well-worn footsteps to scale the protruding ledges. Fortunately, the steepest bit is soon completed and, following this, a more agreeable incline leads further up across the exposed bedrock. Keep gaining height as the continuation route curves around to the NW to pass a series of interesting quartz and mineral veins which run across the surfaces of the rock slabs. The rate of climb continues to vary as you head towards and then pass by a solitary cairn, maintaining your NW bearing.

Then circle around to the R of a lofty, pointed, side pinnacle to head for a distinctive, square-faced marker stone which appears on the horizon above. From here, the craggy, cairned summit of Bencollaghduff lies but a short distance above you to the NW. This top stands at 696 m (2285 ft) and is the highest point of the walk. More splendid scenery may be observed from here during fine weather. Much of this will by now have been committed to memory, but new observations of the westernmost peaks of the Twelve Pins are revealed.

24:2 The craggy eastern panorama towards the Maumturk Mountains revealed from the shoulder of Bencollaghduff

THE WAY BACK TO THE PARKING AREA — MR 819561 (Allow 2½ hours)

Commence your steep descent along a path which zigzags W across rough, rocky terrain, winding across a rocky band positioned between precariously steep slopes — verging on cliff faces — to either side! Take great care on the subsequent, steep scramble down over rock ledges and pitches, keeping your balance under strict control as you stretch in places for footholds which require some agility and confidence to make. Safely at the bottom of this quite demanding descent (it's easier climbing up!), continue to head westwards along the craggy spur to outflank, to the R, the next formidable, rocky outcrop. Following this, a relatively straightforward section follows as you continue to hug the crest of the descending ridge, traversing across more rough, rocky ground on the way down.

Keep heading westwards, working your way along the connecting spur towards the narrow hause ahead. However, just prior to reaching this col, turn full R to continue descending steeply to the NW, selecting less difficult ground of your own choice and planning your way down with care. Bear R lower down to track above the broad, grassy hause ahead to the NNW, making whatever use you can of an intermittent, stony path. Climb down to the bottom of the hollow, which is located at MR 788531, circling around the boggy areas. In clear weather, there are exceptionally good sightings from here of the twin peaks of Bencullagh (An Chailleach) and Muckanaght to the WNW.

Turn R at the hause and head NE down the grassy slopes into the widening valley below. A short distance lower down, you cross one of several merrily gurgling watercourses that eventually spill their contents into the Gleninagh River far below. As you continue to descend across rough, stony slopes, now tracking ENE, you will reach a pointed mound where you are invited to leave a donation. Pass by this spot yourself to find out more!

Lower down, a narrow, faintly defined path develops, and this becomes clearer as you progress along it. A long traverse follows as you progressively surrender height, descending into the wide, attractive valley below, where the Gleninagh River is continually deepening and widening the meandering V-nick cut into its soft, silted-up bed. The debris of a previous landslip then has to be crossed, after which a marker cairn on the far side is passed.

A grassy promontory then leads towards the valley floor, and progress from here continues across soggier, boggier ground where a number of watercourses cross your direction of approach and the path does its best to leave you to it! Areas of bracken are passed as you track NE, heading towards a small group of conifer trees straight ahead. The remains of a collapsed wall are then reached and, beyond this rubble, a path becomes re-established. Then keep to the higher ground on your L to pass by a dilapidated stone hut and enclosure.

More sheep enclosures, these in current use, are passed by further on, and following this the return route connects with the outward way. Finally, retrace your outward steps back to your parked vehicle.

A few words of warning: insects can be a problem crossing this low, waterlogged ground and you are advised to keep as much of your body as you can covered up along here and to liberally apply insect repellent, for some of the bites which may be sustained can be quite nasty!

Alternative Ways

ESCAPES

Once you are committed to reaching the high ground, there is probably no shorter, easier and safer way down! However, one option in inclement weather is to just walk up the valley to the hause at MR 788531 and then to return the way you came.

EXTENSIONS

In good weather conditions at the height of summer, strong, experienced hillwalkers may make extended use of their strategic position on the high ground. Some may opt to climb to the summit of Bencorr, whilst a longer and harder circuit could involve reaching the top of Benbaun and then descending NE along the rocky ridge which leads past several small pools and then over Knockpasheemore. This suggested addition will also take you to a higher altitude of 729 m (2390 ft).

THE MAUMTURK RIDGE

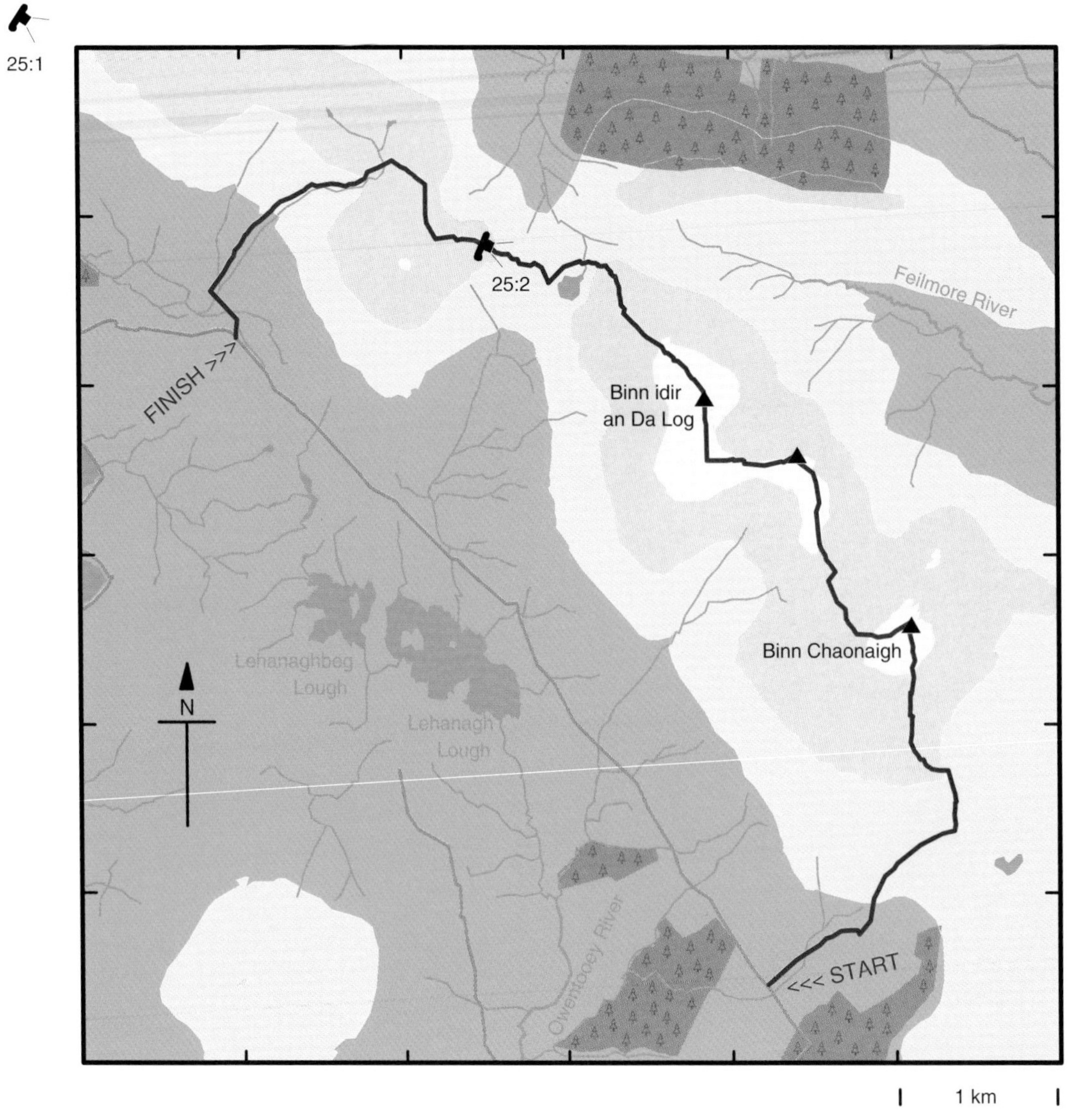

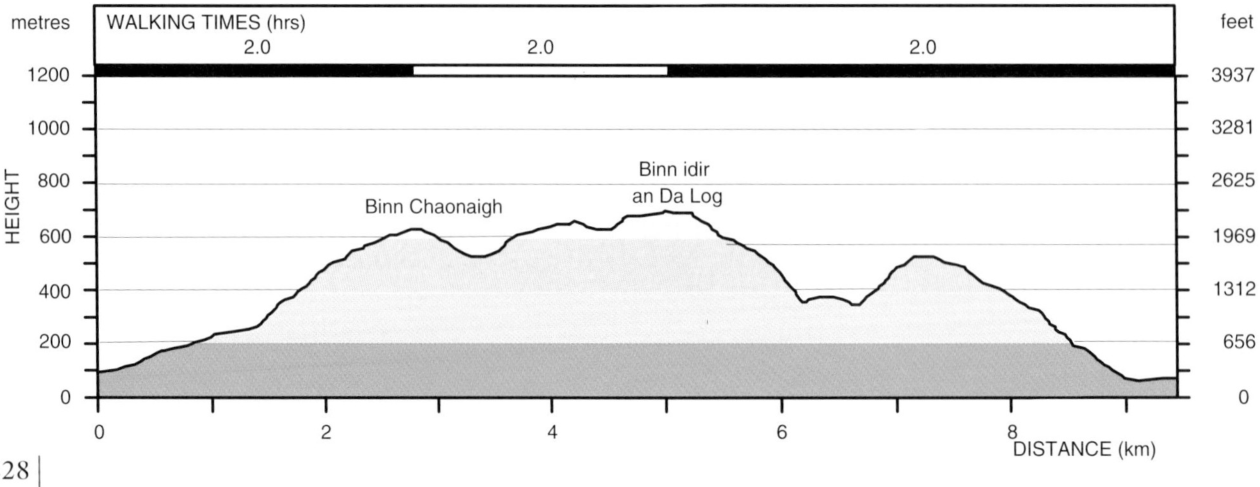

THE MAUMTURK RIDGE

fact file

START/FINISH

Start from the Maumeen turning — MR 892495

Finish further NW along the side road in the vicinity of MR 860533

GRADING

Difficult/strenuous (colour-coded RED)

WALKING TIME ALLOWANCE

6 hours

DISTANCE

9.4 km (5.9 miles)

TOTAL HEIGHT GAINED

940 m (3080 ft)

PRINCIPAL HEIGHTS

- Binn Chaonaigh 633 m (2075 ft)
- Peak (not named) 659 m (2160 ft)
- Binn idir an Da Log 702 m (2305 ft)

digest of walk

PARKING

Parking space for about 15 cars at the start at dedicated parking area. (Note: This is a linear walk and, therefore, ideally two vehicles should be used, the second one positioned beside the road at the finish of the walk.)

OVERVIEW/INTEREST

- The route leads along a wild, wonderful and remote mountain ridge.
- Superb landscapes — both near and far — surround the entire route.
- The trapped waters of two tiny, isolated tarns are visited.
- The sacred place of a Holy Well, St Patrick's Church and the 'Stations of the Cross' is passed *en route*.
- Fascinating rock features and rugged terrain accompany you all the way.

GRADIENTS

The walk starts with a gentle, upward slope to reach the site of the Holy Well. From here, it is continuing steepness for virtually the remainder of the route, alternating up and down. A long, more gradual, final descent will lead you to the finish.

MAPS, FOOTPATHS AND WAYSIGNS

OS DISCOVERY SERIES 1:50 000 — NUMBERS 37 AND 44 (MAYO AND GALWAY)
THE MOUNTAINS OF CONNEMARA 1:50 000
CONNEMARA BY TIM ROBINSON 1:63 360
(The names of the peaks Binn Chaonaigh and Binn idir an Da Log, which are not given on the OS map, have been taken from these additional maps.)

The start is along a wide track which forms part of the Western Way. Above the area of St Patrick's Church, the rest of the route oscillates between a mixture of paths — some of which are clearly defined and some of which are more obscure — and uncharted, rough, rocky ground where there are few indicators to guide you.

There are no signs other than at the start of the walk, but there are some helpfully positioned marker cairns.

GETTING STARTED

Similar to Walk 24, the commencement of this walk is near to the minor R344 road which runs alongside Lough Inagh and which short circuits the western loop of the main N59 road passing through Clifden. The start may be reached either from the N by turning off the R344 at MR 848533 or from the S by turning directly off the N59 at MR 873475. The parking area is located along the side road at the turning to Maumeen, signed 'Tobhair Agus Leaba Pádraic'.

Set off along the broad track which rises towards ENE and which forms part of the Western Way.

SUMMARY DESCRIPTION OF WALK

THE WAY TO BINN CHAONAIGH — MR 900515 (Allow 2 hours)

The walk commences in a wild, remote setting with vast landscapes stretching towards the encircling mountain peaks. The Twelve Pins rise majestically to the WNW, their pearly white domes of quartzite soaring up into the skies above, whilst in the segment between N and E the summits of the Maumturk Mountains (Sléibhte Mhám Toirc), your venue for today, regress in a series of challenging, pointed peaks.

A wide, grassy cart-track rises gently up the slopes ahead as you walk NE towards a gap. The way rises to pass through Maumeen gate where a ladder stile is provided on the R. Continue up rising ground as the surface underfoot becomes rougher through boulders and loose stones infiltrating the grassy way. The track, a former pilgrim's path, snakes further upwards between the high mountain peaks.

The way passes by the Holy Well which is marked on the OS map and hereabouts the 'Stations of the Cross' are located. There are 14 of these, but you will have to divert slightly to inspect them all and you will also need to comprehend the Gaelic language to understand the

25:1 THE NORTH-WEST PASSAGE TOWARDS THE MAUMTURK MOUNTAINS TRAVELLED AT EVENTIDE

narration which is disclosed on the plaques. Climb up the stony, side path to reach the tiny, pointed St Patrick's Church above and to inspect the sombre statue, complete with carved lambs, of the saint contemplating. This is one of the many spots where the immortalised St Patrick is believed to have rested, and his bed is ascribed to a tiny, uncomfortable-looking, rock cavity. The whole site was thoughtfully restored in 1980.

From this sacred spot, head N up the steep, uncharted, rugged mountainside. Bear around to the L following a grassy bank and then use the rocky band which leads upwards to the R of an area of loose scree. Zigzag up the very steep slopes, circling around any particularly difficult rocky ledges or pitches. The steepness of the slopes moderates higher up as heathers cushion your forward footsteps.

Higher up still, circle around to the R to follow the line of a wire fence, thus avoiding more difficult, rocky ground to the L. From this elevated position there are fantastic views in good weather to your rear, these raking down to the indented and island-infested coastline, sections of which are visible between S and SW, many hundreds of feet below you and several miles away. Continue climbing steadily to the NNW, avoiding, by circling around to the L, the more formidable rock slabs which block any more direct ascent ahead.

Still follow the course of the fence, by bearing L, to cross an area of wet, soggy ground before turning full R in accord with the fence to climb up a steeper, grassy incline. At about the 550 m (1800 ft) mark, the upward slope levels off to a gentle gradient. Then, just past a tiny bog pool, a craggy pinnacle provides a grand viewing platform for observing the rugged peaks of the Twelve Pins, way beyond Lough Inagh.

Continue climbing NNE towards the craggy, higher slopes above, treading up a moderate, grassy gradient to approach these. Some — not too exacting — peat hags now have to be crossed and another small bog pool is left behind. Reassuring marker cairns then begin to appear, both directly ahead and to the L of your present position, as you cross an area of almost flat, exposed rock which is littered with a jumble of stones and boulders of all shapes and sizes. This leads to the oasis of a banana-shaped lake, positioned on the OS map at MR 901515.

The lake is relatively well sheltered from the wind and it is, therefore, an ideal spot for refreshments. From here, set off again across the rough terrain, heading NW to reach the summit area, but a short distance higher up, of Binn Chaonaigh. This peak commands a height of 633 m (2075 ft), and from its summit, apart from sightings already mentioned, there are further revealing views to the NW along the undulating, continuation ridge towards the pointed peak of Binn idir an Da Log, the highest point of the route. Also exposed are several significant ups and downs in between, which you will need to traverse to get there.

25:2 Up amongst the crags and tarns of the challenging Maumturk Ridge

THE WAY TO BINN IDIR AN DA LOG — MR 888528 (Allow 2 hours)

Drop down from the summit of Binn Chaonaigh, tracking to your L across loose scree and following an indistinct, stony path. Initially your continuation way is westwards but it then veers progressively more northwards to descend to a broad hause below. On the way down, there are fantastic views to your R of a hanging valley below to the NNE and of the expansive mountain slopes sweeping down into and cradling this.

Another steepish climb follows as you continue to track northwards towards the next peak along the ridge which is unnamed; this is at MR 894526 at a height of 659 m (2160 ft). The path towards this mountain leads up initially along the L-hand side of the connecting spur, and height previously surrendered is quickly recaptured as you climb up these rocky slopes. In this section of the walk between Binn Chaonaigh and Binn idir an Da Log, there are undulations in the terrain which, because of the short distances involved, are not recorded in the contours of the OS map.

More cairns mark the correct continuation route which traverses W before swinging around to the R towards N, and the undulating way forward traverses a modest dip down to cross a peat-covered dell. From here, the route climbs again along a narrow path which deviates to the L to by-pass a difficult, rocky protrusion. This traverse continues for some distance just below and to the W of the crest of the ridge as you continue to head NNW. Rock slabs have to be crossed further on but there are plenty of good footholds, as the route still undulates upwards.

The crest of the ridge is regained, and this leads to the next section of climb along a narrow, rocky ridge which will bring you to another pointed peak which is also unnamed. There are steep fall-aways on both sides now, and further on a narrow cleft to your L is the best way forward to outflank higher ground that you do not need to walk across. This is followed by a short traverse and upward zigzag to your R to regain the apex of the spur, where a line of cairns confirms the correct continuation way. This leads further N. A clear path then crosses another shallow depression before it is upwards once again, and a final steep ascent through rocks will bring you to the summit of Binn idir an Da Log, at a height of 702 m (2305 ft).

More fine panoramas are visible from here in good weather but most of the major sightings in these have previously been positioned. However, there are more revealing and detailed views along the continuation spur but sightings of some of the fascinating ups and downs are, for the time being, baulked by the rounded contours of the much nearer, massive shoulder of the mountain.

THE WAY TO THE FINISH AT THE MINOR ROAD — MR 860533 (Allow 2 hours)

A rugged, lengthy descent, initially northwards but then bending NW, leads eventually to the next trapped corrie lake, located at MR 881537. This section only contains one slight upward undulation, as a clearly defined, stony path guides you down. The path curves to the L-hand side of the craggy, connecting ridge, thus avoiding the crossing of slopes containing areas of loose scree. Part way down, glimpses of the lake reveal its splendid setting, cupped in a rock basin far below.

As you walk across the shoulder of the mountain, you need to be extremely careful to locate and use the correct continuing descent route. This commences to the R and avoids dangerous cliffs directly below your approach position. The start of this descent is marked by a small cairn which is strategically positioned on a rock. A very steep, zigzag drop follows and you need to pace yourself going down, for it is a long, tiring descent before the cool waters of the lake are eventually reached. Be very careful on these extremely steep slopes, as they are covered with loose stones and shattered rock debris which render the ground unstable and difficult to cross.

When you reach the corrie lake you will need to circle around the northern edge of the water and climb over a fence. Then it is up again, now heading W, at first over gently rising, heather-covered slopes and then more steeply into familiar, rocky terrain. Another fence has to be crossed above the lake, and following this allow a stony path to lead you to the next connecting spur. You bear R along this to continue climbing to the NW. Towards the top of the grassy brow ahead, lingeringly look back to register the formidable, steep slopes which you have previously come down! After this, follow the line of a fence down to the hause below to cross over a peat hag at the bottom.

Bear L from here to reach another rocky band which leads upwards, and then veer R and then L to zigzag along a faint path which climbs up an obvious ascent route. This is followed by completing a fairly exposed traverse along a narrow ridge before you turn R to cross easier ground in the form of a flatter ledge. Beyond these features, the climb continues up moderately angled slopes with the aid of an intermittent, stony path. Keep on going up, making further progress to the WNW.

The next formidable summit area is avoided by tracking around to the R, and this will lead you directly to another connecting spur, again a band of rock. A narrow, stony path is used to achieve this easy traverse around the side of the mountain, near to its top, where relatively easy, grassy, side slopes are crossed. These lead to the top of the final steep descent, which commences around MR 871543.

From the top of the ridge, plan your exit way down with some care and choose a safe line of descent, climbing down initially on a NW bearing but then progressively veering L towards W and tracking through stones and stunted heathers. Lower down, make use of a grassy channel which provides both an acceptable rate of descent and more secure footholds. The way leads down to a soggy shelf, and beyond this a miniature waterfall is passed as tiny rivulets begin to form. A wide bowl then opens out below and you track down into this, following the course of the descending watercourse to reach another section of path.

The defined way leads W down into the valley where there is one final steepish slope to negotiate. The continuation route then bears SW to pass through an area of bracken where easier slopes are reached. Trim your final direction of approach to head directly towards the place where you have parked your vehicle or arranged to be collected. This should now be in sight.

Alternative Ways

ESCAPES

Some casual walkers and family groups may be content just to walk to and have a good look around the St Patrick's attractions. Others may wish to climb as far as the first small lake before turning back. However, once you are committed to the main ridge, alternative, safe descent routes are not easy to locate, and you are advised either to continue as described previously or, if you have not reached a point of no return, to turn about and carefully retrace your outward steps.

EXTENSIONS

The obvious extension for strong, fit hillwalkers is to continue along the ridge climbing over Letterbreckaun before descending to the WNW to connect with the Western Way and then use this to walk back along the lower ground, tracking SE to where you have positioned your vehicle or arranged to be collected.

Getting Started and Suggested Itineraries

A lifetime of pleasure could be spent joyously exploring and keeping fit amongst the mountains of Ireland. Those fortunate enough to live amongst the forty shades of green may do just this, allocating a combination of single days, long weekends, part of their annual holidays and eventually some of their retirement time pursuing the healthy, immensely enjoyable and satisfying leisure activity of walking amongst some of the best scenery to be found anywhere in the world.

Dubliners have the expansive Wicklow Mountains sweeping down to their back gardens, and walkers from the city are beginning in increasing numbers to discover the delights of venturing further afield into, for example, the Nire Valley which they are using as a base camp for exploring on foot the Comeragh, Knockmealdown and Galty Mountains rising all around. This delightful area is also within comfortable daily reach of those who live in Waterford and Cork.

The citizens of Cork are particularly well placed because the magnificent, outlying peninsulas of SW Ireland are also within a full day's round trip, with a serious walking interlude separating the road journeys there and back. In fact, we had the pleasure of meeting three high-spirited young ladies from Cork on one occasion near to the summit of Hungry Hill in Beara who were using a precious bank holiday to do just this; having motored over from Cork during the early morning, and after exploring the heights above, they were intent on contributing significantly to the night-life of the city that very evening!

From the Limerick area, keen walkers can head either SW to climb the dizzy heights of the Dingle and Iveragh Peninsulas or NW to clamber over the limestone terracing and pavements of the Burren. The people of Galway may choose to share the Burren with those from Limerick, or alternatively may venture NW into the wild, challenging magnificence of Connemara.

Visitors from abroad intent on discovering the delights of Ireland's mountains will obviously have to reach that country first. Many of these visitors with hillwalking uppermost in their minds, and also more general tourists who enjoy anything from a moderate walk to stretching their legs on an occasional, casual stroll, will start their holiday by disembarking onto Irish soil in the Dublin area, ferry passengers either at Dublin or Dún Laoghaire Ports and those flying to Ireland at Dublin International Airport. Others from abroad will either sail into Rosslare or Cork or fly into Shannon or Cork, before eagerly pulling their walking boots on.

The 25 walks included in this guidebook commence in the Wicklow Mountains, which lie just to the S of Dublin city, and they then tour the other six regions covered in a clockwise direction finishing up in Co Mayo. This presentation presumes that most walkers, both Irish and those from overseas, will venture forth from the Dublin area. However, some people will wish to tour anti-clockwise or will select some alternative variant between these, and, of course, the mountainous circuit may be entered at any point and may be completed or partly completed

An attentive audience listening to words of wisdom from a ranger at Glendalough, Co Wicklow

travelling in a direction of choice — of which there are many. Thus those arriving at Cork may decide to first explore the Nire Valley area or make directly for the Beara Peninsula, whilst walkers from America who descend from a great height into Shannon may elect to head NW for the Burren and Connemara or alternatively may travel SW into Dingle and the other mountainous peninsulas.

I happen to live partly in Cheshire and partly in the Lake District of NW England, and the many trips which I have made to the Emerald Isle whilst researching this book and for other purposes have all involved crossing the Irish Sea by car ferry in order that I could maintain maximum mobility in my own vehicle whilst there. The frequent ferries plying between Holyhead in North Wales and either Dublin or Dún Laoghaire have proved to be particularly convenient for this purpose, and both Irish Ferries and Stena Line have been used. The *Isle of Inishmore*, the big ship now operated on this route by Irish Ferries, takes about $3\frac{1}{2}$ hours for the crossing to Dublin, and its spacious accommodation will give you a real taste of Ireland together with a close encounter with the warm, friendly hospitality which you will later discover appears almost obligatory in this delightful country. The Stena Line HSS skims across the water to Dún Laoghaire in an incredible $1\frac{1}{2}$ hours or just over, and in this enclosed capsule of modern, high-performance technology, you might just about have time to consume a delicious meal, choose your 'duty free' and then dash back to your vehicle for an impressively fast disembarkation onto Irish soil. I have also used the overnight Swansea to Cork route which is operated by a company trading under that very name. This crossing may appeal most to those living in the S and SW of

Britain and also to those island hopping from Continental Europe. If you are making initially for the mountains of SW Ireland it does cut down significantly the amount of motoring along Irish roads. An enjoyable evening meal followed by a good night's rest, weather permitting, are also reliable hallmarks of this crossing from Swansea.

All three ferry crossings are highly commended: the choice is yours, and you should not be disappointed with whichever selection suits your particular needs best. Contact addresses and/or the telephone reservation numbers of these three ferry operators are listed below.

Irish Ferries

IRELAND
2–4 Merrion Row
Dublin 2
Tel Res: 01 661 0511

9 St Patrick's Bridge
Cork
Tel: 021 551995

UNITED KINGDOM
Reliance House
Water Street
Liverpool L2 8TP
Tel Res: 0990 171717

Stena Line

IRELAND
15 Westmorland Street
Dublin 2
Tel Res: 01 204 7777
Call 24 hrs, 7 days a week

Tourist Office
Grand Parade
Cork
Tel: 021 272965

Tourist Office
Arthur's Quay
Limerick
Tel: 061 316259

UNITED KINGDOM
Tel Res: 0990 707070 (travel only)
0990 747474 (inclusive package holidays)
Call 24 hrs, 7 days a week

Swansea Cork Ferries

IRELAND
52 South Mall
Cork
Tel Res: 021 271166

UNITED KINGDOM
Tel Res: 01792 456116

It is confidently assumed that keen walkers living in Ireland will, over the years, complete all 25 walking routes described in this guide, and many more besides, in a sequence and at timings convenient to themselves. At the other extreme, walkers and more general tourists from abroad who are planning their first walking holiday in Ireland, or who have a visit with walking interludes in mind, and who have, say, a couple of weeks available to do this, may decide to explore only two or three of the mountain areas covered in this guidebook in some depth, leaving the delights of venturing into the other regions for some future visits. In this event, to combine a visit to either the eastern or south-eastern region with a trip to one of the contrasting western or south-western areas may prove to be an inspired selection. However, there will be those visitors who even on their first walking trip to Ireland will be keen to sample all of the seven mountain areas covered by the 25 walks — and, I might add, why not?

To meet this latter presumption, two suggested itineraries are listed below for attempting to do just this. The first of these has been compiled with dedicated and energetic hillwalkers in mind who, it is believed, might wish to stand on the top of the several summits above 3000 ft which are described in the book and who, in any event, will probably want to spend as many daylight hours as possible with their boots laced up in active mode. At the other extreme, the second itinerary is targeted at more casual walkers and family groups as well as more general tourists who enjoy walking on lower ground and who may wish to combine this activity with travelling around, sightseeing and even lazing about on the beach. Both of these itineraries cover a two-week visit; it is presumed that 16 days may be squeezed out of this period, that the tour starts from the Dublin area and that the circuit will be followed in a clockwise direction.

EVEN EXPERT GUIDES CONSULT MAPS TO VERIFY THEIR EXACT POSITION AND TO CONFIRM THEIR NEXT INTENDED STEPS, CO GALWAY

Suggested Itineraries

Day	For Dedicated and Energetic Hillwalkers	For Casual Walkers, Family Groups and More General Tourists
1	Arrive in the Dublin area. Motor into the Wicklow Mountains to first overnight destination.	Arrive in the Dublin area. Motor into the Wicklow Mountains to first overnight destination.
2	Complete Walk 2, from Wicklow Gap over Lugnaquillia (above 3000 ft) to Fenton's.	Spend morning around Glendalough, visiting the tourist attractions and undertaking a short walk from the Upper Lake to the waterfalls etc. Visit Lough Dan in the afternoon, using part of Walk 3 to get there and back.
3	Get up early and visit Glendalough. Spend rest of morning and early afternoon travelling to the Nire Valley by the fast route. Explore immediate locality on foot during the evening.	Spend the entire day motoring via the scenic route to the Nire Valley. *En route* visit Avondale Forest Park and stop at the 'Meeting of the Waters'. Indulge in a picnic lunch by the banks of the River Barrow near Graiguenamanagh.
4	Complete Walk 8 in the Comeragh Mountains.	Pass the morning looking around the historic town of Clonmel or have a round of golf on the attractive Clonmel course. Explore immediate locality on foot during the afternoon or evening.
5	Complete Walk 5 to the summit of Galtymore (above 3000 ft).	Motor through the Knockmealdown Mountains, visiting Mount Melleray Abbey if this appeals to you. From the nearby visitor car park, complete the very short 'there-and-back' stroll to Bay Lough. Visit Bay Lough. Irish Farmhouse Cheese on the way back.
6	Motor directly to the Beara Peninsula and travel across Healy Pass part way along the peninsula, stopping to exercise your legs near to the top. Acclimatise yourselves with this fine, craggy countryside and get a feel for the walking possibilities there.	Motor across to Bantry and then on to the Beara Peninsula, adding some scenic loops in to the journey there. It is feasible to include a visit to the Blarney Stone *en route*, with time to kiss it if you are so inclined!
7	Complete Walk 9 to the top of Hungry Hill.	Either sail across to Bear Island and complete Walk 11 or spend the day on the fine beach at Allihies where you can stretch your legs walking along the indented shoreline.
8	Travel into the Iveragh Peninsula and if time permits have a walk into/through the Gap of Dunloe.	Spend the entire day travelling via the Killarney National Park into the Iveragh Peninsula, stopping at a selection of the numerous visitor attractions *en route* such as Moll's Gap, Ladies View, Torc Waterfall, Muckross House and Gardens, and Ross Castle.
9	Stand on the top of Carrauntoohil, at 3410 ft the highest point in all Ireland. Use either Walk 13 or Walk 14 to get there.	Motor around the 'Ring of Kerry', spending some time on the beach and completing a short walk in the vicinity.
10	Complete Walk 15, the Coomasaharn Lake Horseshoe, or have a lazy day should you feel in need of this!	Visit Kate Kearney's Cottage and venture into the Gap of Dunloe either on foot or on the back of a pony. Combine this with a visit to Killarney and either have a leisurely walk along one of the trails in the National Park or take a boat trip on Lough Leane.

Day	For Dedicated and Energetic Hillwalkers	For Casual Walkers, Family Groups and More General Tourists
11	Travel the relatively short distance into the Dingle Peninsula and complete Walk 19 around Inch Point.	Travel the relatively short distance into the Dingle Peninsula and complete Walk 19 around Inch Point.
12	Climb Brandon Mountain (above 3000 ft), following the directions of Walk 16.	Motor around Slea Head, stretching your legs and lungs on the fine, sandy beaches of Ventry and Smerwick Harbours.
13	Get up very early and motor northwards into Connemara via the Burren and Galway, using the Tarbert Ferry to get there. Visit the Cliffs of Moher *en route* and if time permits complete Walk 21, a short climb to the top of Abbey Hill	Get up very early and motor northwards into Connemara via the Burren and Galway, using the Tarbert Ferry to get there. Visit the Cliffs of Moher *en route* and spend some time in Galway City.
14	Select any one of Walks 23, 24 or 25 and extend this as suggested, providing you feel sufficiently energetic.	Complete Walk 22 to the top of Tully Mountain and combine this with a visit to Ocean's Alive Visitor Centre, an aquarium and maritime museum which the children will love.
15	Motor into Co Mayo to stand on the summit of holy Croagh Patrick.*	Motor into Co Mayo and if you can summon up the energy undertake the pilgrimage, as far as you feel you want to, towards the summit of holy Croagh Patrick.*
16	An early start for the journey via Mullingar, which is well worth stopping at, back to the Dublin area.	An early start for the journey via Mullingar, which is well worth stopping at, back to the Dublin area.
17	Back home, arrange next walking holiday in Ireland	

Obviously, bad weather, for it does occasionally rain in Ireland, could influence just how you adopt these suggested itineraries to best suit your own particular needs and preferences. Also, you may decide to have one or more 'rest' days to recharge your batteries somewhere towards the middle of your walking tour. In these situations you will need to either decide just what to miss out or perform some pretty nifty juggling to fit it all in, perhaps even resorting to the aid of a powerful torch to do just this!

Visitors to these shores may also decide to pick and choose from both itineraries, selecting a walking and touring programme somewhere between these two extremes of energy burn-rate!

However, in all cases the overriding objective is to enjoy your walking holiday to the full, to undertake just that 'right' amount of physical activity which suits you best, to visit the interesting places and see the attractions that you want to and at the end of your holiday to feel that, if you live in Ireland, you really want another walking holiday there and, if you are a visitor from abroad, you really want to return to Ireland again for more of the same, this with pristine-clean walking boots placed as a definite priority on your check-list of really essential items to bring back with you.

*This route is not described in this book, but start from Murrisk (MR 919823) and just follow the obvious, wide path worn away by the 'multitudes on the mount' before you.

Summary of Walking Routes

This table provides a concise statistical summary of the 25 walking routes listed in numerical sequence.

Walk No	Name of Walk	Grading: Easy/straight-forward	Grading: Moderate	Grading: Difficult/ strenuous	Walking Time (hours)	Walking Distance (km)	Walking Distance (miles)	Total Height Gained (metres)	Total Height Gained (feet)	Highest Point (metres)	Highest Point (feet)
1	Traverse of the Wicklow Mountains Part 1: Sally Gap to Wicklow Gap			*	8	16.8	10.5	860	2820	849	2785
2	Traverse of the Wicklow Mountains Part 2: Wicklow Gap to Fenton's			*	9	21.8	13.5	750	2460	925	3035
3	Lough Dan and Knocknacloghoge	*	*		5	9.8	6.1	540	1770	534	1750
4	Glendalough, Mullacor and Derrybawn Mountain		*		6	11.6	7.2	560	1840	657	2155
5	Galtymore Mountain			*	8 ½	15.0	9.4	930	3050	919	3015
6	Knockmealdown Ridge		*	*	5 ½	9.6	6.0	720	2360	794	2605
7	Knockanaffrin Ridge		*		5	8.4	5.2	400	1310	755	2475
8	The Gap, Crotty's Rock and Faus Coum			*	7	13.2	8.2	730	2400	792	2600
9	Hungry Hill		*	*	5 ½	9.5	5.9	660	2160	685	2245
10	Knockoura and Knockgour		*		6	11.6	7.2	530	1740	490	1610
11	Bear Island	*			4	9.1	5.6	300	980	258	845
12	Purple Mountain and Tomies Mountain			*	7 ½	14.8	9.2	930	3050	832	2730
13	Carrauntoohil via Devil's Ladder (Tourists' Route)			*	6 ½	10.9	6.8	870	2850	1039	3410
14	Carrauntoohil and Caher			*	7	11.6	7.2	1000	3280	1039	3410
15	Coomasaham Lake Horseshoe			*	7	10.0	6.2	670	2200	772	2535
16	Brandon Mountain from Faha			*	6 ½	10.1	6.3	950	3110	952	3125
17	An Chapán Mór, Croaghskearda and Slievanea		*		5	9.9	6.2	370	1210	670	2200
18	Lough An Scaul and Beenoskee		*		6	11.6	7.2	750	2460	826	2710
19	Inch Strand and Point	*			4	12.2	7.6	20	70	10	35
20	Black Head and Gleninagh Mountain	*	*		6	14.0	8.7	350	1150	317	1040
21	Abbey Hill	*			2 ½	3.9	2.4	160	520	240	785
22	Tully Mountain	*			3	4.9	3.0	360	1180	356	1170
23	The Mweelrea Horseshoe			*	7 ½	14.2	8.8	1140	3740	814	2670
24	Gleninagh and Bencollaghduff (Part of the Twelve Pins)			*	6 ½	10.7	6.7	880	2890	696	2285
25	The Maumturk Ridge			*	6	9.4	5.9	940	3080	702	2305
	Total					**284.6**	**177.0**	**16370**	**53680**		

Useful Addresses

Contact addresses and telephone and fax numbers for selected walking guides, accommodation and ferry operators are listed in the appropriate sections of the book. The following additional contact information may prove useful to walkers either before they go to Ireland or whilst there.

The Automobile Association
23 Rock Hill
Blackrock
Co Dublin
Tel: 01 283 3555
Fax: 01 283 3660

Bus Éireann (Irish Bus)
Broadstone
Dublin 7
Tel: 01 830 2222
Fax: 01 830 9377

Iarnród Éireann (Irish Rail)
Connolly Station
Dublin 1
Tel: 01 836 3333
Fax: 01 836 4760

Independent Holiday Hostels
57 Lower Gardiner Street
Dublin 1
Tel: 01 836 4700
Fax: 01 836 4710

Irish Farm Holidays Association
Head Office
2 Michael Street
Limerick
Tel: 061 400700/400707
Fax: 061 400771

Irish Hotels Federation
13 Northbrook Road
Dublin 6
Tel: 01 497 6459
Fax: 01 497 4613

Mountaineering Council of Ireland
c/o Association for Adventure Sports
House of Sport
Long Mile Road
Dublin 12
Tel: 01 450 9845
Fax: 01 450 2805

National Parks and Wildlife Service
Department of Arts, Heritage, Gaeltacht and the Islands
'Dún Aimhirgin'
43–49 Mespil Road
Dublin 4
Tel: 01 667 0788
Fax: 01 667 0827

An Óige (Irish Youth Hostel Association)
61 Mountjoy Street
Dublin 1
Tel: 01 830 4555
Fax: 01 830 5808

Ordnance Survey
Phoenix Park
Dublin 8
Tel: 01 820 6100
Fax: 01 820 4156

Town and Country Homes Association
Head Office
Donegal Road
Ballyshannon
Co Donegal
Tel: 072 51377
Fax: 072 51207

Wicklow Mountains National Park
Glendalough
Co Wicklow
Tel: 0404 45338
Fax: 0404 45306

TOURIST BOARD, A SELECTION OF OFFICES ABROAD AND REGIONAL TOURISM ORGANISATIONS

Bord Fáilte (Irish Tourist Board)
Baggot Street Bridge
Dublin 2
Tel: 01 602 4000
Fax: 01 602 4100

Irish Tourist Board
150 New Bond Street
London
England
Tel: 0171 518 0800
Fax: 0171 493 9065
(Travel enquiries Tel: 0171 493 3201)

Irish Tourist Board
Irische Fremdenverkehrszentrale
Untermainlage 7
W 6000 Frankfurt Main 1
Germany
Tel: 069 23 64 92
Fax: 069 23 46 26

Irish Tourist Board
Leidestraat 32
1017 PB Amsterdam
Holland
Tel: 020 6 22 31 01
Fax: 020 6 20 80 89

Irish Tourist Board
757 Third Avenue
New York NY 10017
USA
Tel: 212 418 0800
Fax: 212 371 9052

Irish Tourist Board
5th Level
36 Carrington Street
Sydney NSW 2000
Australia
Tel: 02 299 6177
Fax: 02 299 6323

Cork/Kerry Tourism
Tourist House
Grand Parade
Cork
Tel: 021 273251
Fax: 021 273504

Dublin Tourism
Dublin Tourism Centre
Suffolk Street
Dublin 2
Tel: 01 605 7700
Fax: 01 605 7757

Ireland West Tourism
Áras Fáilte
Eyre Square
Galway
Tel: 091 563081
Fax: 091 565201

Midlands-East Tourism
Dublin Road
Mullingar
Co Westmeath
Tel: 044 48761
Fax: 044 40413

North West Tourism
Áras Reddan
Temple Street
Sligo
Tel: 071 61201
Fax: 071 60360

Tourism Division
Shannon Development
Town Centre
Shannon
Co Clare
Tel: 061 361555
Fax: 061 361903

South East Tourism
41 The Quay
Waterford
Tel: 051 875823
Fax: 051 877388

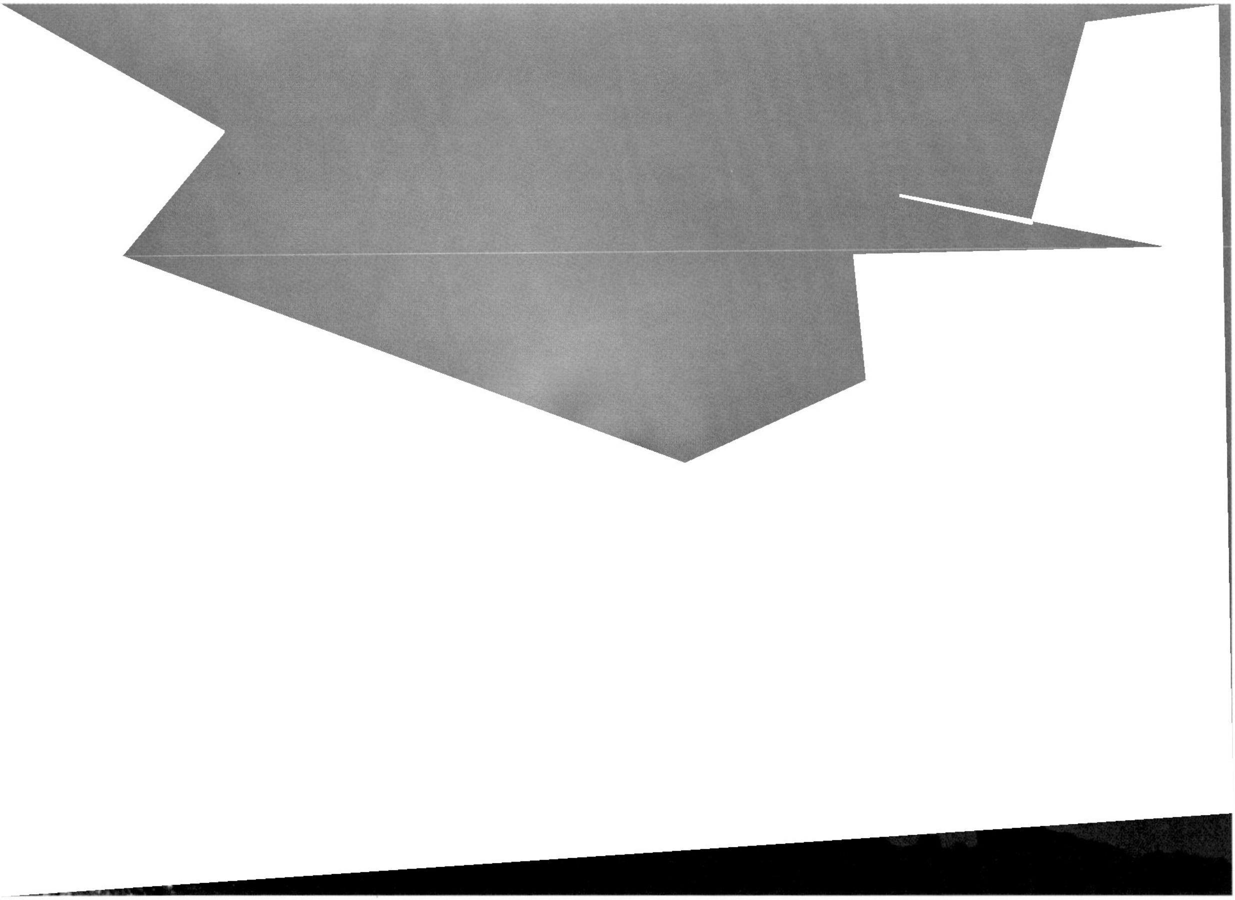

A rare sighting of the mysterious 'Brocken Spectre', complete with its associated 'Glory', observed along the Knockanaffrin Ridge, Co Waterford

INDEX

Numbers in italic indicate photographs.